HISTORY
31st Regiment
Illinois Volunteers

Shawnee Classics: A Series of Classic Regional Reprints for the Midwest

BRIG. GEN. JOHN A. LOGAN.

HISTORY
31st Regiment
Illinois Volunteers

Organized by John A. Logan

W. S. Morris
L. D. Hartwell
J. B. Kuykendall

Foreword by
John Y. Simon

Southern Illinois University Press
Carbondale and Edwardsville

Copyright © 1902 by W. S. Morris
First edition published 1902 by Keller Printing and Publishing Company
Reprinted 1991 by Crossfire Press
New edition published 1998 by Southern Illinois University Press, Carbondale, IL
    62902-3697
Foreword by John Y. Simon, copyright ©1998 by the Board of Trustees, Southern
    Illinois University
Printed in the United States of America
01 00 99 98   4 3 2 1

Library of Congress Cataloging-in-Publication Data
Morris, W. S. (William S.)
        History 31st regiment Illinois volunteers organized by John A.
    Logan / W.S. Morris, L.D. Hartwell, J.B. Kuykendall ; with a foreword by John
    Y. Simon. (pbk. : alk. paper)
            p.   cm. — (Shawnee classics)
        Originally published: Evansville, Ind. : Keller Print. and Pub. Co., 1902.
        1. Logan, John Alexander, 1826–1886. 2. United States. Army.
    Illinois Infantry Regiment, 31st (1861–1865) 3. Illinois—History—Civil War,
    1861–1865—Regimental histories. 4. United States—History—Civil War, 1861–
    1865—Regimental histories. I. Hartwell, L. D. II. Kuykendall, J. B. III. Title.
    IV. Series.
    E505.5 31st.M67 1998
    973.7'473—dc21   97-28956
                                                                              CIP

        ISBN 0-8093-2184-X

Contents.

Index to Illustrations.

Foreword

When Confederate batteries fired the first shots of the Civil War at Fort Sumter in April 1861, North and South divided into warring nations. Lines of division, however, were not foreordained. Contention between Unionists and secessionists brought internal disorder to Missouri and a brief attempt at official neutrality to Kentucky. Nestled between these two states, southern Illinois also experienced the upheaval of a region torn between North and South.

Eighteen counties of southern Illinois formed the congressional district of Democrat John A. Logan, who held political sovereignty. His constituents had given him 80 percent of their votes in the 1860 election, and even his Republican opponent for Congress received a few more votes than presidential candidate Abraham Lincoln. In essence, Logan's district contained a population of hardscrabble subsistence farmers of Southern origin, fiercely Democratic and devoted to Logan, who had established his reputation as a proponent of legislation excluding free blacks from Illinois and as a defender in Congress of Southern rights. Illinoisans gave the name Egypt to the southernmost region, whose people were labeled "ignorant, disloyal, intemperate, and generally heathenish." While acting as state mustering officer at Anna, former captain Ulysses S. Grant noted the stereotypes but was "agreeably disappointed in the people of Egypt" after mustering in the 9th Congressional District Regiment, later the 18th Illinois. If these troops and Colonel Michael K. Lawler refuted the stereotypes, Logan reinforced them.

Usually vociferous in his opinions, Logan maintained an ominous silence during the first two months of the Civil War, a silence interpreted by many as sympathy for the South. In Marion, where Logan had recently become a resident, a public meeting called soon after the surrender of Fort Sumter adopted a resolution pledging adherence "to the Southern Confederacy." The next day, however, other citizens of Marion, influenced by Unionists in Carbondale, repealed the resolution. Concerned about turmoil in Egypt, Illinois Governor Richard Yates responded to a federal call for troops in Cairo by sending them from Chicago, and the first trainload left a company to guard the Big Muddy Bridge above Carbondale, considered the point most vulnerable to southern Illinois secessionists.

In Marion, two local secessionists, Thorndike Brooks and Harvey Hayes, began to recruit for the Confederate Army, assembling about thirty-five men, who marched to Kentucky and eventually joined the 15th Tennessee. Logan's young brother-in-law Hibert Cunningham joined this rebel band, but midway through the war appeared at Logan's headquarters prepared to switch sides. During the Atlanta campaign he served on Logan's staff as captain, apparently given this rank as a family courtesy. In 1866, Cunningham denied that Logan had encouraged him to fight for the South, a statement disputed by Logan's own sister. Although Logan was not involved directly in Confederate recruiting, his name was used and volunteers expected him to command them.

On June 18, Logan finally broke silence under dramatic circumstances. In Springfield an unruly regiment of farm boys from central Illinois, who had already driven one colonel into premature retirement, faced the choice of returning home or entering U.S. service under Colonel Grant, who asked Congressman John A. McClernand to urge the men to enlist. Logan's arrival at camp accompanying McClernand roused apprehension. After speaking, McClernand introduced Logan, whose patriotic sentiments turned the tide. In a public statement a few days later, he continued to condemn "the abolitionists of the North and the secessionists of the South" for bringing war but pledged support to the government and vowed to join the army immediately after a special session of Congress.

True to his word, Logan returned to Marion in August and addressed a crowd in the town square from the platform of a wagon. He began with a denunciation of extremists North and South, but ended with an announcement that the "time has come when a man must be for or against his country." Logan then enrolled for the war and urged those in his audience to join him. By prearrangement with county clerk John H. White, some friends stepped forward, joined by a few converts, but others in the crowd left angrily. A few days later, Logan's mother "upbraided" him for abandoning his principles.

Abandoned by many relatives and friends, Logan plunged into recruiting throughout Egypt. Accepting a coveted commission as colonel from Yates, who believed, as Lincoln did, that placing prominent Democrats in command would demonstrate Northern unity, Logan gave his devoted constituents the opportunity to follow him in war as they had in peace. Eight of the ten companies of his regiment were recruited in Logan's congressional district, and a newspaper reported that of 1,100 men all except twelve were Democrats.

Logan's example and leadership had tremendous effect throughout southern Illinois, and neither he nor his men thereafter questioned the Union cause, however much they may have wavered when war began. Some had once expected Logan to lead a regiment of southern Illinois troops in Confederate uniform; instead the 31st Illinois became a prime component in Grant's western campaigns.

Selected by Brigadier General Grant as one of five regiments for an expedition from Cairo, the 31st fought for the first time at Belmont, Missouri, sweeping the enemy from the field, and being swept off the field themselves when Confederate reinforcements arrived. Williamson County Confederates served with those reinforcements, and the troops knew they had fought their former neighbors. Casualties of ten killed and seventy wounded convinced the 31st that war was serious business.

In February 1862, the 31st embarked from Cairo again, this time for Grant's expedition against Fort Henry on the Tennessee River and Fort Donelson on the Cumberland. Fort Henry fell to a gunboat attack before land forces arrived, but Grant then boldly marched to Fort Donelson, besieging an initially superior Confederate force. On February 15, Confederates under Gideon J. Pillow attempted to break free, achieving initial dramatic success until checked by a stubborn defense which men of the 31st remembered as one of their proudest moments. Fifty-eight died at the battle of Fort Donelson, the highest loss of the 31st in any Civil War battle. Lieutenant Colonel John H. White fell, and Logan received such severe wounds that he was initially reported dead. Logan's valor at Donelson won him promotion to brigadier general, leaving the 31st without a colonel.

His successor, Lindorf Ozburn of Murphysboro, was married to Logan's cousin. At Logan's urging Ozburn had run unsuccessfully in 1860 for the state legislature. A veteran of the Mexican War, where he had served as commissary, he was appointed quartermaster of the 31st Illinois. On April 6, 1862, the regimental officers unanimously selected Ozburn as colonel, and a commission from Springfield followed. The preliminary Emancipation Proclamation of September 22, 1862, angered the enthusiastically partisan Democrat, as it did many in the regiment already restless from extended garrison duty, kindling what Ozburn called "a spark of insubordination" that forced him to send two officers and some twenty men to the guardhouse in a single day. Ozburn's opposition to the Emancipation

Proclamation led Logan to demand his resignation. Logan also resented emancipation but kept his political opinions quiet and continued his metamorphosis from hardshell Democrat to stalwart Republican. Discharged ostensibly for reasons of health, Ozburn returned home. In March 1864, at a banquet provided by citizens of Carbondale for furloughed troops of the 31st Illinois, a soldier who still resented Ozburn's discipline killed him by hitting him on the head with a scale weight.

Ozburn's successor as colonel, Edwin Stanton McCook, named in honor of the man who became secretary of war, came from a remarkable Ohio family: his father and seven brothers served in the Civil War. This family produced two major generals, two brigadier generals, two colonels, two majors, and one private, the last being the father, who died in Ohio of wounds received while repelling John Hunt Morgan's cavalry. At Logan's urging, Edwin McCook, who had attended the U.S. Naval Academy for two years, raised a company in central Illinois for the 31st. He commanded the regiment for a few weeks until a wound in the foot received at the battle of Port Gibson on May 1, 1863, effectively ended his military career. Like Ozburn, he was later murdered when a civilian, in his case while serving as acting governor of Dakota Territory.

As the 31st commenced the final phase of the Vicksburg campaign, Robert N. Pearson took command. Born in Pennsylvania, a twenty-year-old bricklayer in Quincy, Illinois, when the war began, he had enlisted as a private, risen from the ranks to lieutenant colonel and thereafter actually commanded the regiment, although his promotion to colonel dated officially from April 3, 1865, when fighting had virtually ceased. Awarded an appointment as brevet brigadier general after the war, he was among the few former privates who received that honor. Pearson appropriately led a regiment whose twenty-five officers discharged at war's end had all risen from the ranks.

The regiment had marched approximately 2,000 miles under Grant's command, another 2,000 under Major General William T. Sherman, had fought fourteen battles and twenty-five skirmishes, and had participated in compelling the surrender of Confederate armies at Fort Donelson, at Vicksburg, and in North Carolina. Overall, 471 members of the 31st Illinois died in the war, a total equalled by one other Illinois regiment but exceeded by none. Of these, 175 were killed in battle or died of wounds; most of the others died of disease. Farm boys rarely exposed to common childhood ailments crowded into camps where illness flourished. At Cairo, measles struck half the troops. The 37 percent rate for battle deaths in the 31st is consistent with the 30 percent rate for all U.S. forces.

In 1889, veterans of the 31st assembled at Harrisburg, Illinois, for a reunion that became an annual event. They enjoyed reminiscent "Camp fire talks" and an annual address that celebrated the regiment's achievements. They sang "Marching Through Georgia" with the enthusiasm of those who had marched. As years passed, numbers diminished: sixty-two survivors attended the 1894 reunion, thirty-seven gathered in 1896. Yet 150 veterans of the 31st marched with Colonel Pearson in Chicago in 1897 at the dedication of the Augustus Saint-Gaudens statue of Logan. At the tenth reunion, the veterans appointed a committee of three to write the history of their regiment, and the book appeared four years later in 1902. Although William S. Morris entered the copyright and is sometimes credited with authorship, there is no adequate reason to doubt that all three played a role, and some sections read like a book written by a committee.

At age nineteen, Morris had enlisted the day Logan delivered his dramatic address in the Marion town square. His father had followed a common pioneer path from the upper South to southern Illinois, where the son was born on a tobacco farm in Gallatin County. He served through the war, and was discharged as first lieutenant. After studying law with Andrew D. Duff of Benton, who had been arrested for disloyalty during the war, Morris practiced at Elizabethtown from 1870 to 1880, then moved to Golconda. He was elected to the legislature in 1876 and 1880, and won election to the state senate in 1882 and 1884, where he proudly supported Logan for U.S. senator. In old age, he reminisced about an earlier southern Illinois.

Carbondale was a village of shanties, weatherboarded with clap boards, made with froe and axe in the woods.

Cairo was a frog pond and mosquito preserve in the summer time—an ocean in winter. Kaskaskia was tumbling into the Mississippi River. East St. Louis had no record except as a rendezvous for the lawless, and as the *locus in quo* of the Wiggins Ferry Co. . . .

I recall how in the years just after the war a Democrat tried for life or liberty, would not suffer a Republican to sit on the jury if he could help it; so likewise the Republican was equally leery of the Democrat. This condition was fostered by the lawyers, many of whom were practical politicians, but very impractical lawyers. The aftermath of the Civil War had its full effect reflected in Egypt. The Williamson County vendetta, represented by the

Bulliners and Hendersons, the night-riders of Green Cantrell, masked and hooded, who met their overthrow at the battle of Maddox Lane about two miles north of Old Frankfort, the Ku Klux Klan of Hardin County, the warring factions of the Belts and Oldhams, together with numerous killings, assault, etc., are returned in my memory.

Throughout this region of the State these outbursts of lawlessness so frequent from 1860 to 1880 may be traced to antibellum times intensified by hatred engendered by Civil War.

The second committee member, Joseph B. Kuykendall of Vienna, Johnson County, enlisted as a nineteen-year-old private in August 1861, rising to sergeant major, first lieutenant, and adjutant. His father, Andrew J. Kuykendall, a prominent lawyer-politician and longtime member of the legislature, was a Democratic state senator when war came. He gave strong support to the war, served as major of the 31st Illinois until 1862, and, in 1864, was elected as a Republican to Congress. After the war, his son Joseph became a prominent businessman in Vienna.

Lorenzo Dow Hartwell, Jr., of Williamson County, the third committee member, was one of six brothers who served in the Union army, three in the same company of the 31st Illinois. He enlisted at age seventeen, reenlisted as a veteran, received a complimentary commission as second lieutenant after fighting ended but was never mustered at that rank, and was discharged as a sergeant. After the war, he embarked on a career as a Republican lawyer-politician in Marion, where he was city attorney, and was elected county judge in 1890 and state's attorney in 1900, living until 1925.

Appointed thirty-three years after Appomattox to write the regiment's history, the three veterans, who had enlisted as teenagers, were then in their fifties, and their memories remained vivid. Their narrative, however, had deliberate omissions. Since all were now staunch Republicans, the political turmoil in which the regiment originated and the unfavorable reception of the Emancipation Proclamation were unmentioned in the account. Instead, they chose to celebrate the triumphs of their comrades, the heroism of the fallen, and the adventures of soldier life from the perspective of the campfire rather than the officer's tent. By doing so, they captured much of the common soldier's experience of the war.

The story of John A. Logan's famed Civil War regiment, told by its veterans, follows its troops through the battles of Belmont, Fort Donelson, Vicksburg, Kenesaw Mountain, and Atlanta through the March to the Sea and into North Carolina, where southern Illinois farm boys, half a continent away from home, joined in forcing the surrender of the last major Confederate army. Few regiments fought longer or more fiercely, suffered more casualties, or won more victories. This firsthand account of the Civil War, written by its proud survivors, deserves attention from anyone who seeks to understand the American past.

JOHN Y. SIMON
SOUTHERN ILLINOIS UNIVERSITY AT CARBONDALE

Publisher's Note

Civil War regimental histories are unique treasures, and the original editions are very scarce. The rarity of *History, 31st Regiment Illinois Volunteers* is due in part to the fact that it was originally privately printed; that is, the book's production costs were underwritten by the authors, themselves veterans of the 31st's remarkable history.

Although the original text has been reprinted in its entirety, several concessions to modern bookmaking have been made for this new edition. The table of contents and the index to illustrations, originally placed in the back of the book, have been moved to the front and slightly revised for accuracy, and a new foreword has been added.

HISTORY
31st Regiment
Illinois Volunteers

Introductory.

 T the annual reunion of survivors of the 31st Regt. of Ills. Vols. held at Marion, Ills., Sept. 7-8, 1898, the undersigned were selected to write a history of the regiment from its organization to muster out of service at the close of the civil war. In the discharge of this duty, the committee realized that something more than biography was intended by the association; hence the book contains a connected narrative of the military operations in which the regiment was engaged.

This regiment was organized by John A. Logan, in August, 1861, and went into camp at Camp Dunlap, from thence it was sent to Cairo, and mustered into service Sept. 18, 1861. The men met the enemy for the first time at Belmont, Nov. 7, within less than two months after their muster into the U. S. service, and again at Forts Henry and Donelson, in February, 1862. After the fall of these strongholds, it was engaged with the army under Gen. Helleck in the siege of Corinth, and then spent the summer of 1862 in West Tennessee, guarding railroads, and scouring the country round about for the predatory bands of the enemy that infested it. In the fall, the regiment was with Gen. Grant in his campaign from Corinth toward Vicksburg, returning in the winter to Memphis, from whence it embarked March 19, 1863, for Lake Providence, La. After the close of operations there, the regiment crossed the river with the invading army and took part in the battles of Port Gibson, Raymond and Jackson, turning west upon Vicksburg, and joining en route in the decisive battle of Champion Hills, following the retreating enemy to the defenses of Vicksburg, before which it deployed on May 18, 1863.

The men with their comrades dug their way into Fort Hill and on July 4th, leading the division, entered past its breaches into Vicksburg. The regiment was with Gen. Stephenson's detachment to Monroe, La., and upon returning to Vicksburg was put into camp at Black River, where three-fourths of the men re-enlisted, and immediately entered upon the Meridian campaign with Gen. Sherman. Returning to Vicksburg, a furlough of thirty days was allowed, at the end of which, the regiment going by way of Cairo, Clifton, Huntsville and Rome reached the front at Ackworth's Station and entered upon the series of battles fought for the possession of Kenesaw and Atlanta.

After the battle at Jonesboro, when Hood began his northward march through Georgia, Alabama and Tennessee, this was one of the regiments that followed him. Retracing its steps to Atlanta it began the march to the sea with the right wing on the 15th of November, 1864; celebrated Christmas in Savannah, and on the 5th of January, 1865, took passage by sea for Beaufort, S. C. On the 30th of January, 1865, it began the northward march through the Carolinas, that culminated in the capture of Johnston's and Lee's armies. The regiment marched from Raleigh via Richmond to Washington, where it took part in the grand review on May 24. It was mustered out at Springfield, Ill., July 23rd, 1865.

This regiment was efficiently commanded. At the time of discharge there were present twenty-five officers and six hundred and seventy-seven enlisted men. When first organized, there were on the rolls one thousand, one hundred and thirty men, and recruited while in service, seven hundred men. The losses, including those discharged before final muster out, amounted to eleven hundred and twenty-eight men. It had been commanded by four colonels, John A. Logan, Lindorf Osburn, Edwin S. McCook, and Robert N. Pearson. It had first and last, five lieutenant-colonels and six majors. All the officers discharged at the close of the war had been promoted from the ranks except Rev. Jacob Cole, the chaplain. The test of the efficiency, endurance and courage of this fighting machine will be found in the following pages, descriptive of its campaign, including its forty engagements of skirmish and battle with the enemy.

John A. Logan was a member of congress from the Cairo, Illinois district, when the first battle of Bull Run was fought, and in which he took an active part as a common soldier in the ranks. Upon his return to Washington, he

asked and obtained the consent of the President to raise a
regiment in his district. It was given, and in August, 1861, a
sufficient number had enrolled themselves to complete the
organization with the following persons as the field and staff
officers:

John A. Logan, colonel; John H. White, lieutenant-
colonel; Andrew J. Kuykendall, major; Charles H. Capehart,
adjutant; Emery A. Merrifield, surgeon; Jacob Cole, chaplain.

Logan rose through successive grades to the rank of major-general and to the command of the army of the Tennessee.
He had three successors, colonels of the regiment: Lindorf
Osburn, Edwin S. McCook and Robert N. Pearson. Lieuten-
ant Colonel John H. White was killed at the battle of Fort
Donelson, and was succeeded by Edwin S. McCook, John D.
Reece, Robert N. Pearson and William B. Short in the order they are named. Major Andrew J. Kuykendall was succeeded by John D. Reece, Martin V. B. Murphy, Harry Almon
and William B. Short. The adjutants succeeding Charles
H. Capehart were Robert N. Pearson, Joseph B. Kuykendall,
Monroe J. Potts, James W. Seaman and Francis B. Thacker.
Michael F. Swortzcope and Joshua B. Davis were succeeding
quarter-masters after Lindorf Osburn. David T. Whitnell
and Gustave Suhfras succeeded Emery A. Merrifield as regimental surgeons. Rev. Jacob Cole had no successor as chaplain, and served with the regiment till the end of the war.

Company A was organized at Pinkneyville, Perry County, by Captain John D. Reece, whose successors were William
B. Short and Daniel Quillman.

Four first lieutenants, John Campbell, Davidson Moore, Daniel Quillman and James R. Tyler, were borne upon its rolls. Davidson C. Moore, Isham E. Willis and John M. Brown were second lieutenants.

Company B was organized at Harrisburg, Saline County, by Captain Thomas J. Cain. The succeeding captains were Sterne W. Forgy and William W. Largent. The first lieutenants during the existence of the company were Cressa K. Davis, Sterne W. Forgy, Robert Lewis, Joseph B. Kuydendall, William W. Largent and William L. Dillard. Second lieutenants: Sterne W. Forgy, Geo. W. Youngblood.

Company C was organized at Marion, Williamson County, by Captain W. A. Looney, who was succeeded by Captains Geo. W. Goddard and S. C. Mooningham. Its first lieutenants, first and last, were in the following order: Daniel R. Pulley, Philander Jones, Frederick B. Merriman and William S. Morris. Second lieutenants: John H. White, James M. Askew, S. C. Mooningham and Allen H. Wilson.

Company D was enrolled in Massac County by Captain James H. Williamson. The succeeding captains were Levi B. Casey, James P. Anderson, George W. Sanders, and John Toler. First lieutenants were Robert C. Nelson, James P. Anderson, George W. Sanders, Newton Mount, John W. Toler and Howell Y. Mangum. Second lieutenants: Levi B. Casey, James S. Bridges, Jasper Johnson, George W. Sanders, William W. Mount and James M. Bridges.

Company E was from Union County, commanded by Captain Irvin C. Batson. The succeeding captains were Martin V. B. Murphy, John B. Raymond and James Sanders. First lieutenants in succession: Josephus G. Gilliland, William Miller, William V. Sanders, Thomas M. Logan, Surry Steele, James M. Sanders and James Pinegar. Second lieutenants: Robert E. Elmore, Martin V. B. Murphy, Robert Moore, John B. Raymond, and Martin L. Coonce.

Company F was enrolled by Captain John W. Rigby, of Caledonia, Pulaski County. Its captains afterward were: Patrick H. Ayres and John P. Carnes. The first lieutenants, while in service, were: George W. Goddard, Patrick H. Ayers, Phillip Sipple, John P. Carnes and John H. Hunter. Second lieutenants: James M. Hale, John P. Carnes and Lorenzo D. Hartwell.

Company G was enrolled by Captain Willis A. Stricklin, of Harrisburg, Saline County. The subsequent captains were: Simpson S. Stricklin and Monroe J. Potts. Its first lieutenants were Larkin Riley, Simpson S. Stricklin, Monroe J. Potts and William S. Blackman. The second lieutenants: Simpson S. Stricklin, Benjamin Sisk and John W. Stricklin.

Company H was organized by Captain Oramus Greenlee, of Cairo, Alexander County, and was succeeded by Horace L. Boyer, Jesse Robberds and Augustus M. Jenkins. The first lieutenants of this company were Horace L. Boyer, Jesse Robberds, David Culp, Joshua B. Davis and Samuel P. Steele. Second lieutenants: Jesse Robberds, William N. Miller, David Culp, John W. Cole and William A. York.

Company I was formed by Captain Edwin S. McCook, of Pekin, and succeeded by Captains Harry Almon, Carroll,

Moore and Isaac Wirt. First lieutenants: John Mooneyham, Robert R. Towns, John J. Curry, Isaac Wirt and Francis W. Stickney. Second lieutenants: Robert A. Boneman, Carroll Moore and David Wirt.

Company K was organized by Captain Alexander S. Somerville, of Centralia. Its succeeding captains were Thomas Hunter and John W. Stewart. First lieutenants: Charles H. Capehart, Henry T. Snyder, John S. Hoover and Henry C. Lewis. Second lieutenants: Levi E. Morris, Pinkney K. Watts and Mitchell S. Barney.

A considerable proportion of the rank and file of companies I and K came from beyond the borders of Logan's district, a few of them from Chicago, some from adjoining states and one from Montreal, Canada.

W. S. MORRIS,

L. D. HARTWELL,

J. B. KUYKENDALL,

Committee.

MRS. JOHN A. LOGAN

Chapter I.

"*Up many a fortress wall*
They charged—these boys in blue—
'Mid surging smoke, and volleyed ball
The bravest were the first to fall;
To fall for me and you!
These noble men—the nations' pride—
Four hnndred thousand men have died
For me and you!
Good friend, for me and you!"

HE   rank and file of what afterwards became the 31st Regiment of Illinois Volunteers, and later the 31st Regiment of Illinois Veteran Volunteers, as called during and since the Civil War, first became acquainted with each other, as soldiers at Camp Dunlap, near Jacksonville, Illinois.   These men seemed to have been selected at random, from the general mass, and were for the main part composed of the sons of farmers, merchants, and mechanics, all from Southern Illinois, except about two companies.   As they were taken directly from their homes to their first encampment by the company officers they had elected, they presented upon their arrival, clothed in every

conceivable fashion and variety of garment, a novel and striking appearance, in such vivid contrast to the appearance of
organized, equipped and trained soldiers, that the onlooker,
without experience, would have imagined their gathering
at Camp Dunlap as a military burlesque. Here, however,
they mounted guard without guns, slept in the straw without blankets, organized mess clubs, began learning to cook
and underwent the physical examination necessary to en-
able them to pass muster. From Camp Dunlap the officers
and men went by rail to Cairo, where the regiment was organized by Colonel John A. Logan, and on September 18,
1861, the formation being complete, it was mustered into the
service of the United States by Captain Pitcher, U. S. A., to
serve three years or during the war.

Military drill and training began at once, roll call, dress
parade, the manual of arms, and battalion drill was soon the
standing order of the day. Guard mounting became familiar
to all, and the soldiers' camp a short distance up the Mississippi, was encircled by a line of sentries, through which
neither civilian nor soldier could leave or enter without a
pass or the mysterious countersign.

Through the months of September and October, 1861,
the routine of the soldiers' camp life at Cairo found little
change or excitement, except in the arrival of new troops,
news of a recent battle or skirmish, and an occasional hurried and unexpected march to the river landing, or to some
undefined and unknown place up the Mississippi River.

As the government was straining its energies to the ut-
most to feed, clothe, arm and equip the volunteers that
came rushing into the various camps from every quarter of
the loyal half of the union, the men did not receive their uniforms until many of them, who had left home in summer holi-
day attire, were in actual need, before the quartermaster
could honor the requisitions of their captains. Neither could
suitable arms be readily obtained, but after a while clothing
was distributed. The "Queen's arm," a musket with barrel
three inches longer than the Springfield rifle, and that had
been shorn of flint and frizzen, and supplied with cap locks,
was put into the hands of the volunteers who with their
bright new uniforms and these ancient weapons, began to
step about in such soldierly fashion that in a few weeks anyone of them might have been taken for a veritable "cock of
the walk" in almost any quarter of the world.

Thus equipped and uniformed, the training went on. A
few men and officers had seen service in the Mexican war and
they were lookd upon as authority on all military subjects.
The officers of the line were themselves exercised in the manual of arms by Private R. N. Pearson, of Company K, who
afterwards became colonel of the regiment, and they were
also instructed in company drill by him, who from his experience of three months under the first call of the President for volunteers, and his aptness for military affairs, was
even then a competent drill master.

While Colonel Logan was indefatigable in care and attention to the discipline and wants of his men, the battallion

drill and complicated movements of the parade ground were mostly conducted by Lieutenant-Colonel John H. White, who had been a soldier of the Mexican war and who, by temperament and soldierly bearing and instincts, was not only eminently fitted for his position, but also fully qualified to take high rank as a leader in the stirring and trying scenes soon to be encountered.

After a while the regimental and company commanders became possessed of pocket editions of "Hardee's Tactics," and as the improved training went on, instead of hearing a captain on the parade ground command his company in a subdued tone: "Boys turn right 'round this stump, here," we might hear his, "Company, file left," in a clear, confident and ringing voice.

So passed the months of September and October, and as the interest in military duty increased and as the intensity of the struggle then impending grew clearer, the volunteers began to tire of camp life, its incidents and monotony, and many began to express their desire to meet the enemy known to be not far off, his heavy batteries barring the navigation of the Mississippi River below Columbus, Ky., his flag flying defiantly on the Cumberland and Tennessee Rivers from head to mouth, and his hostile bands roaming at pleasure through Eastern and Southern Missouri. It was known to the least informed among the volunteers at Cairo, that the relative positions of the opposing forces could not be long maintained without a shock of arms that would definitely determine the mettle of these hostile Americans, who had become

BRIG.-GEN. ROBERT N. PEARSON.

enemies because political party lines had so nearly become fixed by geographical lines. There existed also a feeling of anxiety and suspense that grew with information of every skirmish or battle, and men began to inquire what part they were to play in the wonderful and soul-stirring drama now opened and spread out before the astonished gaze of the civilized world. The volunteers were asking themselves whether they in triumph should plant their victorious banners upon the strongholds of the Confederacy, or would these Confederates cross the northern boundaries of the seceded states and levy tribute upon the people of those states that now stood firmly by the old Union? Events were shaping an answer to the impatient questioning of the eager volunteers.

Within the period of camp life at Cairo, rumors of a Confederate attack had reached the camp, insurgent bands had prowled about the country between Cairo and Charleston, Missouri, only a few miles away, and the lower Mississippi being in complete possession of the secessionists, an attack upon Cairo and the Federal camp was within the scope of reasonable conjecture.

Gen. Grant had command of southeast Missouri, with headquarters at Cairo. Hostile demonstrations by Gen. Polk had induced him to seize Paducah on the 6th of September, then occupied by Gen. Tighlman, his staff and a company of recruits, that hurried out of town on his approach.

On the 1st of November Gen. Grant had by direction of the president sent about three thousand men under Colonel Richard J. Oglesby to scour the country in the direction of

the St. Francis River, to look out for reinforcements being
sent by Polk from Columbus, to Price in Southeast Missouri,
to make a diversion in favor of Oglesby's column. Grant
was ordered to make demonstrations toward Columbus on
both sides of the river and thereby distract the attention of
the Confederate commanders, in order to accomplish the protection that Oglesby might need. Hence on the evening of
the 6th of November, Gen. Grant with thirty-one hundred and
fourteen men on steamers, including a section of artillery,
two squardons of cavalry and five regiments of infantry
(among them the 31st regiment in its new uniform, armed
with this dangerous old musket, that at every discharge
"kicked" in its recoil so vigorously that the soldiers
cursed the day they made its acquaintance) proceeded
nine miles down the river and made a feint of landing on the Kentucky shore, thus giving color to a maneuver
of Gen. Smith who menaced Columbus from the northeast
as if about to attack. Hearing that Oglesby was in danger,
Gen. Grant determined to convert his "demonstrations" into
an attack, and at six o'clock the boats moved down the river
and the troops were landed at Hunter's Point in Missouri,
just beyond range of the batteries at Columbus and within
three miles of the enemies' camp at Belmont, and there, the
Confederates, protected by fallen timber, surrounded by a
dense forest, that in places was almost a jungle, silently
awaited the forward movement of the attacking column.

And now the volunteers are about to realize the wish
for an actual battle, and learn what war means. With the ex-

ception of a guard left to protect the landing and the boats, the entire column marched out about one mile where skirmishers deployed to the front, became immediately engaged with the enemy. Among the regiments so deployed was the 7th Iowa, or portions of it. As the firing increased Colonel Logan rode forward, leaving the regiment standing at a halt, under the temporary command of Lieutenant-Colonel White. It was now nearing ten o'clock and when the order came to move forward in line, not a little confusion followed the effort of officers and men to dress the line and present an even front, for in addition to the thick growth of timber the forest land was cut up in slashes by sloughs and ravines that made it impossible to maintain a perfect line. In some way, however, the men, encouraged by their chiefs, struggled forward, sometimes jammed in bunches and sometimes scattered as skirmishers during the advance. The firing increased and the musket balls were falling uncomfortably near as now and then a comrade fell in death or was stricken down with wounds. But fortunately for the attacking column the enemy fired too high and many balls went wide of the mark. Again the brush and timber that checked the advance afforded protection to the assailants so that when these Western men were told to "take trees and fight Indian fashion," their nerves grew stronger and with more freedom of action they became more formidable to their foe. The artillery fire of the enemy should be called ineffective, though much damage was sustained from it, most of the shots going high overhead. To new men the scene was the strangest they had

ever witnessed. The peculiar screeching of the shells and
whistle of the bullets, mingled with the boom of cannon and
the commands of the officers, made strange music in these
hitherto peaceful forests.

Finally the outer edge of the abatis was reached and the
men still dodging forward from tree to tree, and from cover
to cover, some single, others in groups, broke through the
camp with a rush, drove out the defenders, captured and
broke up the camp, chased the enemy to the brink of the
water below the river bank, and took several hundred prisoners and all the artillery and baggage. The victory was
complete, but the want of discipline became immediately em-
barrassing. The men began to plunder the camp, loading
themselves with small arms, baggage and even horses. To
stop it the camp was set on fire which drew the attention of
the artillerists in Columbus, and they began to drop their
shell in and about the camp. Meanwhile Polk hurried a fresh
brigade across the river as reinforcements, and these troops
and those hitherto protected by the river bank moved under
its cover to a point on the river between the Federal troops
and the transports that had brought them hither. When informed of this, Logan declared that "we must cut our way
out as we had cut our way in," and the return movement was
instantly begun. The 31st regiment acting as a rear guard
passed the enemies' right flank in safety, after the main column, with but little opposition, being confronted by the men

they had driven out of their camps in the morning. But before reaching the boats, the enemy attacked, and a running fight was kept up to the landing.

The officers experienced some difficulty in getting the men on board the transports, Colonel White being among the last to leave the landing. His horse was forcibly pulled down the river bank on his haunches and dragged across the stage plank on to the boat. Under the musket fire of the enemy now pressing on with shouts of defiance, safely on board, the men returned the fire, and as the transports slowly rounded out in mid stream, the gunboats Lexington and Tyler opened upon the defiant Southerners with grape, canister and shells, at a distance of fifty or sixty yards, cutting them to pieces and utterly routing them. Here, however, they sent a storm of shot at the boats, but they passed for the most part over the hurricane deck and did but little damage.

By five o'clock in the afternoon the boats were all out of range and the rank and file were highly elated with the idea of having gained a great victory.

From the reports of Gen. Pillow who had immediate command at Belmont, he must have brought into action on that day not less than seven thousand men of all arms. The Confederate loss was six hundred and forty-two, the Federal loss four hundred and eighty-five in killed, wounded and missing. One hundred and seventy-five of the wounded fell into the hands of the enemy. The Federal troops took with them one hundred and seventy-five prisoners and two cannon. Four guns were spiked and left on the battlefield.

The volunteers had met the enemy; they returned to Cairo, rejoicing in their achievement, self-reliant and confident, and for months thereafter, upon the drill ground or elsewhere, all that was necessary to rouse the enthusiasm of the regiment was to command "Belmont charge," and with a wild cheer the men would move forward in line at the double quick, in a way that won the respect and admiration of the officers, and that afterwards became a sign of fearful warning to their foes.

After returning to Cairo, camp life proceeded about after the old fashion. The drilling and training went on. The leisure hours were enlivened by stories of the battle that sometimes took a serious turn, when the names of those who had fallen were mentioned, or as the task of war became more clearly defined and its tremendous and overwhelming possibilities were more distinctly revealed and comprehended.

On the 9th of November, 1861, Gen. Halleck superseded Fremont and assumed the command of the department of the Missouri, including Arkansas and Kentucky west of the Cumberland River. For two months thereafter there was no forward movement in the department, but organization, company and battalion instruction, and drill continued in the camp at Cairo. Early in January, 1862, Gen. McClellan, then commander-in-chief of the army, directed Halleck to begin military operations in his department, and by the latter's direction a force of six thousand men under McClernand was sent out by Gen. Grant from Cairo and Bird's Point towards Mayfield and Murray in Western Kentucky. The 31st was with this expedition. After the movement was begun the order was countermanded by Halleck, but as the troops were well on their way, they proceeded to the accomplishment of their object, which was to divert the attention of the Confederate chieftains from certain operations of Gen. Buell in the department of the Cumberland. The troops were out more than a week and suffered much from cold, rain, sleet and snow, and very many were injured in health from the severe exposure. There was no fighting.

Gen. Thomas, commanding under Buell, had fought and won the battle of Mill Springs in Eastern Kentucky, so that notwithstanding there was some murmuring among the men and more grumbling. The object of the movement was accomplished.

Matters again went smoothly at Cairo where the troops, now quartered in barracks, made of plank boards and set up like box houses, managed as best they could to shield themselves from the weather. The signs around and near the volunteers at Cairo were ominous and threatening. The Confederates occupied at that time a defensive line extending from middle Kentucky, on their right, to the Mississippi at Columbus, on their extreme left. They dominated the Cumberland and Tennessee Rivers and all the country behind and adjacent thereto. One hundred thousand men stood ready to defend or reinforce this defensive line. Gunboats could and were being built on these rivers. The fortifications were strong at Columbus and defended by one hundred and forty guns, works were in pro-

cess of building at Dover on the Cumberland, and Forts
Henry and Heiman on the Tennessee, and at other strong
points on these rivers.

We have called the Confederate line a defensive line.
Might it not be converted into a base, and the host that defended it be turned into an offensive force? The military
captains of that day were discussing probabilities: Before
the green grass shall again appear to decorate the hills and
valley of the Northwest, a solution will be found in the grim
renewal of the clash of arms.

LIEUT.-COL. JOHN H. WHITE.

Chapter II.

I knew him I tell you! and also I knew,
When he fell on that battle swept ridge,
That the poor battered body that lay there in blue
Was only a plank in the bridge,
Over which some commander shall pass on to fame
That shall shine while the bright stars shall shine!
Your hero is known by an echoing name,
But the man with the musket is mine.

O N the 22nd of January, 1862, Gen. Grant had received information that the capture of Fort Henry on the Tennessee was necessary and could be accomplished, and he immediately requested Halleck to give him permission to make the attempt. The permission was given on the 30th, and on the second day of February Gen. Grant with seventeen thousand men on steamboats, convoyed by seven gunboats, steamed away from the landing at Cairo and bade what subsequently proved to be to the soldiers a long farewell to their camp at Cairo. A few days before starting a new sutler had pitched his tent and displayed his wares in the camp. The men were mostly out of money, but the accommodating sutler proposed selling on credit till

pay day and most of the men supplemented the contents
of their haversacks by additions of sausage, cheese, canned
goods and tobacco, to various amounts, ranging from twenty-
five cents to two dollars. That sutler has never called to collect his bills.

Until February, 1862, the regiment was a part of General McClernand's brigade, who had now become a division
commander. He was succeeded by Oglesby and both accompanied the expedition. The 31st was put on board the steamer Minnehaha. The upper decks were screened, and all within were packed together like sardines in a box, many being
stowed away in the hold, who did not see the sky until the
boat reached Paducah, at the mouth of the Tennessee, where
they crawled out to see what was then known as a Confederate town.

On the 4th of February the debarkation began at Bailey's Ferry on the east bank of the Tennessee and out of
range of the guns of Fort Henry, three miles away.

As Logan's regiment marched across the bow of a boat
between the one that brought them up the river and one lying at the landing, they piled up the "Queen's arms," and
each received a new Enfield rifle with its accoutrement.

The camp at Bailey's landing in the woods, on the hills
by the river, was chill and uncomfortable and the men bivouaced that night around the camp fires without tents, exposed
to the fall of snow and rain.

About daybreak in the morning of the 6th, the gunboats
began to put themselves in readiness to attack Fort Henry,

and by eleven o'clock the army and navy were moving in the direction of the fort and its defenses. McClernand's orders being to place his troops " on the roads to Fort Donelson and Dover and hold them in readiness to storm the works on receipt of orders."

Fort Heiman had been evacuated the night before, and every effort was made by the enemy, to save Fort Henry which was defended on the river front by batteries containing seventeen heavy guns. The country back of the river was covered with a dense growth of timber and the approaches to the river covered by rifle pits, field batteries and a tangled mass of fallen timber.

The fort was reduced in about an hour and a half by the gunboats, and before the troops had reached their position it was surrendered to the naval commanding officers by Gen. Tighlman and staff, with about sixty men who had operated the big guns. The principal force had made good its retreat on the roads to Dover and were beyond the reach of cavalry sent after them. Detachments of the 31st regiment brought in two cannon that had been abandoned in the flight to Dover. The men quartered at night in the abandoned barracks, some of which contained supplies of corn meal, salt pork and potatoes, which were immediately taken, cooked and eaten. The barracks were log cabins built in regular order with company parade grounds between. Some of the Confederates had left their uniforms and extra clothing in these cabins, and many of the men who had waded a slough up to their necks clothed themselves in the gray and dried their uni-

forms by the fires. It was no fault of the officers and men
that the Confederate retreat was not impeded or cut off. The
roads from Bailey's landing were very muddy, the ground
soft and spongy, the miring of horses, artillery and wagons
on the march rendered it slow and toilsome, notwithstanding
the efforts made to go forward. The column was frequently
halted and soldiers were detailed to assist in pulling the cannon out of the mud, and in moving obstructions out of the
road. These halts made intervals in the column, and the almost constant cry of "Close up! close up," continually fell
upon the ears of the toilers through the mud.

The scene within the fort, about the barracks and camp,
was one of destruction and ruin. A big gun in the fort was
struck in the muzzle by a shell which exploded and split it
like a rail cut. Bloody and mangled bodies were scattered
about the guns. Some of the log houses struck by shells
were utterly demolished, others knocked to pieces looked as
if they had stood in the path of a cyclone. The soldiers were
happy, the enemy was gone and the navigation of the Tennessee River opened up for many miles.

From the 6th to the morning of February 12th the regiment remained in camp at Fort Henry. The weather was
wet and dismal and the river and tributary streams overflowing. On the eleventh of February Commodore Foote, with his
gun boats having in charge a number of steamers loaded with
troops, started to Fort Donelson by way of the Ohio and
Cumberland Rivers. McClernand's division moved out several
miles towards Dover on the same day, and on the morning of

REGIMENTAL FLAG AT VICKSBURG.

the 12th the main army under Gen. Grant, fifteen thousand strong, with eight field batteries, took up the march for Donelson, twelve miles from Fort Henry, on the Cumberland. The position was known to be well fortified, the approaches covered by all manner of obstruction, within which the Confederate leaders had assembled more than twenty-one thousand men, commanded by Floyd, Pillow and Buckner. The water batteries were formidable in position, men and guns. The country between Henry and Donelson had been shorn of much of its heavy timber for making charcoal to supply an iron furnace that had been operated about mid-way between the two rivers and on the line of march. In place of this timber a dense undergrowth had covered the hills and valleys so that military men have perplexed themselves with the question of why the enemy did not avail himself of these natural defenses, by there fighting the battle for Donelson, or by such defensive measures as would delay, harass and discourage the Union troops who must have forced their way through it, if at all, with great loss and discomfort to themselves and animals. The number of wagons taken, however, had been reduced to the minimum, as the greater part of the baggage and all the tents were left in charge of a garrison of twenty-five hundred men at Fort Henry. On the evening of the twelfth the troops approached the Confederate position and there was a sharp skirmish, in which part of the 31st and 29th Illinois regiments were engaged. The Union troops drove in these skirmishers, supposed to belong to Forrest's command of mounted men, as they left double-barrel shot guns and powder horns scattered about in the bushes.

The night of the 12th was spent in getting the men around to points opposite the center and left of the Confederate lines, the left of the Federal position resting well down to the Cumberland, where communication was maintained with the gun boats.

Some lively skirmishing was kept up during the 13th and the novel warfare of "Birges' sharp shooters," each with a squirrel tail in his cap and a Henry rifle in his hand, in his own way from behind a rock, tree or other cover, picked off the enemy with his rifle. By such means and a pretty general shelling from several batteries, the Confederates were kept close by within their rifle pits.

On the night of the 13th the lines were extended still further to the right, but owing to high water in the Cumberland, backing up into the sloughs south of Dover, a lodgment could not be effected on the river above the town. An incident of the movements on the night of the 13th was the accidental firing of some of the Union troops into the ranks of the 29th Illinois, from which firing several men were killed and wounded.

The relative position of the two armies remained pretty much the same throughout the 14th, but at one time during the day the brigade was massed against the Confederate left and moved close up to the works among the fallen timbers, so close that the enemy could be plainly seen, drawn up in line behind his rifle pits. The purpose was apparently to assault, but fortunately the troops were withdrawn and went into camp where they remained during the night.

Up to this time about three hundred men of Gen. Grant's army had been killed and wounded. The gunboats had on this day made an unsuccessful attack upon the water batteries, from which they were repulsed. Several of the boats were badly disabled, the commodore wounded, and fifty-four of his men disabled by death and wounds. The night of the 14th was cold and bitter. The rain fall of the early evening changed into sleet and snow, that was driven with a brisk north wind across the Federal bivouac, where the men without tents and without fire rolled themselves in their overcoat and blankets in the snow, or tramped around in a vain effort to counteract the cold. All night long, more or less firing could be heard, and the noise in and about Dover and the landing, plainly indicated some unusual commotion within the enemies' lines.

At daylight on the morning of the 15th, before the men could cook and eat their rations of bacon and crackers, and while preparing their coffee for breakfast, the Confederates who in the night had massed their strength for an attack upon McClerand's division, came out of their works, and deploying rapidly to our right, burst upon McClernand's division with loud and defiant yells. The attack was supported by a tremendous artillery fire from the Confederate field batteries, advancing with the infantry. Shrapnel, grape and canister, supplemented the musketry with fearful precision and deadly effect. Several guns of Schwartz's battery on the

right of our regiment were instantly dismounted, and most of
the horses and many of the men killed or disabled. At the
beginning of the firing, Colonel Logan, in order to bring his
men to the crest of the hill in front of his line, had ordered
the line to move forward forty paces. Here they dropped upon
their knees in the snow and here at very close range they received and gave their first fire, and here the ranks were torn
by canister and plowed by bullets. The officers of the line
held and encouraged the men to hold their ground by every
form of command and entreaty known in modern warfare,
while the commander of the regiment and his staff fearlessly
and almost to a man remained on horseback close up to the
line, presenting themselves as targets to the Texans and Ten-
nesseeans who swarmed about the front and right of the line
with their rifles, double-barrel shot guns, and muskets, yell-
ing like tigers in the intervals of firing. Confident of success and without wavering or blinking, in the very path of a
whirlwind of bullets that swept from the front of our line,
the soldiers loaded and fired at will. Nothing could be
heard above the deadly clash, clamor and roar that was
sweeping over hill and valley, through which wound the Charlotte road, for the mastery of which this battle was fought.
Men and officers were falling rapidly. Some lay where they
fell in the snow, others were conveyed to the rear.   The
colonels could not see their regiments from flank to flank as
the smoke hung over the dense underbrush and enveloped
the battle like a cloud.   Within less than two hours the
cartridges were becoming scarce. The right of the brigade

MAJ. S. H. ALMON.   LIEUT.-COL. JOHN D. REECE.
CAPT. W. B. SHORT.

being turned, the men were doggedly retiring to avoid the flanking fire. Colonel Logan about this time was severely wounded in the shoulder and reluctantly allowed himself to be assisted to the rear. The right was giving way and the attacking columns seemed about to effect a permanent lodgment on the coveted road. The 11th and 31st Illinois regiments alone presented an unbroken front, but they also failed before this withering blast. The confident enemy having now found themselves on the ground occupied by the regiments of the right wing, began enfilading our line also. Lieutenant-Colonel White, alive to the danger, ordered a change of front to rear to meet the new attack. Riding among the men and conducting the movement, he was shot from his horse and fell upon the snow, being killed in the moment of saving his regiment from the loss of many men who in their exposed position would have been destroyed or captured almost to a man. Notwithstanding the loss of their chiefs, the men, assisted by such of the company officers as remained on their feet, returned bullet for bullet, and right manfully in the wooded gorge where they were so greatly outnumbered, they continued the struggle till out of ammunition, and then in tolerable order, were retired to the left and rear, as reinforcements reached them from Wallace's division. But we did not again engage in the action, but were conducted at night fall to the rear of the left flank of the army, camping upon a hill side covered with snow. Here the men had an opportunity to cook and eat, many not having tasted a morsel in forty-eight hours, and here the tired fellows again biv-

ouaced in the snow, without tents, many without over coats
or blankets. But as the artillery had ceased its fire on both
sides and there was no longer danger of being shelled, the
camp fires burned brightly through the long night, being fed
from the forest where there was abundant timber that also
afforded some protection from the cold.

On the evening of the 15th, and soon after Pillow had
planted his flag upon the Charlotte road, Gen. A. J. Smith had
been directed to storm the position in his front, much weakened by the massing of the enemy on their left for the attack on McClernand, in the morning. Smith and his men
nobly performed their task, and when, on the evening of that
eventful day, they planted their victorious flag upon the Confederate breastworks, they put it there to stay. At dark, on
that night, all the Confederate troops that remained to defend Fort Donelson were cooped up within their intrenchments and a white flag fluttered above the ramparts of this
grim fortress on the Cumberland. On the morrow the Confederate army had surrendered.

The general officers immediately established headquarters in and about Dover, and many of the troops went into
camp within the Confederate lines. Soon thereafter, our
regiment took permanent quarters in the old log cabins near
the main water batteries at Fort Donelson, that the garrison
had erected for barracks. They were provided with floors
made of rude plank or puncheons, and some of them had fire
places and bunks—a sort of frame work attached to the
walls—on which the men spread their blankets and bedding.

Here we had comfortable quarters, and as there were quite a number of well disposed citizens in the neighborhood, commercial relations with them were established, and coffee, sugar, rice, etc., was exchanged with them for corn meal, eggs, butter and other products that the farmers brought in for that purpose. The regiment remained on garrison duty at Fort Donelson till spring. While here many were visited by friends and relatives from the north, and many sight-seers came to look at the famous battlefield and pick up incidents of the campaign. The wounded had been sent away as rapidly as possible, and the prisoners had been immediately sent north to Chicago and Rock Island.

While on garrison duty the regiment was paid off, and commerce with the natives was stimulated by the circulation of greenbacks given in exchange for such delicacies as they had to sell, principally eggs, milk and butter.

The men had been once paid at Cairo, and it is a noteworthy fact that they received from the paymaster gold and silver coin, and the bills of state banks, some receiving Kentucky state bank bills in payment of their wages.

This regiment had suffered severely in the battle of Fort Donelson. It is remembered, that every mounted officer present in the action was killed or wounded, and of the company officers, the majority had met death or wounds.

The men who fought in the ranks so stubbornly and survived the conflict, well remember the shortened line as it now appeared at roll call or parade. Hardly a home in Southern Illinois but was bereft of some member of it, or some friend attached to it.

Some idea of the terrific magnitude and grandeur of this battle may be had when it is remembered that its thunders were heard through all the counties of Southern Illinois, startling its peaceful citizens as far north as Benton, the county seat of Franklin County.

The importance of the victory will be appreciated when it is understood that the navigation of the Cumberland River was secure from its mouth beyond Nashville, and a way opened through Tennessee and Kentucky to the interior of the South where lay the strength of the Confederacy.

The story is admirably summed up in Gen. Grant's congratulatory orders to his troops two days after battle in which he says: "For four successive nights, without shelter, they faced an enemy in large force, in a position chosen by himself. Though strongly fortified by nature, all the safeguards suggested by science were added. Without a murmur this was borne, prepared at all times to receive an attack, and with continuous skirmishing by day, resulting ultimately in forcing the enemy to surrender without conditions.

"The victory achieved was not only great in breaking down the rebellion, but secured the greatest number of prisoners of war ever taken in one battle on this continent up to that time.

"Fort Donelson will hereafter be marked in capitals on the maps of our re-united country, and the men who fought the battle will live in the memory of a grateful people."

With no disparagement whatever to the gallant officers and men who stood upon the right and left of our regimental battle line on that eventful day, we accept Gen. Pillow's estimate of the regiment as among the highest enconiums, when he declared on that day that "had it not been for that regiment of regulars clothed in short blue jackets he would have made a Bull Run of it." Pillow was mistaken. We were not regulars, but we did wear blue pea jackets and barred his passage to the Charlotte road.

In garrison on the Cumberland, the experience of officers and men was, in the main, such as is ordinarily witnessed in routine camp life. The tactical exercise necessary to more perfectly fit the soldier for his duty, was not overlooked by the officers, and almost every soldier had learned to appreciate the importance of training.

Colonel Logan had been made brigadier-general. White was dead. Major Kuykendall and Captain Rigsby alternately had commanded the regiment until near the time of leaving Fort Donelson, when Colonel Lindorf Osburn, who had been promoted from quartermaster assumed command.

During the latter half of March, 1862, the Federal leaders had been busy organizing and concentrating troops on the Tennessee River, particularly about Savannah and Pittsburg landings, with the evident intention of opening the Tennessee River to its source, and with the apparent design of pushing military operations into the States of Alabama and Mississippi. Nor had the Confederate leaders been idle. Real-

izing the importance of keeping possession of the Tennessee
River, they were rapidly concentrating a large army at Corinth, Miss., with the evident intention of resisting the further progress of the Federal arms, and in this position guarding and covering Memphis and the country behind them, or
with gathered resources, by a bold and powerful push, recover the ground and prestige lost at Forts Henry and Donelson.

From these movements it was clear that a great battle
was to be fought on the Tennessee and near the Mississippi
state line, as indeed it was fought on the 6th and 7th days
of April, 1862.

It is not within the scope of our present task to sketch
the battle of Shiloh. The story has been often told by eye
witnesses and chief actors in that memorable drama, and the
critical reader who desires a clear comprehension of it may
consult with pleasure and profit Gen. Badeau's Military
History of Gen. Grant, the memoirs of Gen. Sherman,
the very able and entertaining articles of Gen. Lew Wallace and Gen. Grant on the side of the Federals, and those of
the Confederate officers, particularly Gen. Jordan, adjutant-
general to Gen. Beauregard, who drafted the battle order for
the attack at Shiloh. These historical master pieces will be
found in the war series of the Century Magazine and have
attracted the eyes of the reading public, throughout the
world, to that great struggle where the Western men of the
hostile sections constituted the principal body of strength
and courage, that for two long days surged and wrestled in
deadly combat, amid the brush, mud, ravines and thickets on

the banks of the Tennessee, between the now historic streams of Lick and Owl creeks.

Thousands of patriotic men and women, from all sections of our common country, annually make their visit to this wonderful battlefield and there, by the flow of the inland river, whence the fleets of iron have fled, they scatter the flowers of spring upon the graves of the blue and gray, and together rejoice in the present and future of our united country, trust-each other that

> " No more shall the war cloud sever
>   Nor the winding rivers be red,
> They banish our anger forever
>   When they laurel the graves of our dead."

Chapter III.

W E heard of the battle of Shiloh while on garrison duty at Fort Donelson. Immediately thereafter, we were transported by steamer down the Cumberland again, passed Paducah and up the Tennessee to Pittsburg landing, the only incidents of note on the way being a few volleys from the muskets and carbines of roving bands of the enemy who fired upon the boats from the bluffs between Ft. Heiman and Pittsburg landing, as they passed up the river, that resulted in wounding some of the men who occupied every part of the boats from the boiler decks to the top of the hurricane roofs. Arriving at Shiloh the men were put into camp near the right center of a large army and near the Purdy road. The great conflict had left its mark and impress upon every visible thing in field and forest. About the river bank and landing, baggage wagons, caisons, broken muskets, battered tents and dead animals were promiscuously strewn together, and further out, great trees were cut down or torn to pieces by the heavy batteries that had sent their shot and shell screeching and howling among the branches. About

MONUMENT ERECTED TO COL. JOHN H. WHITE.

the Shiloh church and spring, the fire of musketry had
gnawed and scarred every object that could be seen, while
further to the left, about the "hornets' nest," the undergrowth was cut away as with a scythe. Long trenches filled
with the dead told where the storm of conflict had raged
during the dreadful hours of battle. No man beholding the
scene expressed his wonder when told that the great northwest was draped in mourning for its sons who had fallen on
this fateful field. Illinois, Missouri, Tennessee and Mississippi were the chief mourners, but Wisconsin, Kentucky, Iowa
and Texas had had a hearing and their bravest sons had
here their full share in this baptism of blood.

There was now collected in and about the Shiloh battlefield a great army under the immediate command of Gen.
Halleck which was divided into three large army corps under
the respective commands of Thomas, Pope and Buell, supported by an army under McClernand, called the "Reserve Army
of the Tennessee," of which Logan's brigade and his old regiment formed a part.

The whole face of the earth seemed to be covered with
men, and every conceivable thing attendant upon a mighty
host. Sutlers and civilians also swarmed about the camps,
curiosity hunters, speculators, spoilsmen and loafers, which,
added to tents, baggage and provisions made a vast collection
of impediment in and about the camps.

The Confederate army was in force at Corinth not twenty miles away where with pick and spade and shovel, they
followed the directions of their engineers and crowned every

hill and piece of commanding ground in and around their camp with extensive intrenchments and rifle pits.

Halleck seemed paralyzed by the onslaught of the hosts at Shiloh and did not appear to desire another pitched battle. He fell to digging and ditching. Immense siege guns were brought up and drawn by cattle over the mirey roads of McNary County, sometimes going forward as much as two miles in twenty-four hours, while the men built roads, bridges and embankments and talked of redoubts, rifle pits, embrazures, bastions and traverses and vaguely conjectured the meaning of all this expenditure of engineering skill and muscular force. An occasional skirmish, a mere affair of out posts varied the routine, but the siege of Corinth, as it is called, went on.

On the 30th of May Halleck announced to his chiefs that "There is every indication that the enemy will attack our left in the morning." Accordingly the army was drawn out for battle on the next day, only to find that instead of an attack Beauregard had, with his army, slipped out of Corinth, leaving his formidable works crowned with wooden cannon. But Halleck amused himself by rejoicing over his great victory and marched his army into the evacuated town and encampment.

An army of one hundred and twenty thousand men had advanced fifteen miles in six weeks; had thrown up miles of earth works, while its enemy had constructed defensive works still more elaborately and then left them.

A master mind had suffered temporary obscurity and a guiding hand had been withdrawn from the direction of the Federal army in the west. When the curtain is again drawn the scene will open with the beginning of a system in which the objects of the war will be more clearly defined.

During this period Gen. Halleck in assuming command of operations in the field had left Gen. Grant as second in command, but his command was only nominal, and although the corps commanders were his inferiors in rank, orders were frequently sent to them without making Gen. Grant acquainted with their contents. He had recommended an attack by the extreme right of the Union line before the 30th of May, but Halleck declined, and nothing but the empty honor of taking Corinth succeeded as a sequel to what seemed to have been some great design. Soon afterward Gen. Pope went to Virginia. Halleck superceded McClellan and Gen. Grant was left in command of the district of West Tennessee.

The 31st regiment went with its brigade to Bethel by way of Purdy and from thence marched by the wagon roads to Jackson, near the Forky Deer river in West Tennessee. Here for portions of the time it again experienced the routine of camp life, but was not in action for any considerable length of time, on the contrary scouring the country to Brownsville and in the direction of Bolivar, was frequent, and some of the companies were for some time used in guarding important points on the railroad north of Jackson, where in the summer of 1862, they were attacked by greatly superior forces, but beat off the enemy and held their ground till reinforced by Col. Osburn, who himself hastened to the scene on a hand car from Jackson.

While at Jackson the brigade was for a part of the time commanded by Brigadier General Mike Lawler and afterwards by McPherson.

Immediately after Beauregard's retreat from Corinth, a great many troops were withdrawn from Gen. Grant's command, Memphis having been taken by the naval forces in June, was within his department, where for a part of the time he made his headquarters, and part of the time at Corinth. Bragg had invaded Kentucky, Pope and McClellan were relieving each other from time to time in Virginia and the Union cause was dangerously threatened in many quarters so that Gen. Grant whose duty is was to protect his territory, particularly the positions at Corinth, Jackson, Boliver and Memphis and the railroad north which was his only means of supply, was practically on the defensive.

On the 19th of September Rosencrans fought the battle of Iuka and drove off the assailants, but the enemy was simply checked, not beaten.

The attack at Iuka was made by Vandorn, Price and his Confederates were in force at Ripley and Lagrange, and it became apparent to Gen. Grant from the movements of their cavalry that Boliver or Corinth would be the place of attack. He therefore established his headquarters at Jackson so as to direct support to whatever point it might be most needed.

COLONEL WHITE'S ACCOUTREMENTS.

Gen. McPherson, by direction of Grant, got a brigade together, including the 31st infantry and marched to the support of Rosencrans at Corinth.

On the night of October 3rd McPherson's command went into bivouac within ten miles of Corinth and at early dawn were aroused by the roar of cannon that announced the opening of the battle of Corinth. As soon as could be McPherson's column resumed its march and reached the vicinity of Corinth before the battle was over, but unable to reach the garrison in any other way McPherson marched his brigade around the Confederate flank, bringing it in on the right of Rosencrans. Later in the day the regiment marched into and through Corinth and passed Fort Robinet around which there had been a deadly struggle.

On the morning of the 5th we began the pursuit, but by some mistake took the road toward Chewalla instead of that farther south, by which the enemy had moved. The mistake was soon discovered and the column turned toward the Hatchie. At the first attempt of Confederates to cross this stream they were headed off by Ord and Hurlburt and driven six miles further up the stream. Here we fell in with their rear guard and after the capture of a couple of guns the 48th Illinois, by a brilliant charge, secured the bridge and a large number of wagons and baggage that obstructed the road for a mile beyond.

In this wreck was found a large quantity of plug tobacco which the men "confiscated," and "all went merry as a marriage bell," as they plodded forward to the ascent of the high hills beyond the Hatchie.

At this time the regiment composed the vanguard, but moved at rout step with flankers on each side of the road, and scouts in front, but the enemy were not overtaken again, and upon reaching Ripley rations were found to be exhausted. The men eat fresh pork without salt, coffee or hard tack, and after proceeding a few miles beyond Ripley the return movement began.

It seems proper at this point to refer more specifically to the conditions of military affairs as then understood in this department. Gen. Grant chafing at the thought of maintaining defensive operations had suggested to Gen. Halleck, then in supreme command, the propriety of seizing Vicksburg and opening up the Mississippi River. The general in chief had gained experience and he also longed that something be done that would result in victory to the Union arms.

Gen. W. T. Sherman was in command at Memphis, and it was conceived by Gen. Grant that with control of the river to that point, and by seizing and holding the Mississippi Central railroad further south, an army of thirty thousand men might operate successfully against the rear of Vicksburg, or by drawing out its garrison, beat Gen. Pemberton in the open, and thereby compel the abandonment of that stronghold on the great river, or after crippling it sufficiently, carry it by assault, and thus cut the Confederacy into two parts and deprive its eastern half of its great supplies of beef from Texas without which they could not (the whole southern coast being blockaded) long maintain the contest. Gen. Halleck lent free and loyal support to this plan of operations.

Early in November the movement for securing the Mississippi Central railroad and compelling a battle outside of Vicksburg began. The Confederates held Grenada, Lagrange and Holly Springs. The column to which the 31st was attached moved toward Lagrange, which was abandoned on the approach of the Union troops. Here we were rested for a few days and then continued the march toward Holly Springs which the cavalry occupied on the 13th of November. Later infantry and artillery passed through the town and the Mississippi Central was in possession of the Union troops as far south as the Tallahatchie River where Pemberton had strongly intrenched himself. These works could scarcely have been carried by direct assault, but as Gen. Grant was about to turn them, Pemberton withdrew to the south side of the Yallabusha, while we continued the pursuit through and beyond Oxford, the home of J. Q. A. Lamar.

A comic incident occurred in the streets of Oxford. The men of the 31st had clothed an army mule in full uniform and drove the solemn looking animal through the town at the head of the column, singing "We'll hang Jeff Davis, etc," and shouting: "Here's yer mule" to the great amusement of themselves if to no one else.

The army was now a long way from its principal base of supplies. A good supply, however, including munitions of war had been stored at Holly Springs.

The cavalry was at Coffeyville, only eighteen miles from Grenada, but it seemed impracticable to proceed further. Sherman and McClernand had gone down the Mississippi to attack the Yazoo bluffs, and the unprotected country in our rear invited attack. On the 20th of December Van Dorn's cavalry dashed into Holly Springs and captured the garrison with all its stores. The commandant, Colonel Murphy, though warned of the impending attack, made no effort to defend the post and the government lost more than a million dollars in army supplies and stores. Colonel Murphy was dismissed from the service, but the army south of Holly Springs suf fered great hardship for want of food.

The men, however, made shift to subsist, Gen. Logan commanding the division directed his command to make lye hominy. The country was scoured for corn. The wagons brought it to camp, the men skinned it with lye from the ashes of their camp fires, and we were all reminded of the good old days of "hog and hominy," without the hog. For a while we got ONE cracker per day for each man.

Soon the retrograde movement began, and woe to the luckless chicken, goose or gander that crossed the path of the soldier as he marched in the direction of Uncle Sam's store houses.

The columns were headed toward Memphis. Sherman and McClernand had been repulsed at the Yazoo, because the works were too formidable for assault.

But the campaign against Vicksburg was not abandoned. Grant had made up his mind and his superiors had agreed

MAJ. ANDREW J. KUYKENDALL.

that Vicksburg should feel the weight of the national forces intended for its destruction, and so the long lines stretched out day by day, through part of the months of December and January, without regard to rain or snow and by the 10th of January the headquarters were at Memphis. The camp of the 31st regiment was pitched a few miles south east of the city and here, in the snow, Mrs. Mary Logan at an evening dress parade, walked down the line, shook hands with the men, calling many of them by name, and encouraging them in their devotion to the cause of their country.

A few months before her gallant husband in reply to a letter from O. M. Hatch, then Secretary of State for Illinois, who had requested Gen. Logan to become a candidate for congress-at-large. Writing from Jackson, Tenn., he said among other things in declining the nomination: "In making this reply, I feel that it is unnecessary for me to enlarge as to what were, are, or may hereafter be my political views, but would simply state that politics of every grade and character are now ignored by me. Since I am convinced that the constitution and life of this republic—which I shall never cease to adore—are in danger. I express all my views and politics when I assert my attachment to the Union. I have no other politics now, and consequently no aspirations for civil place and power. * * * I have entered the field—to die if needs be—for this government and never expect to return to peaceful pursuits until this war for preservation has become a fact established." Gen. Logan was with his command at Memphis. The men had imbibed his sentiment. The

one universal aim was the preservation of the Union, and
the work of preparation for the reduction of Vicksburg and
the opening of the Mississippi river, was pushed forward as
rapidly as possible.

Less than one hundred years before the Spaniards had
denied the right to the free navigation of this continental
stream. It was now a question whether it should be free to
all Americans alike, or be dominated by an exclusive Southern Confederacy.

Chapter IV.

EAVING Memphis in the beginning of March, 1863, the regiment embarked on steamers, proceeded down the river to Lake Providence, Louisiana. Here and about Young's Point and Miliken's Bend were collected an army of fifty thousand men, encamped on low, flat lands, subject to overflow, so that the camps had to be frequently removed to escape the rising floods. Heavy details were kept at work upon a canal intended to turn the channel of the river through Lake Providence and Bayou Tensas and the Red river, to afford a passage below for troops and gunboats. This had been a favorite scheme for sometime, but life in the swamps soon proved to be not only irksome, but dangerous and unhealthy also. Many men sickened and died. By the 5th of April the canal project had proved to be a failure and was afterwards abandoned. All around us every effort possible had been and was made by the navy and the army to secure a passage for the men and fleet so as to concentrate an attacking force at some point below Vicksburg on the east side of the river.

In these attempts Admiral Porter's gunboats were well nigh lost by proceeding through a bayou with thickly wooded banks. The Confederates felled the timber in front and rear of them at a point where the muzzles of the guns were three feet below the banks, so that they could not be effectively used, and thus, wedged in with the fallen timber, they would have been captured but for the land forces sent to their relief. These drove off the enemy and released the boats from their perilous position.

At length it was determined to move the army to the east side of the river and the experiment of running the Vicksburg batteries was fallen upon, which, being repeated, it was thought to be possible to send transports laden with supplies past the batteries and this was finally done. In the meantime troops were moved lower down the river to Milliken's Bend. From thence, our division proceeded to Hard Times where it arrived on the last day of April.

On the 30th of April, preparations having been completed for the transportation of the men across the river, the 13th corps was crossed over to Bruinsburg. A diversion had been made causing much firing at Haine's bluff. The sudden appearance of the national forces on the east bank of the river created a great alarm in the camps at Vicksburg and the defenses below.

Gen. Bowen, immediately, with the idea of holding the Union forces in check, marched out of and abandoned his defenses at Grand Gulf and selected a strong defensive position near Port Gibson and the bayou Pierre. The 13th corps was in front of this position on the morning of May 1st, while Logan's division was rapidly advancing to its assistance. Our regiment had remained at the landing for rations, but hearing the firing eight miles away, decided to go forward hungry, and pushed as rapidly as possible to the support of the men already engaged.

The weather was intensely hot, the roads covered with dry sand. Many fell by the wayside overcome with heat. Arriving at the battle ground, and after a momentary halt, the regiment took its place in John G. Smith's brigade, on the left of the line and to the left of the road to Port Gibson. Preparations were made to charge and under the eyes of Grant, McPherson, Governor Yates, Gens. Logan and Smith, the brigade dashed through the sedge grass and gulleys of an old field upon the right flank of Bowen's line (commanded by Gen. Tracy who was killed in the battle) capturing many prisoners. The rout of Bowen's line was complete, numbers of prisoners and stragglers being captured. Bowen's force amounted to about seven thousand men, but he was greatly outnumbered and suffered heavily. He was pursued but a short distance. We camped that night on a hill side so steep that the paths where we slid downward, in the effort to sleep, had a decided rearward tendency as they appeared on the following morning.

Gen. Grant's loss in the battle of Port Gibson, or as better known by our men—Thompson's Hill—was one hundred and thirty-seven killed and seven hundred and eighteen wounded. The losses of Bowen were about the same, but our force had captured six hundred and fifty prisoners and six field guns.

It should be remembered that soon after beginning operations at Lake Providence and Milliken's Bend, Gen. Grant had directed Gen. Hovey, then at Memphis, to send Colonel Grierson with five or six hundred picked men, to cut the rail- roads east of Jackson and then cut his way south, destroying everything he could, and reach some point on the Mississippi River. This feat had been accomplished to the great conster- nation of the people of the interior, which accounts, in part, for the want of concert in the movements of the Confederate force defending Vicksburg.

We passed through the town of Port Gibson on the morning of May 2d, crossed a stream called the South Fork on temporary bridges while the engineers were repairing the one fired by the Confederates.

Gen. McClernand's column—the 13th corps—was moved in the direction of Edward's Station, the object then being to keep the left wing close to the Big Black so as to move directly on Vicksburg.

During the 2d and 3d our regiment, with the whole or other portions of Logan's division, was almost constantly in line, skirmishing about Ingram heights and beyond. We were then a part of the right wing of the army commanded by Gen. McPherson.

Gen. Sherman's corps, the 15th, was still on the west bank of the Mississippi River and did not cross till the 5th of May, when his command became the central column.

After some skirmishing about Willow Springs, it was learned by the commanding general that Pemberton was concentrating and fortifying at Edward's Station; also that efforts to reinforce him would be made from the direction of Raymond and Jackson. To counteract these efforts McPherson's column was directed toward Raymond, the intention now being to avoid a battle with the main army of Pemberton till reinforcements should arrive, but in the meantime to attack and defeat any detached army or part of an army that might be in a position to succor him.

On May 10th McPherson marched to a point seven miles west of Utica. Sherman had now arrived and he and McClernand moved on nearly parallel lines along and to the east of the Big Black, while we, with McPherson's command, moved to the north and east of the rest of the army.

The marching columns of Grant's army on the east side of the river numbered now about thirty-five thousand men and twenty-five field batteries. General Grant said, "When I crossed the river the means of ferriage were so limited and time so important that I started without teams and an average of two days' rations in the haversacks."

On the 11th of May Gen. Grant severed his connection with the rear and informed Halleck he would not again communicate with Grand Gulf. Strangely enough on the same day Halleck telegraphed him to return and co-operate with Banks. The telegraph being cut, he did not, of course, get the order, in fact, never got it till communication was opened with the fleet above Vicksburg. On the 11th of May Mc-

Pherson was still on the road to Raymond. Logan's division
led the advance. On the 12th and by eleven o'clock we came
up with the enemy about five thousand strong. They came
from Port Hudson as reinforcements for Pemberton, and
were well posted by Gen. Gregg with two batteries of artillery, the infantry to the left of the road on rising ground and
among timber in front of the hill.

As the 31st regiment hurried to the front it was assigned to the right of the line, which it reached by passing
through a tangled wood and across a deep ravine, neck deep in
water, which was crossed in some places on logs or by wading. The east bank of this ravine was skirted by an open
field and the bank served as a breastwork behind which the
regiment formed its line of battle. As it did so a heavy roll
of musketry broke over the woods to our left.

The position had scarcely been taken when the Confederate infantry came across the field obliquely in our front, at a
quick run, as if bent upon the seizure of something to our
left. The companies fired in a manner resembling the firing
by file, for as they came first within range of the right of the
line they encountered a continuous fire till they reached the
left. The battle at this point was over in less than twenty
minutes. The men fired at will after the first round, but it is
believed that, after running the gauntlet of the first vollies,
they were soon out of range or under cover. Our men
cheered loudly as these fellows ran across and against their
front. It seemed an ambuscade, but it is probable that neith-

Major S. H. Almon.

er part knew the position of the other, till the enemy made his wild dash across the field.

Gregg fell back, retreating through Raymond on the Jackson road, our troops pursuing. In this short but rather lively battle, the Federal loss was sixty-nine men killed, forty-one wounded, and thirty-one missing. Gregg's loss was one hundred killed, three hundred and five wounded, four hundred and fifteen prisoners, and two pieces of cannon. The enfilading fire across the field had contributed powerfully toward the result.

Gen. Grant's army was now between that of Pemberton and whatever force Joe Johnston had at Jackson, Mississippi, which, together with reinforcements hurrying toward Jackson from other points, would, when combined, outnumber the Federal forces on the east side of the river more than two to one.

Gen. Grant, to prevent a junction, now determined to march directly upon Jackson and ordered Sherman and McClarnand to follow McPherson toward Clinton. McPherson's column began the movement at daylight on the morning of the 13th, the very day that Johnston arrived at Jackson and assumed command, not only at Jackson but of all the Confederate troops in the state. He at once, and on the same day, ordered Pemberton, who had massed his troops at Edwards' Station, to attack Grant in rear at Clinton immediately. We reached Clinton with McPherson on the evening of the 13th, ten miles from Raymond and ten miles from Jackson, in the afternoon, tore up the railroad track and destroyed the telegraph. Here, dispatches from Pemberton to Gregg were captured, from which it appeared that Pemberton was still expecting an attack at Edwards' Station.

The movement on Jackson began at four o'clock on the morning of the 14th. By nine o'clock the advance division met the Confederate pickets five miles out from Jackson. They were immediately driven in.

Our corps under McPherson was on the left of the Clinton road, completely detached from Sherman's troops, their left flank being two miles away.

Crocker's division of the 17th corps composed our front line, Logan's division the reserve. A brilliant charge by Crocker, supported by Logan, dislodged the enemy in front. At about the same time, Sherman was getting into their works. Shortly after we entered the city and our regiment bivouaced on capital square. The troops of Joe Johnston were driven beyond supporting distance of Pemberton, and the armies meant for our destruction were now worse scattered than immediately following the battle of Port Gibson and were moving in opposite directions.

The loss in McPherson's command was thirty-seven killed and two hundred and twenty-eight wounded. He reported Johnston's loss at eight hundred and forty-five, including prisoners.

Johnston retreated in the direction of Canton and again ordered Pemberton to attack our rear.

During the evening, or that night, it was learned that Pemberton was at Edwards' Station with eighty regiments of infantry and ten field batteries and still advancing. Our division made a night march on the Bolton road toward the Big Black, drenched in rain. On the morning of the 16th the men were halted in a field to the right of the road and ordered to spread their poncheas in the sun and dry their cartridges.

The troops in advance had come up with Pemberton's army near Baker's Creek, in a strong position with the left of his line on Champion Hill, which takes its name from the farm house that stood upon it.

The division did not have long to remain at rest. Heavy firing was soon heard six miles to the front, which soon reached the proportions of battle. Hovey was hotly engaged. Logan was ordered to follow Hovey with his column. The cartridges were soon replaced in the boxes and the men urged forward as rapidly as their strength would admit, being ordered to the double quick. They trotted forward with guns and luggage till a pause for breath became indispensible, when they would again resume the march. The weather was dense and hot, the men tired and warm. But all had learned that a waste of leg force was really a life of preservation. That rapid movement secured advantages and saved men, so all went cheerfully forward, while nearer and more deadly rose the sound of battle. As quickly as possible we were brought up to the rear of Hovey, and as the column moved in his rear to take position in his extreme right, we could hear the wild Confederate yell, as they swept up to Hovey's line in headlong charge.

Passing rapidly to the right of the line, the brigade came to a front, looking across the Champion Hill farm house and the high ground where field batteries were in position to defend the extreme left of the Confederate line of infantry drawn up in double column. They crowned the hill, that with its abrupt northeastern face covered with timber, presented a formidable barrier to any force that might assail it. Behind the brigade was an open field; far off to the right the flat bottoms of Baker's Creek. The men here slung their knapsacks and lay flat upon the ground in line. Major Stahlbrand pushed his twenty-four pound Howitzers several yards in front of our position and opened at close range with shell and shrapnel, cutting his shell at a second and a half. The guns on the hill added their music and sent their missiles tearing across the narrow valley at Stahlbrand's guns. The Major observed from his position at the guns a line of infantry moving down the hill. He turned round and riding up to Gen. J. E. Smith, commanding the brigade, said: "Sheneral Schmidt dey are sharging you mitt doubled column. By damn it they vant mine guns." Smith looked to the right and left of his line and replied grimly: "Let 'em come, we're ready to receive them." He commanded, "Attention brigade," and the line stood upon its feet. Again he looked steadily up and down the line and bawled out "Fix bayonets." The bayonets flashed from the scabbards and the jingle of the steel rattled along the line. Logan and McPherson dashed up. The corps commander smilingly rode along the line, saying: "Give them Jesse boys, give them Jesse." Logan straightened him-

MAJ. DAVID T. WHITNELL, SURGEON.

self in his stirrups and said: "We are about to fight the battle for Vicksburg." Appealing to his old regiment he cried out: "Thirty onesters remember the blood of your mammas. We must whip them here or all go under the sod together. Give 'em hell." Smith gazed earnestly at his brigade and seemed to measure with his eye the distance to the crest of the hill before him, and then in a long drawn voice he commanded: "Forward—double quick—march." The line plunged into the valley among the brush, struck and became commingled with the first line of the enemy at the ravine at the base of the hill, and with loud cheers drove them up the hill beyond their batteries and through the double formation that had now lost all semblance of order, and fled every man for himself, across the fields and woods in their rear. The assailants chased them without stopping to load or fire. The Confederate battery was now behind them and hundreds of prisoners threw down their muskets and "skedaddled" to the rear of our lines, many of them wholly unattended by their guard or captors.

Those who mounted the hill could see to their left, dense masses of infantry, the bulk of Pemberton's army. Logan's division had gained its left flank and rear, but was recalled and the pursuit was checked. Had the true situation been then known, we might have captured Pemberton's army en masse upon the battlefield.

The road being now open, the two armies began the race for Vicksburg. Between us and that stronghold were the

strong entrenchments and garrison at the Big Black. The
columns of McClernand's and McPherson's corps were headed that way and the advance divisions marched with all the
speed they were capable of exerting, during the fore part of
the night, going into camp tired, hungry and covered with
dust.

Early on the 17th the march was resumed and at length
the firing was again heard at the Black River. Mike Lawler
who held the advance found a point where his men could
wade the river; hurried them across, charged the enemy
from the rear, capturing nearly all of them and all their
heavy guns. While Lawler was fighting his battle, our regiment was in the lead of the brigade, frequently at the double
quick. We heard the quick rattle of the guns, the wild
cheers of the men. A lull, then another cheer. Our pace
was slackened. Lawler came riding down the road, wearing
his famous sword belt of two gun slings; with one leg
thrown across the pummel of his saddle, he said to Gen. Leggett who rode at the head of our column: "Let your men
rest General, let 'em rest." "Did you get any of them?" said
Leggett. "Whole acres of them, whole acres of them,"
growled Lawler and then the men began cheering which was
caught up successively as it rolled backward.

On the 18th we took the road to Vicksburg, McClernand's corps being directed to the left, Sherman to the right
and McPherson to the center. Before nightfall Sherman was
at Haines Bluff where he could see the fleet and the Mississippi River. McClernand was well up on the left and stretch-

ing out toward the river below Vicksburg, while McPherson formed his line across the central road running past Fort Hill into Vicksburg, Logan's division fronting the main fort. These divisions were mere skeletons, thousands of men being scattered in the rear toward the Big Black and Champion Hill. They were neither cowards nor skulkers, but overcome with fatigue and heat. They sat down by the road or leaned against a tree, where sleep bound them in its strong embrace, oblivious alike to the tread of marching columns or the sound of distant battle.

As the attenuated lines were drawn about the defenses of Vicksburg on May 18, 1863, many of the companies could not put more than five or six men in line of battle. The scene within the Confederate lines was similar. Thousands had thrown away their guns and luggage and swarmed about the city and landing in an aimless sort of way, or slept where they had sat down, overcome by their long struggles and dispirited by their defeats. But the Confederates had enough to man their works. Batteries were put in position on that day and opened from several parts of the line. The enemy replied to them. We watched the white puffs of smoke from their guns and fell upon our faces to avoid their missiles that screeched red hot in the sultry Mississippi sun.

All that the soldiers could see clearly in front were the ground earthworks and frowning batteries. To reach them they must pass over deep gullies, through tangled masses of fallen timber; over zig-zag hill and deep gulches that were of such irregular formation that they seemed to mock at the points of the compass.

Among these hills with videttes thrown to the front, the army slept that night. Not more than five days' rations had been issued to the army since May 1st, and everything along the line of march from water mill to farm house had been eaten. Everything that grunted, squaked, gobbled, or cackled had found its way into the mess pan, or had been stewed in the camp kettle, or roasted on a ramrod, for the soldier must eat before he can march or fight. The country had been stripped from Port Gibson to Jackson, and thence to the Mississippi; hence, all felt a yearning for Haines Bluff where supplies from the Mississippi and the Yazoo would now be brought. Sherman was there standing on the very bluff from which he had been repulsed six months before. Chickasaw landing, at the base of the Walnut Hills, was now made the base of supplies, and roads were cut and bridges built to distribute them to the army.

It was twenty days since the campaign had begun. Two Confederate armies had been whipped in five battles. Eighty-eight cannon had been taken, twelve thousand five hundred men had been killed, captured and wounded. The conquering army had lost one-third as many; had drawn five days' rations during the campaign, and was now getting itself together for the final struggle with the grim and formidable batteries that stretched between it and Vicksburg. In these achievements the 31st Illinois infantry had borne a conspicuous

Adj. Joseph B. Kuykendall.

part; all had distinguished themselves, the killed, the wounded and the fit for duty.

On the 19th an assault was ordered from the respective fronts of the three corps, upon the supposition that the enemy was badly demoralized, and that a lodgment could be effected within his lines. The men struggled bravely and well, crossing the obstructions at many points of the line. Some reached the top of the parapets but could not cross over. They held their positions close up to the ditches until night, then drew back a few yards and began to cover themselves with rifle pits.

On the 20th it was determined to renew the assault and preparations were made to escalade the works. On the 22d batteries were put in position to cover the advance of the storming columns, that were to be preceded by forlorn hopes, carrying planks with which to cross the ditch.

The ground in front had been cleared as much as could be. When the assault began, the advance parties moved forward at a run, and by ten o'clock all the uproar and fury of the 19th was again repeated with added intensity. The tangled abatis and other obstructions were so great that in many places the regiments could not be fully deployed into line, these attacked by heads of columns. In some such way our own regiment advanced, saddlebagging the road directly east of Fort Hill. This road ran along the top of a narrow ridge east and west. This ridge was swept with canister and bullets. The picture, here, was much like the others on the right and left. The Confederates rose up behind their parapets and at point blank range poured in a destructive fire. Their batteries from every hill top and rising ground filled the air with their destructive shell and shrapnel. The steep declivities and spurs of ground afforded momentary respite from the deadly work. But the works must be taken or the assault would fail as on the 19th, so now some of the men crossed the ditches and mounted the escarpment to be stricken down or captured. Strong columns planted their standards within a few yards or a few feet of the embankments only to see them riddled. The attack failed; by mistake, it was renewed, with the result of increasing the list of the dead and wounded. By this means it was demonstrated that the defenses of Vicksburg were too strong to be taken by direct assault, and the fire slackened.

It can hardly be said that the men were withdrawn. Strong points, entrenched and defended by batteries, were permanently held within from one to two hundred yards of the hostile works. Other position were held even nearer.

On the 23d the army had settled down to a regular siege. Entrenching implements had been brought up from the Yazoo. Engineers were making profiles and marking positions to be secured. A parallel was opened on the rear, along the north side of the road leading out toward the Big Black. It soon became deep enough and wide enough for an army wagon and six mules to pass through. The parallel was protected by traverses that spanned it every few yards. These traverses were a protection against an enfilading fire and were for the most part made of baled hay and cotton.

As the work progressed, every day became alike. Details were made daily to work on the entrenchments. Behind other divisions, parallels, similar to the one described, ran from front to rear. From each side of these parallels, and running lateral to them, rifle pits were opened confronting those of the enemy. These grew up every night, always encroaching toward the front. They were marks for the enemy who used them for target practice. Our men defended them and from time to time crept closer.

When it was desired to extend the parallel toward the enemy, sap rollers were used, being rolled toward the front. Behind this the men, with spade and pick, dug away, pushing the parallel closer and closer till the head of the sap finally touched the Confederate works.

The rifle pits were mounted with head logs and through the space between the dirt and logs the soldiers fired. These head logs were laid in the notches of smaller ones that ran rearward across the trench. When knocked off it rolled backward over the heads of the men. Our regiment camped and worked along the north side of the road leading east toward the Big Black, taking its turn in the rifle pits and in the work of the siege. Details gathered material for sap rollers, gabions and head logs.

The skirmish lines were the pickets thrown a few yards to the front at night. These protected themselves by lunettes that sheltered them from the fire in front, opening to the rear and thus affording a safe retreat when necessary. The enemy were occupied in the same way and the men were close enough to talk with each other and exchange tobacco and coffee.

Through the remainder of the months of May and June the siege progressed. Reinforcements came to assist us. Joe Johnston closed upon our rear about Edwards' Station and on the Big Black. The army was digging into the ene- mies' position in front, inclosing him in a semi-circle, with a line of rifle pits and batteries extending from the river above to the river below him. Batteries were mounted on the west side of the river. These and mortars, from floating batter- ies on the river, threw their shells into the rebel lines east of the city.

The intrenchments to our rear were as elaborate as those in front, presenting an insurmountable barrier to Johnston without.

The Federal army occupied an entrenched camp entirely surrounded in the direction of its base about the Walnut Hill. Every day the list of casualties was increased.

Skulkers, who earned the expressive name of "cane breakers," were hustled from their hiding place and put to extra work on the approaches.

Sometimes at night the sky would be lit up by lurid flashes of musketry, and the red glare of the batteries' mor- tar shells crossed and recrossed each other, resembling shoot- ing meteors.

The videttes of both armies saw each other at their posts at night. They were instructed to hold their fire unless ap proaches were made in force.

Capt. Thos. J. Cain, Co. B.

By the 25th of June the heads of saps, at many places, ran into the defensive works. Angles of earth works almost touched each other. Mines and countermines were driven by the sappers and miners on both sides. Grenades were fre quently thrown by the enemy into the heads of saps.

On the 25th of June a furious cannonade was begun from every elevated position of the Federal line. Blood spurted from the nose and ears of men at the big guns. Some put their hands to their ears; the sound seemed to penetrate the brain. It was a crash, expectancy was at its height. Men caught the idea of sublimity. The mine under Fort Hill was sprung; the earth trembled as if an earthquake were passing. There was a momentary pause, a loud yell of triumph, and in- fantry with fixed bayonets dashed into the crater made by the explosion. The enemy had anticipated this event. A new re- doubt had been built in the rear of the old one. This redoubt was yet the strong defense of Fort Hill. The Confederates would not let it go. The crater would not admit more than two companies at once. The 56th and 31st Illinois regiments fought here by turns. Details relieved each other. There was here a large log on the new redoubt. It was gnawed by bullets and pierced by bayonet thrusts. The Confederates threw grenades over the embankment; the Union soldiers threw them back. Shells from the twenty pounders were thrown by hand. Men pitched muskets at each other. Some had rifles snatched out of their hands. The front line with their backs to the redoubt raised the breech and depressed the muzzles of their rifles so their balls might reach the foe

on the other side. The rear line faced their comrades and
loaded for them. Then men were encouraged by their officers
who animated their efforts. The ground in the crater became
slippery with blood. The men called it "the slaughter pen."

When the fort was blown up a negro was blown on our
side of the line and was not hurt, but badly scared. Part of
our regiment who were engaged here, slept that night in the
ditch behind the angle in the redan, a few rods to the right
and rear. Two pieces of artillery fired nearly all night, from
a position a few yards from where they slept soundly, some
of them dreaming of home.

Two twenty pounders, double shotted and unlimbered,
stood within the parallel to sweep the crater. At one time
the enemy swept over the crest to drive our men out. It
was then the twenty pounders were put in place.

This was the battle of Fort Hill. It cannot be painted
by brush or pen. If once seen, it can never be forgotten. It
was a hell within a radius of five hundred feet. The Confederates held the hill. The "Yankees" encircled it. The garrison inside was nearing starvation. The inhabitants made
chambers in the abrupt sides of the hills to shelter themselves from the shells. Many of these chambers were neatly
furnished and carpeted.

At one time, Pemberton attempted to build enough boats
of a light draft to cross the river to the west side. The batteries there would head them off or sink them.

Sherman kept Johnson on the east side of the Big Black
and Grant kept Pemberton inside his works at Vicksburg
where mule meat was selling at a dollar a pound.

Each succeeding day was in many respects like the former. The sap rollers crept up near and nearer. New mines were sprung; batteries opened their fire from unexpected places, but the heroic garrison, whose devotion merited a better cause, still clung to the trenches with the spectre of starvation mocking at the sacrifice.

The hardships were not confined to Pemberton's lines. Continuous watching and exposure, scarcity of water, and a broiling sun annoyed and sickened the assailants. The horrors of the siege were everywhere visible.

On the 1st of July the approaches reached the ditches at ten places along the lines. The heads of column could be brought within a few rods of the Confederate works. The 4th of July was fixed upon as the time for a final assault. The heads of approaches were prepared so that the columns, moving by fours, could quickly pass over the ditches, filling them with bags of pressed cotton or placing planks across them. But no assault was made. Pemberton on the 1st of July held a council of war. Two of his generals advised a surrender. On the 3d he sent Gen. Grant a request for an armistice, and an interview was arranged for the two hostile commanders that afternoon.

At three o'clock in the afternoon Pemberton attended by Gen. Bowen and Col. Montgomery, came to his front. Gen. Grant accompanied by Generals Ord, McPherson, Logan and A. J. Smith met them within two hundred feet of the Confederate works south of the main road leading into Vicksburg.

The interview was within sight of our camp. The appearance of the generals and the white flags wrought a magic change. The deep mouthed thunder of the cannon was hushed. The hostile forces, without arms, showed themselves above and upon the ramparts. They rose up out of their trenches like apparitions and the blue and the gray gazed at each other in mute astonishment. In places, they were not over two rods apart.

The interview between the generals closed the campaign against Vicksburg. By the terms of surrender the Confederate soldiers marched out of their works and stacked their arms in front of the positions they had so gallantly defended.

It was at ten o'clock on Saturday, July 4th, Independence Day, that the Confederates streamed across the trenches along the whole front and laid down their colors with their arms, sometimes on the very ground where so many of their assailants had fallen, and then, in sight of the Union troops, they recrossed the parapet, prisoners of war, to remain within our lines until paroled.

Gen. Grant rode into the town with his staff, at the head of Logan's division, which had approached nearest the Confederate lines, about the center. We marched with the division. The flag of the 55th Illinois was planted on the Court House in Vicksburg and the free navigation of the Mississippi was assured.

It was a glorious Fourth. Dispatches brought the news of Meade's great victory far away among the hills of Pennsylvania. The throb of the National pulse became stronger and wise men saw the beginning of the end. The Fourth of July was vindicated in the eyes of the world.

GROUP OF OFFICERS.

Chapter V.

AFTER the surrender of Vicksburg, the regiment went into camp on a high hill inside the Confederate lines and to the northwest of Fort Hill, overlooking the graveyard road. Along this valley road supplies were passed from Vicksburg to Pemberton's left wing during the siege. In this valley our sharp shooters had killed "Price's camel," used as a pack animal by the Confederates. His skeleton was picked up and his bones made into finger rings and other ornaments and sold to curiosity hunters from the North. When the supply was exhausted, the bones of cattle slain for beef were substituted, the souvenir fiend being fully satisfied they were a part of "Price's camel."

The tree under which Grant and Pemberton met was dug up, every root and limb carried away as keep-sakes and mementoes of the great event. Blocks and limbs from other trees found their way into the curiosity market and were readily accepted as parts of the famous tree.

The importance of the great campaign was recognized at Washington. Gen. Halleck wrote to Gen. Grant as follows:

"Your report dated July 6, of your campaign ending in the capitulation of Vicksburg, was received last evening. Your narration of the campaign, like the operations themselves, is brief, soldierly, and, in every respect creditable and satisfactory. In boldness of plan, rapidity of execution, and brilliancy of routes, these operations will compare most favorably with those of Napoleon about Ulm. You and your army have well deserved the gratitude of your country, and it will be the boast of your children that their fathers were of the heroic army which re-opened the Mississippi River."

The greatness of the achievements are better illustrated by the comparative losses of the two armies. Confederates: Prisoners, 42,000; killed and wounded, 12,000; stragglers, 6,000; total, 60,000.

Gen. Grant's total loss in killed and wounded did not reach 10,000.

The enemy never recovered from the hard blow struck at Vicksburg. The prisoners who were paroled were lost to the Confederacy, and nearly all of them escaped the possibility of exchange. They had had enough, and communicated their demoralization to other parts of the army and to the inhabitants of the South. The Union troops, on the other hand, were correspondingly elated with victory, and their spirits mounted to high water mark. The privations had been great, but their faith in their cause, themselves and their chiefs, had been sublime. Gen. Badeau thus describes the soldiers of that army: "The rank and file, especially, were not fighting for fame. They knew that most of them could have no chance for promotion, although here and there, those who distinguished themselves might rise, and did rise. Yet, doubtless, gallant deeds were done that never found a chronicler. Doubtless, undeveloped talent lay hidden during all these campaigns under many a private's coat. Doubtless, glory was often won, and the costly price not paid. This the soldiers knew had been and felt must be again. Yet they fought, and marched, and worked and died as willingly as those to whom the great prizes were incentives. They did this not only under the stimulating enthusiasm which drove them to the field in the first days of the war, but in the weary months of the long spring of 1863, under the piercing blasts and pelting storms of Donelson, and in the scorching heats and sickening atmosphere of Vicksburg. Without the excitement of danger, as well as in the very presence of quick coming death, they persisted in doing all that was necessary to accomplish the end they set out to gain."

Within a week after entering the Confederate lines, the work of paroling thirty-two thousand men had been completed and without arms, in sad dejection they passed out of their camps in charge of their officers to the parol camps assigned them. All hope was gone and their humiliation wrung tears from the eyes of the victors.

Port Hudson had fallen on the 8th of July. Sherman went after Joe Johnston, pushing him through Jackson, across the Pearl River and beyond. It was desirable to broaden the area between the two halves of the Confederacy and expeditions for that purpose moved out from different points

on the river east and west. The 31st regiment was with one
of these expeditions sent out under Gen. Stephenson to Monroe, La., late in the summer of 1863, which proceeded as far
as Monroe and the Wachita River. The march out and the return was without incident save the suffering from the autum-
nal heat and the want of water. The river bottoms in most
places were dry and men drank water from the loathsome la-
goons and bayous along the line of march. Stagnant water
from pools, and even horse tracks where it was held, was
drunk by thirsty soldiers. At the Wachita, better water from
the clear rippling river was procured. Here a warehouse of
Louisiana rum was found, and, in spite of all precautions by
the officers, was appropriated by the men, who, in their exhil-
eration lit up the banks of the Wachita with bonfires around
which they cooked their rations, told stories, sang songs and
drank their rum, with evident satisfaction. We returned to
Vicksburg by the route we had marched out. The entire
country along the line of march was uninviting, even repul-
sive. In the open fields the cotton stalks and cockle burs
stood six feet high. The air was oppressive and the sun's
rays dense and sickening. We returned to the old camp at
Vicksburg, where, soon after, a fearful malady called break
bone fever spread over the camp. Hospitals were so crowded
that many got such treatment only as could be afforded in
their camps. At one time there were not five men in the
company fit for duty. Weeks were required before the
victims of this fever could walk without pain, after a pro-
tracted convalescence.

W. W. Largent, Captain Co. B.

The regiment was afterwards removed to a better camp twelve or fifteen miles east on the west side of the Big Black River, the scene of Lawler's battle of May 17. The Confederate cavalry occupied camps a few miles out on the east side. The time occupied here was in the main pleasant and profitable. Here the men were paid off and were constantly occupied in battalion and brigade drill. So proficient had the men become in these exercises that a match was arranged between Col. Pearson and the colonel of the 124th Illinois for a competitive drill. Constant preparations were made for the event and every effort put forth for the attainment of that excellency in movement, soldierly bearing and intelligence in comprehending the movements of the battalion and the commands of superiors as must insure success. When the day came a great crowd of people, in addition to soldiers from the division camps and general officers, were present to witness the movements of the competing regiments. The two colonels proud of their skill and the skill of their commands did all they could to win the prize—an elegant silk banner. Each had sent orders for paper collars for their men and the colonel of the 124th got his order filled. Colonel Pearson, of the 31st, was not so fortunate and the 124th carried off the banner. The judges held that each regiment was perfect in the drill, but the men in paper collars excelled in soldierly appearance. The defeated cursed those paper collars, and the men of the 31st who are now living will have nothing to do with them, even to this day.

While we were in camp at Black River, provisions were made for the voluntary re-enlistment of those whose terms of enlistment would soon expire. A bounty of four hundred dollars was offered to each soldier and a furlough for thirty days. This liberal offer of the government, and the consideration of the great danger confronting the Union cause throughout the vast theater of war, caused the men to respond to the call by tens of thousands and the old 31st was not behind its sister regiments on the 5th of January, 1864. About three-fourths of the men fit for duty re-enlisted as veterans.

The reorganization as a veteran regiment was completed late in the afternoon and then a torch light procession for Brig.-Gen. Force was immediately improvised. The regulation candle was lit, put into the sockets of the bayonets, and the regiments marched to the front of the General's headquarter tent. He was called upon for a speech and responded in a neat and patriotic manner in which he extolled the men for their patriotic devotion to the country in the present, trying hour, as well as for their past valor, and closed by calling for three cheers for the 31st. As no other body of men were present, the regiment stood mute, when Force again complimented the men for their modesty and added, "I command you, cheer, cheer yourselves, boys, hip, hip, etc." The cheers were now given with a will and the men then volunteered a tiger and three groans for the Confederacy. Next day a large amount of lager beer, brought up from Vicksburg, was put on tap and the day was devoted to unobstruct-

ed levity within the camp. As the men were not used to in-
toxicants, many were the worse for wear, with headaches next
day, but the joy of perfect freedom for a day was appreciated
by all. The men were greatly recuperated by camp life at
the Big Black; many were visited by friends and relatives.
Sutlers were in the camp, and tobacco, stationery, canned
fruit, dried beef, etc., could be purchased, at a high price it
is true, but the price was not considered by the soldiers who
had money. Small change was scarce. Hard money was unknown and the men not infrequently tore a new green back
dollar bill in two to make change. The holders of odd halves
were afterwards losers, as the government properly refused
to honor the mutilated bills.

While here the men lived in "dog tents," but they made
their quarters larger and more comfortable by making walls
of boards and covering the top with the "dog tents," used as
flies, four put together, making very comfortable quarters.
Sometimes they were still further enlarged and rude fire
places constructed and attached to them. Our comforts were
not to be of long duration. The climate was favorable to
winter campaigning. The battles about Chattanooga and
Lookout Mountain had been fought on the 23d and 25th of
November, 1863. Bragg had retired into Northern Georgia.
Knoxville had been relieved and Longstreet was in winter
quarters in East Tennessee. The severity of the winters in
East Tennessee and Northern Georgia are such as to make
military operations exceedingly hazardous in the mountains
at this inclement season. So it was determined that Gen.

Sherman should make an expedition march from Vicksburg
to Meridian, utterly destroy all the railroads east and
south of that place, uncover Mobile, and, if a favorable opportunity was presented, to invest and capture it.   This
movement was to be supported by a large cavalry force from
Corinth and Memphis, which moving south upon Meridian,
would form junction there with Sherman's army.   The
cavalry was commanded by Gen. William Sody Smith, but he
never reached Meridian and ended his campaign in disgrace.

The Vicksburg column began the movement on the 3d
of February and skirmished almost continuously with the
divisions of Loring and French who sought to form a junction at Jackson with Lee's cavalry.   The movement was so
rapid that they were not permitted to accomplish their purpose. We pushed through Jackson and across the Pearl River
as rapidly as possible and took the most direct roads to Meridian, where the troops arrived on the 15th, and on the following day a systematic work of destruction was begun. For
five days, ten thousand men were at work with crow bars,
hammers, and axes, tearing up the tracks, burning the railroad ties and bridges, heating and twisting the rails, tearing
up the trestles and doing all manner of damage to public
property within sixty miles east and south of Meridian. It
was impossible, without the cavalry, to overtake the enemy
on the east of the Tombigbee River; hence on the 20th we began the return march on the main road with McPherson,
while another column moved north of us in the same direction to feel for Sody Smith and his cavalry.   He was not

W. A. LOONEY, CAPTAIN CO. C.

found, having been whipped by Forrest, he had hastened back
to Memphis. The Meridian expedition, however, had cleaned
out Mississippi, not only of armed enemies, but of nearly
everything else. We were in and about Canton on the return till about the 3d of March and returned thence to Vicksburg where the veterans on the 19th of March, 1864, received their promised furloughs and were at once transported
by steamers to Cairo, thence by the Illinois Central railroad
to the various stations most convenient to their homes.
There is no record of their history while at home, save that
which is held in dim but delightful memory by survivors,
relatives and friends. To most of them it was a continuous
gala day for one whole month; visiting, feasting, love making,
renewing of old family ties and meetings with friends and
school mates that had been separated during these years of
fateful strife. The veterans on furlough were welcomed everywhere they went, and whether at church, the public meeting, or the gathering of the young folk at the evening party,
every mark of appreciation was shown them. They were
proud of themselves and their work. But the scene was not
unmixed with sadness. Many families were in mourning and
many households had a vacant chair. Wives, mothers,
sisters, brothers, and fathers inquired for the missing ones
who were at rest on distant battlefields. To them the old
Union of the fathers was even dearer than before it had been
consecrated in the blood of their families and friends, and
they realized that great progress had been made in the struggle for preservation. They remembered also that the Con-

federate armies were still in the field, proud, defiant and determined, and that before there could be full restoration of
the seceded states to the Union, other battles must be fought
and these hostile armies destroyed, dispersed or captured,
their resources broken up and their power overthrown; that
these sons must soon return to set their faces again toward
the foe. No period could be fixed for their return again to
their families and homes, with diminished ranks and shortened line, but the fathers and mothers, wives, sweethearts
and sisters bore themselves proudly and firmly when the part-
ing came and spoke brave and confident words as they pronounced the long farewells. The veterans gathered at Carbondale where an excellent entertainment and dinner was
given them and, the last greetings being pronounced again,
boarded the cars for Cairo, and were transferred to steamers that conveyed them up the Ohio and Tennessee, where on
May 1st, 1864 they rendezvoused at Clifton on the southern
banks of that historic stream.

Gen. Grant had assumed command of all the armies of
the United States. Sherman had succeeded to the command
of the military division of the Mississippi and was already
at the front.

Lee with the army of Northern Virginia had pitched his
cantonment south of the Rapidan, screened and defended by
the wilderness. Grant with the army of the Potomac was
on the north side confronting Lee.

Joseph E. Johnston occupied the mountains of Northern
Georgia, covering Atlanta, and Sherman was securing his

positions and making maps and plans of campaign, while thousands of the returning veterans from the North were streaming toward the front by every conceivable and known means of transportation.

It had been announced that the armies of the Union would move forward from every available position on their long lines from Virginia to the Mississippi River, so that a close observer of the situation on the 1st of May, 1864, might have readily surmised that the closing act and final scene in the great drama of the Civil War were about to burst upon the astonished gaze of the civilized world.

On the 3d of May Gen. Grant crossed the Rapidan at Germania Ford and other points, the heads of his long columns turned in the direction of the wilderness where the lion of Northern Virginia had determined to defend his native jungle. Sherman's army was bracing itself against the mountains of Georgia and preparations for the grand attack were all complete.

What followed, in so far as is within the scope of this task, will be the subject of another chapter.

Chapter VI.

N the latter part of April, 1864, Gen. Legget, our division commander, had his headquarters at Cairo and went with his division to Clifton. Here also the division of Gen. Crocker was brought. The headquarters of the army of the Tennessee was then at Huntsville. As we have already hinted the beginning of the spring campaigning had been timed for May 1st.

In brief, the leading features were that Gen. Grant himself should cross the Rapidan and assail Lee in the Wilderness with his army of the Potomac. Gen. Butler with the army of the James to operate against Richmond from the south side of the James River. Gen. Sherman with the armies of the Cumberland, Tennessee and Ohio to move against Joseph E. Johnston, then strongly entrenched at Dalton, and follow him whithersoever he might go, till his army was dispersed or destroyed. Gen. Canby, with all the troops that could be spared from the trans-Mississippi department, was to take Mobile. All other military operations were merely auxiliary and the whole movement contemplated the utter destruction of the Southern Confederacy.

The purpose of the campaign is clearly outlined by the following letter from Gen. Sherman to Gen. Grant:

"Headquarters Military Division of the Mississippi,

"Nashville, Tennessee, April 10, 1864.

"Lieutenant General U. S. Grant, Commander in Chief, Washington, D. C.

"Dear General: Your two letters of April the 4th are now before me, and afford me infinite satisfaction, that we are now all to act on a common plan, converging on a common center, looks like enlightened war. Like yourself you take the biggest load and from me you shall have thorough and hearty co-operation. I will not let side issues draw me off from your plans in which I am to knock Joseph Johnston and do as much damage to the resources of the enemy as possible. I have heretofore written to General Rawlins and to Colonel Comstock (of your staff) somewhat of the method in which I propose to act. I have seen all my army corps and division commanders and have signified only to the former, viz: Schofield, Thomas and McPherson, our general plans, which I inferred from the purport of our conversation here and at Cincinnati.

"First, I am pushing stores to the front with all possible dispatch, and am completing the army organization, according to the orders from Washington which are ample and satisfactory. It will take us all of April to get in our furloughed veterans, to bring up A. J. Smith's command and to collect provisions and cattle on the line of the Tennessee. Each of the armies will guard, by detachments of its own, its rear communications. At the signal to be given by you, Schofield, leaving a select garrison at Knoxville and London, with twelve thousand men will drop down the Hiawassee and march around Johnston's right by the old Federal road. Stoneman, now in Kentucky, organizing the cavalry forces of the army of the Ohio, will operate with Schofield on his left front, and it may be, by pushing a select body of about two thousand cavalry by Ducktown or Elijah, toward Athens, Georgia, Thomas will aim to have forty-five thousand men of all arms, and move straight against Johnston wherever he may be, fighting him cautiously, persistently, and to the best advantage. He will have two divisions of cavalry and take advantage of any offering. McPherson will have nine divisions of the army of the Tennessee. If A. J. Smith gets here, in which case he will have fully thirty thousand of the best men in America, he will cross the Tennessee at Decatur and Whitesburg, march toward Rome, and feel for Thomas. If Johnston falls behind the Coosa, then McPherson will cross over and join Thomas.

"McPherson has no cavalry, but I have taken one of Thomas' division, viz: Garrard's, six thousand strong, which is now at Columbia, mounting, preparing and equipping. I desire this division to operate on McPherson's right, rear or front, according as the enemy appears. But the moment I detect Johnston falling behind the Chattahoochie, I propose to cast off the effective part of this cavalry division, after crossing the Coosa, straight for Opelika, West Point, Columbus or Wetumpka, and to break up the road between Montgomery and Georgia. If Garrard can do this work well, he can return to the Union army, but should a superior force interpose, then he will seek safety in Pensacola and join Banks, or after rest, will act against any force he can find east of Mobile, till such time as he can reach me. Should Johnston fall behind the Chattahoochie, I will feign to the right, but pass to the left, and act against Atlanta, or its eastern communications, according to developed facts.

"This is about as far ahead as I feel disposed to look, but I will ever bear in mind that Johnston is at all times to be kept so busy that he can not in any event send any part of his command against you or Banks.

"If Banks can at the same time carry Mobile, and open up the Alabama River, he will, in a measure, solve the most difficult part of my problem, viz, 'provisions.' But in that I must venture Georgia has a million of inhabitants. If they can live, we should not starve. If the enemy interrupt our communications I will be absolved from all obligations to subsist on our own resources, and will feel perfectly justified in taking whatever and wherever we can find.

"I will inspire my command, if successful, with the feeling that beef and salt are all that is absolutely necessary to life, and that parched corn was once fed to Gen. Jackson's army on that very ground.

"As ever your friend and servant,

"W. T. SHERMAN, Major General."

On the 28th of April Gen. Sherman was at Chattanooga.
Gen. McPherson's troops were rapidly arriving by rail and by
marching. Thomas was out with his advance toward Ringold. Schofield was moving toward Coosa Springs. On the
5th of May Sherman rode out to Ringold and the grand movement began. The General says in his memoirs: "My general
headquarters and official records remained back at Nashville,
and I had near me only my personal staff and inspector general with about half a dozen wagons and a single company
of Ohio sharp shooters at headquarters or camp guard. I
also had a small company of Alabama cavalry used mostly
as orderlies and couriers. No wall tents were allowed, only
the flies. Our mess establishment was less in bulk than any
of the brigade commanders, nor was this an indifference to
the ordinary comforts of life, but because I wanted to set
the example and gradually convert all parts of that army
into a mobile machine, willing and able to start at a moment's notice and to subsist on the scantiest food. To reap
absolute success might involve the necessity even of drop-
ping all wagons and to subsist on the chance food which the
country was known to contain. I had obtained not only the
United States census tables of 1860, but a compilation made
by the comptroller of the State of Georgia, for the purpose of
taxation, containing in considerable detail the 'population
and statistics' of every county in Georgia. One of my aids
acted as assistant adjutant general, with an order book, letter book and writing paper that filled a small chest not much
larger than an ordinary candle box. The only reports called

S. C. MOONINGHAM, CAPTAIN CO. C.

for were the ordinary tri-monthly returns of 'effective strength.' As these accumulated they were sent back to Nashville and afterwards were embraced in the archives of the Military Division of the Mississippi, changed in '65 to the Military Division of the Missouri, and I suppose they were burned in the Chicago fire of 1870. Still, duplicates remain of all essential papers in the archives of the War Department."

Thus it will be understood that, from the general to the private, every man was stripped for the conflict and put into the best possible condition for quick and unimpeded movement. This vast army numbered about one hundred thousand men of all arms, with two hundred and fifty-four cannon. The animals, including the cavalry horses, were seventy-five thousand.

From our camp at Clifton, we moved with our division, under Gen. Leggett, and with Crocker's division, to Huntsville, Alabama, crossing the Tennessee River at Decatur on pontoon bridges and thence proceeded in the direction of Rome, Georgia. For part of the time the regiment was engaged in guarding and helping to drive a large herd of beef cattle to feed the army. While our divisions were drawing nearer and nearer to the main army, it had fought its way from Dalton southward and had turned the Confederate positions at Dalton, Resacca, New Hope Church and Dallas; had here and at other places fought obstinately, but all the time guarded and protected its long line of communication back to Nashville.

About the 9th of June our division joined the main
army at Ackworths' Station, and took its position in the line
of the Seventeenth Army Corps, army of the Tennessee, composed of the 15th, 16th and 17th corps, commanded respect-
ively at that time by Gens. Logan, Dodge and Blair.   Its
ranks according to Gen. Sherman were formed of "the best
men in America."

The regiment was in the skirmish firing and fighting
about Big Shanty and Brush Mountain. At the latter place
our brigade formed about the base of this steep spur of Kenesaw Mountain and under a tremendous artillery fire, clambered up its steep and rocky sides, entering the rifle pits at
nightfall, and facing Kenesaw, lay in line of battle on the
crest all night.

The position of Johnston's army on the 10th of June,
1864 was on three prominent elevations known as Pine, Kenesaw and Lost Mountains.   Each was covered with rifle pits
defended by numerous artillery and provided with signal stations. His connected line was ten miles long and was defended by 60,000 men.   The army of the Ohio curved around
the north base of Kenesaw.   The army of the Cumberland
held the center facing Pine Mountain, and Schofield with the
army of the Ohio faced Lost Mountain to the south.   Every
camp of the Federal army was entrenched.   The railroad to
the rear was strongly guarded and at important points block·
houses had been built and manned to protect important
bridges, trestles and the like.   At this season of the year the
Georgia mountains are the scene of thunderstorms that

burst among them, swelling the small streams into torrents, and making the otherwise miserable roads impassable, so that the armies in these mountains in June, 1864, cooped up inside of their mud embankments, or feeling their way forward through mud, across streams and through tangled underbrush and projecting cliffs, could hardly be said to be a body of gala day excursionists in search of pleasure. On the contrary, every day was filled up with the grim realities of war, exposure and death, and could the ten thousand dead, who were buried near by or around the bases of these mountains tell the story of their sacrifices, their devotion, daring and death, it might furnish a chapter for future peace conferences to consider, while debating and formulating their schemes of universal peace.

By the 14th of June the Federal lines, completely entrenched and conforming to the curves and angles of those of the enemy, stretched out in irregular form over hill, dale and stream, for more than ten miles, from right to left. On this day occurred the death of Maj. Gen. Polk. Heavy skirmishing had been indulged in during the day, about the base of Pine Mountain. Sherman happened to be riding along his line at this point, observed a group of men on the crest about eight hundred yards away and ordered a battery near by to fire upon it. Among the group of men upon which the fire was directed were Gens. Hardee and Polk. The latter was killed by this fire and the fact of Gen. Polk's death was soon known along the whole line. The men of our signal service caught and read the signals from the Confederates

on Pine Mountain.   One of them when   translated read:
"Send an ambulance for Gen. Polk's body."   In this way the
secrets of the enemy were sometimes made known.   They
obtained intelligence the same way.

Lost Mountain was abandoned on the 16th and our right
wing swung toward the rear of Marietta.

It rained heavily on the 17th and 18th, but the men toiled
away at their work strengthening the left and center.   On
the 19th of June the Confederates fell back on their flanks
and for a time it was supposed they were crossing the Chattahoochie River.   This was a mistake.   They were concentrating for the better defense of Marietta and their railroad.
Johnston had simply refused his two flanks, covering them
with parapets and adding strength to Kenesaw.

About the 20th of June a strong force of the enemy's
cavalry passed our flanks to the rear to destroy the railroad.
There was heavy fighting on the greater part of the lines on
the 22d, 23d and 24th, in fact, it continued till the 27th, when
assaults were made from the respective fronts of Schofield,
Thomas and McPherson in a vain effort to dislodge the enemy
from Kenesaw.   No man can describe this battle.   It extended along a front of ten miles and was supported by artillery
at every point.   The men skirmished in the woods, clambered
up the steep sides of the mountain where they encountered
every form of defense, musketry, artillery, etc. At places the
enemy had loosened great rocks from their anchorage.
These plunged or rolled down the steep sides of the mountain, smashing whatever they struck.   Shells and balls

W. S. Morris, First Lieut. Co. C.

scalped the high points of rocks and hills, and richocheted among the tree tops of the valley. The army of the Tennessee fought around Marietta and the eastern sides of Kenesaw. Some companies of the 31st Illinois secured and covered with rifle pits a spur far up the mountain. Other companies were in action to the left, midway between those on the mountain and Marietta.

It was a fateful day, the enemy for the most part could not be seen. Secure and invisible, he fired with deadly aim, or loosened the ragged rocks and rolled them down. We did not capture Kenesaw. The men were not driven away, and did not run, but we were recalled and the old mountain, grim and terrible, "dark in its glory, frowned down on the flag of the free," while its assailants gathered themselves within their entrenched lines to await the further orders of their chiefs. Sherman estimates his losses in this battle at twenty-five hundred men, killed and wounded, while Johnston puts his at eight hundred and eight. Gen. Sherman now abandoned the idea of attacking Johnston in his entrenched lines about Kenesaw. Before July 1st Schofield had attained a threatening position towards the left rear of the Confederate lines and Stoneman's cavalry was still further to our right about Sweetwater.

On the night of July 2d, McPherson drew out of his lines and passed to the rear, stretching out down Nick-a-Jack Creek, but the movement was detected by the Confederate leaders and Johnston abandoned his strongholds at Marietta and Kenesaw. Gen. Sherman says that from the 10th of June to the 3d of July, his operations and that of the enemy were really one continuous battle. He estimated his losses during the period at a total of seven thousand, five hundred, and those of Johnston at three thousand, nine hundred and forty-eight.

The movement by McPherson, to the right, compelled Johnson either to attack the strongly entrenched line of Thomas in his front, or move to the rear to protect his crossing of the Chattahoochie and his railroads. He choose the latter alternative but did not, as was then supposed, immediately cross the Chattahoochie, but retired to strongly fortified lines on the north side of that stream and again faced his relentless enemy. Thomas ran up against these works, but they were too strong to be carried by assault.

Sherman says in his memoirs: "During the night Johnston drew back all his army and trains inside the tete-du-pont at the Chattahoochie which proved one of the strongest pieces of field fortifications I ever saw. We closed up against it but were promptly met by a heavy and severe fire."

During the whole of the fourth of July we were in line of battle with the brigade, and moving forward in line, with skirmishers deployed to the front. The firing was noisy throughout the long, hot day, and when, at night, we halted on the bluffs of a deep and rocky creek, the enemy met us with an artillery fire, disputed the passage of the stream and denied our rights to it as a watering place. None had coffee that night unless he surreptitiously retired to a dark ravine to the rear to make it, for the officers prohibited the building of fires that night, as it would have drawn the attention of the artillerists on the opposing bluffs.

By the 6th of July our army had reached points on the Chattahoochie above and below Johnston's entrenched camp. From the high grounds along the river the houses could be seen in Atlanta, nine or ten miles away. Sherman's right, now under McPherson, was at Turner's Ferry. Thomas fronted the entrenched lines with his left below at Paice's Ferry. Preparations for crossing were in progress. Stores were collected at Allatoona and Marietta. On the 13th McPherson was ordered to move his command to the crossings at Roswell, cross over, entrench his camps and prepare and protect the bridges for those who were to follow. The 17th corps remained temporarily at Turner's Ferry, where it was replaced by Stoneman's cavalry on the 15th, when this corps also moved to the crossing at Roswell. In the meantime Johnston again withdrew from his works on the Chattahoochie. Most of Sherman's army had followed at the several crossings, and by the 18th the entire army was moving at a general right turn, forming a line facing Peach Tree Creek. Thomas was on the right, Schofield on his left and McPherson still to his left and toward the railroad, between Stone Mountain and Decatur. He reached the railroad on the 18th and faced west toward Atlanta and began tearing up the railroad toward Decatur. McPherson's column joined Schofield on his right, but between Schofield's right and the left of the army of the Cumberland, there was a wide gap of a mile and a half. This space was still unoccupied on the 19th, at which time McPherson's army was moving in line along the railroad, Schofield along a public road leading to Atlanta, while Thomas was crossing Peach Tree Creek, all converging towards Atlanta. The Richmond Government had become tired of Joe Johnston's mode of warfare. The admirers of the tactics and strategy of Lee and Stonewall Jackson looked at the depressive policy of Joe Johnston as suicidal to their most cherished hopes. They argued that Sherman would have found his Thermopylea in the mountain fortresses of Northern Georgia, had their armies there been commanded by men of the Lee and Stonewall type, who instead of abandoning these natural defenses, would have defended their defiles with small numbers against a direct advance, and with their main force, or large columns of attack, march out through the natural salley ports of the mountains to the flank and rear of the invading army and beat it in successive battles, or so interrupted its communications as to compel its withdrawal. These arguments had due weight with the Confederate Government. President Davis visited Atlanta, removed Joe Johnston on the 17th, and Hood assumed command on the 18th. He then held the rank of lieutenant-general; had been a class-mate of McPherson, Schofield and Sheridan, and was known as an impetuous, daring and accomplished officer, who had lost his leg in a brilliant and successive charge at Chickamauga. Sherman's entire army, perhaps, knew of this change on the 18th. I know that we of the left wing knew it, and Sherman took measures

LEVI B. CASEY, CAPT. CO. D.

to close the gap between Schofield and Thomas. Hood immediately assumed the offensive on the 20th. About noon he made a furious attack upon Thomas.

The report made by Gen. Featherstone, of the Confederate army, of the battle of Peach Tree Creek, contains very full information. Relating to it, he says: "The plan of battle, as explained to me, was as follows: The attack was to begin on the extreme right of the army. General Hood's old corps and Hardee's were both on my right. The troops were to advance enechelon by division, beginning on the extreme right, the first division advancing some three hundred yards to the front, before the second moved. The same order was to be observed down the entire line, from right to left, extending through all three of the army corps. Each division, when it reached Peach Tree Creek, was to oblique to the left and sweep down the creek, and thereby make the attack upon the enemy, one upon his front and left flank at the same time. My orders were to fix bayonets and charge the works when we reached them; to stop for no object, however formidable, but to make the attack a desperate one. I was informed that the same orders had been delivered by the commander-in-chief, General Hood, to each and every army corps. I thought the battle well planned and heard it spoken of by my associates in arms in terms of commendation. The whole corps, so far as I heard an expression of their opinions, anticipated a brilliant victory. * * * Had the attack been vigorously made by all the troops on our right and the plan of battle been strictly carried out, I then believed and still believe, the victory would have been a brilliant one, and the Federal forces on the south side of Peach Tree Creek would have been all either killed, wounded or captured. The orders seem to have been misunderstood by our troops on the right, or, for some cause, not fully carried out."

General Hood says his order to corps commanders, delivered to them in the presence of each other, was "to drive the enemy back to the creek and then towards the river into the narrow space formed by the river and creek; everything on our side of the creek to be taken at all hazzards."

Cleyborn claims that he was hampered by Gen. Hardee's warning to look out for breastworks. Sherman says: "General Thomas happened to be near the rear of Newton's division, and got some field batteries in a good position on the north side of Peach Tree Creek, from which he directed a furious fire on a mass of the enemy which was passing around Newton's left and exposed flank. After a couple of hours of hard and close conflict, the enemy retired slowly within his trenches." It were idle to conjecture what might have happened had Hood's orders been explicitly obeyed. Most of the men who have survived that conflict would incline to the opinion that Thomas—"the Rock of Chickamauga"—would have held his ground with the same stubbornness by which he had succeeded in former conflicts, no matter how well timed and persistent Hood's assault might have been made. But it was not our purpose to go into the details of the battle of Peach Tree Creek, but for the purpose of connected narrative and to observe that the new general commanding

the Southern soldiers about Atlanta did thus clearly make
known his ability and readiness to strike swift and hard
blows in defense of the "Gate City;" that in so doing he did
not mean to remain on the defensive, but having been trained
in what he called the "Lee and Jackson School," he would as
often as he deemed it expedient, take the initiative and
deliver his attacks without waiting for his adversary to
attack him. So within lines drawn more closely around the
City of Atlanta, he marked the progress of McPherson on
the night of the 20th and on the day of the 21st of July, to
see whether in that general's efforts to destroy his railroads,
he might not deliver him a staggering blow.

Every member of the 31st regiment of Illinois volunteers
will remember that we rose from the bivouac in the woods,
a mile and a half east of Atlanta, on the morning of July 21st,
1864, at early dawn, and in a drizzling rain and as the men
were ordered to "take arms," the bullets began to drop into
the ranks. Between this bivouac and Atlanta the Confederates had constructed rifle pits that were defended by artillery, infantry and sharp shooters. These rifle pits in our front
ran along a ridge covered with a skirt of timber, and between
our line and this timber there was a cornfield gently sloping
to the east, the green corn nearly ready to blossom. We
arose from the camp in line of battle and moved forward
with the division and brigade in the same order. The front
of the brigade was swept by a close fire of musketry and a
field battery, directly in front, added its volleys of shrapnel
and grape in rapid succession. We could see the gunners

load and fire and could distinctly hear the "Confederate yell" which our men answered with a cheer. We crossed the cornfield and entered the woods within a few yards of the rifle pit. An order was given for a movement by the left flank, and was obeyed by the greater part of the brigade, but some companies or regiments on the right gave way, and portions of our regiments, mistaking the movement by the flank for an order to charge, pressed forward to the rifle pits. Here less than a hundred men held the reverse of this rifle pit till near night when they rejoined the regiment to the left of "Leggett's Hill," so named in honor of our division general, whose troops had taken it. On the night of the 21st we reversed the rifle pits taken, and threw up others extending to the left of Leggett's Hill, and looking west to Atlanta. Traverses were thrown up along the rifle pits on the flanks of each company at proper intervals. Leggett's Hill was well fortified during the night with parapet and ditch, and cannon mounted within.

The fifteenth army corps, under Logan, was similarly covered with rifle pits and field batteries, fronting Atlanta from the right of Leggett's Hill, and parallel almost with the railroad. The seventeenth extended south from Leggett's Hill, (the nearest approach to Atlanta), with the left bent a little backward, while one division of Dodge's sixteenth corps formed at right angles with the seventeenth. In military parlance the sixteenth corps was refused.

What the enemy was doing on the night of July 21st, and the purpose in view, may be readily understood by the fact that McPherson was about to seize the Macon road and his position on the east side of Atlanta rendered it insecure, so that it was desired to crush him by a decisive battle. Hood says of his purpose in his book entitled "Advance and Retreat," 176-177: "I had summoned moreover to my headquarters, Hardee, Stewart and Cheatham, together with Major-General Wheeler, commanding cavalry corps, and Major-General G. W. Smith, commanding Georgia State troops. The following minute instructions were given in the presence of all assembled, in order that each might understand not only his own duty, but likewise that of his brother corps commanders. By this means I hoped each officer would know what support to expect from his neighbor in the hour of battle. Stewart, Cheatham and G. W. Smith were ordered to occupy, soon after dark, the positions assigned them in the new line around the city and to entrench as thoroughly as possible. General Shoupe, chief of artillery, was ordered to mass artillery on our right. General Hardee was directed to put his corps in motion soon after dark; to move south on the McDonough road, across Entrenchment Creek at Coob's Mills, and to completely turn the left of McPherson's army and attack at day light, or as soon thereafter as possible. He was furnished guides from Wheeler's cavalry, who were familiar with the various roads in that direction; was given clear and positive orders to detach his corps, to swing away from the main body of the army and to march entirely around and to the rear of McPherson's left flank, even if he was forced to go to or beyond Decatur, which was only about six miles from Atlanta."

The reader should be reminded that owing to the dissimilarity in the organization of the Confederate and Federal armies in the West, a Confederate division was in numbers, infantry, artillery and equipment, equal to a Federal army corps; hence the three divisions of Hardee's corps were the equivalent of the army of the Tennessee. From these considerations it will be seen that Hardee's attack was formidable in numbers and equipment, and that to stem the tide of battle about to burst unlooked for upon McPherson's exposed flank and rear, would be no child's play, but must test the skill and courage of commanders, no less than the bravery, intelligence and powers of endurance of the men. The attack thus planned began a short time before noon. Firing was heard first in the direction of our rear extending toward Decatur. Some of our men, picking blackberries in the fields towards Atlanta, were driven in by sharp shooters and skirmishers, and our regiment was ordered to "take arms," while the sergeants were dividing rations among the men. As we did so, loud and rapid volleys were resounding in the woods directly behind us, whither General McPherson had gone to detect the movements of the enemy. As the men fell into line an orderly from Leggett or General Force dashed up and directed Colonel Pearson to move to the rear in column left, in front. The Colonel quickly formed his men, who followed him as the regiment filed right, in columns of fours, into the dense woods behind our line of rifle pits. By the time we had moved twice the length of the regiment, we encountered a heavy fire from every quarter, seemingly. Some of the officers ordered the men to hold their fire, think-ing we had been fired on by our own men. The flag bearer was told to shake his flag. He did so, and was answered by more bullets and the Confederate yell. A right face brought us to front, looking south, but the enemy was in front, be-hind us, and rapidly enveloping the left flank. Another right face, and forward, put the head of the column in the direc-tion of the rifle pits just left. In this order we passed through the woods, regained the works, taking the reverse or Atlanta side where line was formed at will, and the men with their backs to Atlanta prepared for their defenses. They had been closely followed through the woods. Many had heard the "Halt you d—d Yankee S—of a B—." As the assailants pressed on, a battery sent showers of canister and shell through the woods as the men passed, while bullets fell like rain.

Here, while we held these works, we were furiously as-saulted from the east. A Confederate flag went down with-in a rod of our front and was brought into our lines by two or three men who seized it amid a deafening din of musketry and loud cheering in our lines. The volleys sent from this position where the men had formed from three to five deep were too terrible for the enemy to face and they retired be-yond range. The respite, however, was brief. A heavy col-umn now assailed us from the west toward Atlanta. The men sprang over their works, faced to the west, and a few

well directed volleys sent the new assailants reeling backward whence they came. This attack was meant to be sim-
ultaneous with the first. Had it been so timed the result
would have been fearful. A third and enfilading attack now
came from the south, and the entire left wing of the army
of the Tennessee became involved.

A strong column moved along the railroad cut in front
of Logan's fifteenth corps which they fiercely assaulted,
broke through a part of the main line, captured two guns of
Degress' battery and turned them upon the men of that
corps. General Logan, however, who since the death of General McPherson in the morning, had command of the army
of the Tennessee, was near the gap made in his line of the
fifteenth corps, and in person rallied and led the men who
had been driven out of position, and, with Wood's division,
not only re-established the line, but striking the enemy in
flank, swept them back into Atlanta, re-capturing the guns
that had been lost, and adding other trophies to his victory.
At the same time the sixteenth and seventeenth corps having effected a new alignment with the right at Leggett's
Hill, the line now stood at right angles with that of the morning. While it was in this position it was fiercely assaulted
along the south front and about Leggett's Hill, the enemy
planting their standards on the works and repeating their
efforts at every point where it seemed possible to reach the
line, but were at each assault repulsed and driven backward
to the brush.

J. N. Sanders, Capt. Co. E.

The repulses of the confident enemy on the front of the fifteenth corps, and about Leggett's Hill, were the turning points in the battle, and as the July sun sank to the west in fiery splendor, as seen through the smoke that hung low over the field of battle, the attacking columns gradually drew back and night closed upon the scene of blood and slaughter. The men lay down where night overtook them, some among the dead and wounded of both armies, for in this strange discordant conflict, friend and foe had fallen together, or near the same spot, making a strange commingling of blue and gray in ghastly composure as they lay in death around the batteries on Leggett's Hill. Here the men of the 31st fought last on that day. Here they piled their knapsacks and other obstructions in the embrazures of the fort, and standing in front of our own guns repelled the headlong assaults of the enemy with their muskets, and when night brought them respite, they crowned Leggett's Hill, and many seated themselves upon the parapet to catch a breath of air and ponder over the incidents of a hard won victory.

As there is much conflict of opinion respecting this battle, we give here, the report of General Logan to his commanding general, made on the spot while the incidents were fresh, which is regarded as pertinent to the subjects treated, and will be read with interest by every survivor of that conflict:

"Headquarters Department and Army of the Tennessee, before Atlanta, Georgia, July 24, 1864.

"Major-General W. T. Sherman, commanding Military Division of the Mississippi:

"General: I have the honor to report the following general summary of the result of the attack of the enemy on this army on the 22d inst. Total loss, killed, wounded and missing, thirty-five hundred and twenty-one, and ten pieces of artillery.

"We have buried and delivered to the enemy, under a flag of truce sent in by them, in front of the third division, seventeenth corps, one thousand of their killed, the number of their dead in front of the fourth division of the same corps, including those on the ground not now occupied by our troops. General Blair's reports will swell the number of their dead on his front to two thousand.

"The number of their dead buried in front of the fifteenth corps, up to this hour, is three hundred and sixty, and the commanding officer reports that there are at least as many more yet unburied, burying parties being still at work. The number of dead buried in front of the sixteenth corps, is four hundred and twenty-two. We have over one thousand of their wounded in our hands, the larger number of the wounded being carried off during the night after the engagement by them.

"We captured eighteen stands of collars and have them now. We also captured five thousand stands of arms.

"The attack was made on our lines seven times, and was seven times repulsed. Hood's and Hardee's corps and Wheeler's cavalry engaged us. We have sent to the rear one thousand prisoners, including thirty-three commissioned officers of high rank. We still occupy the field and the troops are in fine spirits. A detailed and full report will be furnished as soon as completed.

RECAPITULATION.

Our total loss	3,521
Enemy's dead thus far reported buried and delivered to them	3,220
Total prisoners sent north	1,017
Total prisoners wounded in our hands	1,000
Estimated loss of the enemy, at least	10,000

"Very respectfully, your obedient servant,

"JOHN A. LOGAN, Major-General."

Gen. Hood says in his history of the siege of Atlanta: "My failure on the 20th and 22d, to bring about a general pitched battle, arose from the unfortunate policy pursued from Dalton to Atlanta and which had wrought such demoralization amid rank and file as to render the men unreliable in battle."

In a letter by Gen. Blair to Major Austin, of New Orleans, on February, 1875, color is given to General Hood's statement in these words: "The Confederates were very much scattered and did not make a very vigorous attack and they were fatigued by their long and swift march." General Blair in the same letter says, speaking of the beginning of the battle: "I was only able to reach my line by making a detour to the right and reached it at a point where it joined the fifteenth corps to find the whole of my line fighting from the reverse of my entrenchments."

The retreat of Johnston from the mountains of Georgia and the natural defenses of those regions, was, no doubt, a bad policy, but it is not true that he led a demoralized army into Atlanta, neither was there any lack of vigor in the assault of the 22d. If the one thousand dead that fell in front of our third division around Leggett's Hill could be heard they would tell a different story. The writer of this page saw in the rifle pit of one company of our regiment three Federal and two Confederate dead. This rifle pit from right to left was not over forty feet in length. One of those Confederates lay on top of the traverse where he fell. All around this place, on every side, the ground was thickly strewn with the dead of both parties, and I dare say that those of my comrades who stood before Buckner on our right at Donelson, who charged with Smith at Champion Hill and composed the storming party along the road to Fort Hill, never met a more determined and heroic foe than the men of Cheatham's and Hardee's commands in the woods in and around Fort Leggett, on the east of Atlanta on July 22, 1864. They were soldiers of an heroic mould. Their valor was not surpassed on any field of modern warfare, their cause aside. Every one of them is entitled to the laurel wreath, and of their soldierly qualities all Americans should be proud. They fell proudly in the forefront of battle, some of them on top, or within our works, and the "stars and bars," of which they sung and for which they shouted, fell within our lines and became trophies of the battlefield. What more could they have done?

JAMES PINEGAR, LIEUT. CO. E.

Chapter VII.

BOUT the time the battle of the 22d of July was fought, General Sherman says he was advised to look out for reinforcements being sent to Hood. Continuing he said: "I therefore resolved to push matters, and at once set about the original purpose of transferring the whole of the army of the Tennessee to our right flank, leaving Schofield to stretch out, so as to rest his left on the Augusta road, then torn up for thirty miles eastward, and as auxiliary thereto, I ordered all the cavalry to be ready to pass round Atlanta on both flanks; to break up the Macon road at some point below so as to cut off all supplies to the Confederate army inside."

This movement would compel the enemy to evacuate or risk another battle outside his works.

General Howard succeeded McPherson to the command of the army of the Tennessee, which occupied pretty much the same position as before Hood's assault on the 22d, but on the 27th the army of the Tennessee was moved to the rear of the army of the Cumberland, and by making a rapid night march, the three corps, fifteenth, sixteenth and seventeenth, were in position on the extreme right flank of Sherman's army on the morning of the 28th, and partially covered by logs and rifle pits hastily thrown up. The line thus formed stretched north and south, west of Atlanta, and faced to the east, occupying the high wooded grounds near Ezra Church.

That Gen. Hood was aware of the purpose of Sherman in extending his right is apparent from the following extract:

"Gen Wheeler started on the 27th of July in pursuit of the Federal cavalry, which had moved around our right, and Gen. Jackson, with the brigades of Harrison and Ross, was ordered the following day to push vigorously another body of the enemy's cavalry which was reported to have crossed the river at Campbellton, and to be moving, via Fairburn, in the direction of the Macon road. On the 28th it was apparent that Sherman was also moving in the same direction with his main body. Lieutenant-General Lee was instructed to move out with his corps upon the Lickskillet road, and to take the position most advantageous to prevent or delay the extension of the enemy's right flank. This officer promptly obeyed orders and came unexpectedly, in the afternoon, in contact with the Federals in the vicinity of Ezra Church, where a spirited engagement ensued. The enemy was already in possession of a portion of the ground Lee desired to occupy, and the struggle grew to such dimensions that I sent Lieutenant-General Stewart to his support. The contest lasted till near sun set, without any material advantage having been gained by either opponent. Our troops failed to dislodge the enemy from their position and the Federals likewise to capture the position occupied by the Confederates."

General Logan's report of this battle is as follows:

"Headquarters Fifteenth Army Corps,

"Before Atlanta, Georgia, July 29, 1864.

"Lieutenant-Colonel William T. Clark, Assistant Adjutant-General, army of the Tennessee, present.

"Colonel: I have the honor to report that, in pursuance of orders, I moved my command into position on the right of the seventeenth corps, which was the extreme right of the army in the field. During the night of the 27th and morning of the 28th, and while advancing in line of battle to a more favorable position, we were met by the Confederate infantry of Hardee's and Lee's corps, who made a determined and desperate attack upon us at 11:30 a. m. of the 28th (yesterday.) My lines were only protected by logs and rails hastily thrown up in front of them. The first onset was received and checked and the battle commenced and lasted till about three o'clock in the evening. During that time six successive charges were made, which were six times gallantly repulsed, each time with fearful loss to the enemy.

"Later in the evening my lines were several times assaulted vigorously, but each time with like result.

"The worst of the fighting occurred on General Harrow's and Morgan L. Smith's fronts which formed the center and right of the corps. The troops could not have displayed greater courage, nor greater determination not to give ground. Had they shown less they would have been driven from their position.

"Brigadier-Generals C. R. Woods, Harrow and Morgan L. Smith, division commanders, are entitled to equal credit for gallant conduct and skill in repelling the assault.

"My thanks are due to Major-Generals Blair and Dodge for sending me reinforcements at a time when they were much needed.

"My losses were fifty killed, four hundred and forty-nine wounded, seventy-three missing. Aggregate five hundred and seventy-two.

"The division of General Harrow captured five battle flags. There were about fifteen hundred or two thousand muskets left on the battle ground. One hundred and six prisoners were captured, exclusive of seventy-three wounded, who were sent to our hospital and are being cared for by our surgeons. Five hundred and sixty-five Confederates have, up to this time, been buried, and about two hundred are supposed to be yet unburied.

"A large number of their wounded were undoubtedly carried away in the night, as the enemy did not withdraw till near daylight. The enemy's loss could not have been less than six or seven thousand men.

"A more detailed report will hereafter be made.

"Your obedient servant,

JOHN A. LOGAN,

"Major-General commanding fifteenth army corps."

General Howard in transmitting this report added:

JOHN P CARNES, CAPTAIN CO. F.

"I wish to express my high gratification with the conduct of the troops engaged. I never saw better conduct in battle. General Logan, though ill and much worn out, was indefatigable, and the success of the day is as much attributable to him as to any one man."

During the battle of the 28th our regiment was partially detached and for some time lay in support of a battery of the fifteenth corps that drew the attention of the enemy's field artillerists who converged a very heavy fire upon it. Toward nightfall we were moved forward into a wood and, after some skirmishing, threw up light works of dirt and logs. The two or three days following were spent in getting nearer to the works defending Atlanta. Our final position here was near the foot of a gently sloping hill side covered with gulleys and sedge grass, where strong rifle pits were dug, batteries mounted and the regular siege work begun. We were in point blank range of the batteries, but firing upon our position was in the main ineffective, the depression being too great to allow their shots to strike our line. We were also in close rifle range, as men were frequently killed and wounded five or six hundred yards to the rear when passing in that direction for supplies. During these operations in the latter part of July and the first of August serious disaster had befallen cavalry expeditions operating in the rear of Atlanta and toward Macon. Wheeler had disturbed our communications to a harassing extent, far to our rear, but to offset these, General Kilpatrick and his troopers had ridden entirely around Atlanta, bringing trophies of guns and prisoners, after having destroyed railroads, rolling stock and army supplies, but it had become apparent to the commanding general that nothing less than the effort of the main army could take and permanently hold the railroads leading into the Confederate camps. Their works were too strong to be taken by assault, but if their lines of supply could be permanently taken and held, they must then either whip Sherman's army or abandon their positions around the city, hence the army of the Ohio was now stretched out to our right, and reached the Sandtown road, the twentieth army corps being withdrawn and entrenched about the bridges and crossing of the Chattahoochie and other dispositions made for a movement by the right flank to the left and rear of the strong trenches about Atlanta.

Sherman says in his memoirs: "I now became satisfied that cavalry could not, or would not, make a sufficient lodgment on the railroad below Atlanta, and that nothing would suffice but for us to reach it with the main army. On the 4th of August I ordered General Schofield to make a bold attack on the railroad anywhere about East Point."

The execution of this order was necessarily delayed and the real movement did not begin till the 25th. By the 31st we were within a short distance of the railroad near Jonesboro, and went into line with Hazen on a ridge looking to the southeast, and hurriedly threw up works in a sort of zigzag shape, conforming to the shape of the ground. In this position the line was assaulted, but the front resistance and a charge on our left shattered the attacking columns and the battle of Jonesboro was over.

Mistaking in part the movement by the right flank the Confederates, about this time, attacked the position of General Slocum on the Chattahoochie and were repulsed. On the following day Hood abandoned Atlanta. Lee's corps marched from Jonesboro to Rough and Ready, while we followed the enemy as far as Lovejoy Station.

The news of the fall of Atlanta was hailed with delight throughout the whole country and the President sent to headquarters the following dispatch:

"Executive Mansion, Washington, D. C., Sept. 3, 1864.

"The national thanks are tendered by the President to Major-General W. T. Sherman and the gallant officers and soldiers of his command before Atlanta for the distinguished ability and perseverance displayed in the campaign in Georgia, which under divine favor has resulted in the capture of Atlanta. The marches, battles, sieges and other military operations that have signalized the campaign must render it famous in the annals of war, and have entitled those who participated therein to the applause and thanks of the nation.   "ABRAHAM LINCOLN,

"President of the United States."

General Grant paused long enough to add the following testimonial:

"City Point, Virginia, September 4, 1864, 9 p. m. "Major-General Sherman:

"I have just received your dispatch announcing the capture of Atlanta. In honor of your great victory I have ordered a salute to be fired with shotted guns from every battery bearing upon the enemy. The salute will be fired within an hour, amid great rejoicing.

"U S. GRANT, Lieutenant-General."

These dispatches were communicated to the army in general orders and were received by all with grateful thanks and joyful acclamations. Our arms had been victorious elsewhere. Admiral Farragut had entered the harbor of Mobile. Grant was pounding away at Lee with relentless energy. The core of the Confederacy had been found and would now be speedily eaten up, but there was still grim work ahead. The enemy even in the hour of his dissolution was capable of dealing hard blows and was still entitled to such respect as the vicissitudes of war suggest. After some skirmishing about Lovejoy the troops were withdrawn. The army of the Cumberland went into camp at Atlanta, the army of the Ohio at Decatur, and the army of the Tennessee at East Point. Here the troops found needed rest, and while here, the interesting correspondence between Sherman and Hood, relative to the removal of the inhabitants of Atlanta and the exchange of prisoners, was conducted with apparent acrimony. Sherman's assertion that "war is cruelty and you cannot refine it," may be accepted as true.

The purpose of war is, without needless cruelty to cripple your adversary in all his resources with this limitation: Whatever act, aside from wanton cruelty, tends to weaken or destroy his power, is but the exercise of lawful war, and is justified by the law of nations. Judged by their surroundings and purposes, Sherman and Hood were both actuated by proper motives in this controversy, and each played well his part in the game of war, including the policy claimed as justifiable by one and disputed by the other.

While we were at East Point the several armies under Sherman having been located in their respective camps as heretofore recorded for the employment of rest, our antagonists to the south of us were grouped about Palmetto. The interval, though of seeming inactivity, was not really so. The exchange of a few thousand prisoners had been effected.

The condition of the Federal prisoners at Atlanta had been the subject of anxiety both to Generals Sherman and Hood. The latter had at General Sherman's request consented that a considerable quantity of soap and underclothing, with twelve hundred fine tooth combs and four hundred pairs of scissors might be sent through his lines to these suffering men. The same were promptly shipped by Mr. James E. Yeatman, of St. Louis, but in consequence of subsequent events, the supplies did not reach them till after their removal to Jacksonville, Florida. Military records only show five enlisted men of our regiment to have died at Andersonville, up to this time. How many were, actually, at any one time, confined there, we are unable to state.

General Hood was preparing to move northward, leaving Sherman's army south of him, and had sent Forrest and Wheeler with their cavalry to the rear to destroy our railroads.

President Davis visited Hood at his headquarters at Palmetto on the 25th of September and told his followers that their general should lead them back into Tennessee, recover their lost ground and plant their victorious banners upon the banks of the Cumberland and Ohio. It is worthy of note that by means of spies in Hood's camp this speech was telegraphed by General Sherman to the President of the United States within two days after its delivery.

It seems that General Hood had already anticipated this determination of the commander-in-chief of the Confederate troops. Three days previous, September 21st, he had said in a dispatch to General Bragg:

"I shall—unless Sherman moves south—as soon as I can collect supplies, cross the Chattahoochie River and form a line of battle near Powder Spring. This will prevent him from using the Dalton railroad, and force him to drive me off or move south, when I shall follow upon his rear. I make this move as Sherman is weaker now than he will be in future, and I as strong as I can expect to be. Would it not be well to move a part of the important machinery at Macon to the east of the Oconee River, and do the same at Augusta to the east side of the Savannah River? If done it will be important to make the transfer so as not to interfere with the supplies for the armies."

A glance at the map of Georgia will show that if Hood should succeed in marching his army from Palmetto to Powder Springs and "form line of battle," he would thus interpose himself between Sherman and his base of supplies, and the position of the army at Atlanta would immediately become untenable. Hood well knew that Sherman's army was much weakened. General Thomas was at Knoxville and his army of the Cumberland was scattered among the mountains of Tennessee and Georgia guarding important points. Forrest and Wheeler, with some ten or twelve thousand cavalry, were eternally operating upon railroads to our rear, and a more reckless and daring "batch of devils" were never turned loose upon the earth.

The army under Sherman had been shorn of all useless material. The non-veterans, whose time of enlistment had expired, had been discharged, the sick and wounded sent to hospitals far northward, or furloughed and sent home. In brief, the army about Atlanta was stripped for a fight or a foot-race. The development of Hood's campaign proved that this preparation was necessary. Seven days after the big speech at Palmetto, October the 2d, Hood telegraphed to Bragg: "To-night my right will be at Powder Springs, with my left on Lost Mountain. This will, I think, force Sherman to move toward Augusta. All available troops should be sent there with an able officer of high rank to command."

Hood proceeded to carry out his plans with vigor. On the 4th some of his command, under Stewart, captured Big Shanty Station with about one hundred and seventy prisoners, and General Loring, on the same day, took Ackworth Station with two hundred and fifty prisoners. By the 5th of October Hood had destroyed ten miles of the railroad north from this point, over which we had passed in May and June.

General French, on the same day, demanded the surrender
of Allatoona, where was stored a million of rations for Sherman's army, which we left on the 25th of September to follow the movements of Hood.

Sherman became aware by the 1st of October that the
Confederates were in his rear, between him and Dalton and
his supplies, and he now determined to abandon Atlanta and
march to the sea; hence was about to be witnessed two opposing armies that, after having confronted each other for
six months, have at length turned tail to each other, and are
marching in opposite directions as fast as their legs could
carry them. But the rapid development of facts delayed this
event. Hood must be driven from the railroad so that additional supplies could be brought forward for the men and animals. On the 3d of October Slocum was ordered to hold Atlanta and the bridges on the Chattahoochie and the rest of
the army, retracing its steps of June and July, moved rapidly
to Marietta. Generals Logan and Blair having gone home to
look after elections, our corps, the seventeenth, was commanded by General Ransom, the fifteenth by General Oster-
haus. On the 3d of October these corps camped in and about
our old camps at Smyrna, north of the Chattahoochie. On
the 4th and 5th we passed Kenesaw and Marietta, the scene
of former battles, and crossing a mountain road in the direction of Allatoona, witnessed over the heads of French's division, his sanguinary battle with General Corse who had hurried up from Rome with twelve or fifteen hundred men in

L. D Hartwell, Second Lieut. Co. F.

box cars to assist the little garrison, where he arrived in time to receive French's demand for surrender.

As the dispatches between these generals deserve and will have a permanent place in history, I here produce them. The demand of French was in these words:

"Around Allatoona, Oct. 5, 1864.

"Commanding Officer United States Forces, Allatoona:

"I have placed the forces under my command in such position that you are surrounded, and to avoid a needless effusion of blood, I call on you to surrender your forces at once and unconditionally.

"Five minutes will be allowed you to decide. Should you accede to this you will be treated in the most honorable manner as prisoners of war.

"I have the honor to be very respectfully yours,

"S. G. FRENCH,

"Major-General Commanding forces Confederate States."

Five minutes was ample time for convincing Corse that he and his comrades did not wish to be "treated in the most honorable manner as prisoners of war." He replied:

"Headquarters, Fourth Division, Fifteenth Corps.

"Allatoona, Georgia, 8:30 a. m., October 5, 1864.

"Major-General S. G. French, Confederate States, etc.:

"Your communication demanding surrender of my command, I acknowledge receipt of, and respectfully reply that we are prepared for the 'needless effusion of blood" whenever it is agreeable to you.

"I am very respectfully your obedient servant,

"JOHN M. CORSE,

"Brigadier-General Commanding forces United States."

The attack began at once, on the reception by General French of this reply, from front flank and rear. The signal flag officer from his station flashed the intelligence to General Sherman over the heads of friend and foe—in response to his anxious inquiry for him—"Corse is here." Sherman replied: "Hold the fort for I am coming." The conflict was heroic and the words of French and Corse and the actions of their men have become historic, while the signal response of Sherman has passed into music and song familiar to the church and Sunday school.

French outnumbered Corse three to one, but the position was a strong one and the million rations were saved.

On the 6th Corse sent his dispatch to Sherman in which he said: "Among other things I am short a cheek bone and an ear, but am able to whip all hell yet."

General French, before quitting the ground, converged a heavy artillery fire on a block house on Allatoona Creek, about two miles from the fort, set it on fire and captured its defenders, four officers and eighty-five men.

The 31st regiment marched over the battleground and witnessed the wreck and havoc of the battle, the details of which we have not purposed to write. General Sherman made it the subject of a spirited general order and recommended that our troops, when attacked, should imitate the heroes of Allatoona.

The breaks made in our railroad were serious and extensive, and ten thousand men were set to work to repair them.

The troops of Hood continued their work of destruction, and Resacca and other places on the line were menaced and attacked, but not with the vigor that French displayed on the 5th. By the 10th of October we were in the neighborhood of Rome, marching in the direction of Kingston, sometimes parallel with Hood, sometimes on his flank. He crossed the Coosa River ten miles below Rome and seemed to be bound for Tuscumbia, Alabama. His real destination was Tennessee, but he desired to make Alabama and Mobile his bases of supplies and control the railroads that were to draw them to him.

Forrest had reached the Tennessee River during these operations, and with his field pieces and cavalry, captured two gunboats and five steamers, a brilliant feat of arms for cavalry. Subsequently, however, he had been forced to recross the river at Florence.

Hood was in the Chattanooga valley on the 13th and on the next day our army passed through Snake Creek gap, much obstructed by fallen timber. The marching each day, camping at night, and occasional skirmishing assumed much the appearance of routine work. Each was, in its main features, a repetition of the preceding day. We passed down the Chattanooga valley to the Coosa River in the direction of Gadsden, Alabama, and came to a halt, finding plenty of forage in these rich valleys. By the 19th of October the breaks in the railroad were nearly all repaired. A few days thereafter we left the valleys of the Coosa and Chattanooga, marching back in the direction of Rome. On the road to this place Gen.

Ransom, who commanded our corps, became seriously ill, and when no longer able to ride in an ambulance was carried on a litter. He died at a farm house on the road side near Rome. From Rome his body was sent to Chicago for burial.

Toward the last of October Hood was about Decatur, Alabama, but moved to the south side of the Tennessee, about Florence to gather supplies for his intended invasion of Tennessee and Kentucky. These supplies must reach him from Mobile, Selma and Montgomery, by way of Meridian and Corinth—a tortuous route. The work of repairing railroads still progressed, and from the 2d to the 10th of November the different corps of the army stretched out again on their march from Rome to Atlanta, during all of which time the trains were pouring in to Atlanta ammunition and rations for the intended march through Georgia. As said before the army had been stripped of every thing but its fighting and marching weight, all but the able bodied having been eliminated.

Perhaps more has been said, sung and written, about the march from Atlanta to the sea than about any eventful march of the war, and the great majority of our countrymen have ever been and are yet wholly unable to comprehend it. That the project itself was unique in modern military annals may be admitted.

The dangers attending it were at the time wholly misconceived. The purpose of it, except by a few of General Sherman's closest co-adjutors (not over three), was wholly misunderstood. The wisest heads of the Confederacy were

CARROLL MOORE, CAPTAIN CO. I.

equally puzzled; the world was dazzled and amazed at it, but could not comprehend it. The purpose was not the capture of any particular town, city or stronghold of Georgia, but the primary object was to transfer the fighting machine, the army, to the sea coast; open communication with our fleet; establish a new base of supplies, and march upon the Confederate capital from the interior. The primary object was the capture and dispersion of the public functionaries of the Confederate Government at Richmond, and the overthrow of the strong man whose legions had so long and well defended it. To the unprofessional and uninitiated observer, at the time, the scheme must have appeared chimerical. In the light of results and experience, the strategy, grand in conception, was simple in execution. That results could have been different, no one at this writing would believe. Officers and men had learned in the Vicksburg campaign that an army continually moving might subsist on the country without a base of supply. This experience would now be put to a more severe test.

We have stated the primary purpose of the march to Savannah and through the Carolinas to Richmond. There was also an incidental purpose, or rather there were purposes. These were to mislead, capture or destroy any force that might oppose us. To eat up the means of subsistence in the hostile states to be traversed; to parade a conquering army before the very doors of the inhabitants of all classes; to break the delusive spell that had given them faith in the prestige of Confederate leaders; to scatter and disarm this warlike people, dispel its dream of empire, compel the surrender of their great chieftains, on the march or wherever found and thus assure the fall of the Confederate capital.

The march from Atlanta to Savannah, until within thirty miles of the latter city, was in the main, one long, continuous gala day, devoted to a grand review of Sherman's army. There was nothing in our front that could withstand this army in combat, one single hour, outside of Savannah.

We have said this march was a means to an end, in fact, the Georgia and Carolina campaigns are one, but for the latter, the first would not have found a place in history. The first stage was a gala day, the second stage was equally as severe and terrible as that in which Napoleon accomplished his celebrated passage of the Alps.

The distance from Atlanta to Savannah, as marched by the seventeenth corps, is 290 miles. From Savannah to Goldsboro, by the same corps, 478 miles. Goldsboro to Washington, 353 miles.

On the way through Georgia the weather was fine, and there was hardly enough infantry fighting to delay the laying of a pontoon for an hour. The roads were for the most part in good condition.

From Savannah to Goldsboro the rain was incessant, the roads abominable, the enemy active, and the weather continuously bad. Streams overflowed, swamps were converted into lakes, and all that nature and a vigilant enemy could do to make us miserable, seemed to have been done.

But to return to our narrative. The march from Atlanta to the sea will be the subject of the next chapter.

Chapter VIII.

HE southward march from Atlanta began on the morning of November 15, 1864. The seventeenth corps moved with the right wing toward Jonesboro, the left wing east by Decatur and Stone Mountain. The first objective point was Milledgeville, the capital, distant about one hundred miles. The army was expected to make an average of fifteen miles per day. The right wing was the army of the Tennessee, commanded by General Howard, the left wing, the army of the Ohio, then commanded by General Slocum, consisting altogether of (in round numbers) sixty thousand men of all arms. The habitual orders of march prescribed by General Sherman in field orders, were so far as practicable, to be by four roads, as nearly parallel as possible, but converging at specified points from time to time as might be designated. Behind each regiment should follow one ambulance and one wagon, ammunition wagons and provisions following each brigade. These wagons were loaded with ten days' rations and ammunition enough for one great battle in case of such emergency. The wagons were to have the right of way in difficult places, when the sappers and miners should cut parallel roads to the right and left so that columns might keep properly closed up. Regular details for foraging purposes, under competent officers, to be sent out daily to the right, left and front of each brigade, the forage to be brought to camp for equal distribution. Horses and mules to be taken along the route of march for the cavalry, artillery and baggage wagons. To corps commanders and none others, was delegated the power to destroy such property as might be used for hostile purposes. Promiscuous foraging was prohibited. The prohibition was not always obeyed. The army had twenty-five hundred six mule wagons, six hundred two-mule ambulances. Each soldier carried forty rounds of cartridges and the wagons two hundred additional rounds to the man. A pack mule was usually allowed to each company, but, for the most part, the men carried their cooking utensils. They arranged themselves usually into messes of six. A coffee pot, a camp kettle and frying pan constituted the outfit, as each man carried his own tin cup and mess knife with his other baggage. The knapsack contained underclothing and an overcoat, to which was strapped a blanket, and a section or fourth of a "dog tent." In bad weather, the tent was put up for shelter, but when it was fair, it was used for bedding. This is a brief description of the soldier's burden. These sixty thousand men were in fine condition, inured to toil, and they believed themselves invincible. The initial movement through and out of Atlanta

CARROLL MOORE, CAPTAIN CO. I.

presented an imposing and spectacular scene. I will let General Sherman describe it:

"About 7 a. m. of November the 16th we rode out of Atlanta by the Decatur road, filled by the marching troops and wagons of the fourteenth corps. On reaching the hill, just outside of the old Confederate works, we naturally paused to look back upon the scenes of our past battles. We stood upon the very ground where was fought the bloody battle of July 22, and could see the scope of wood where McPherson fell. Behind us lay Atlanta smouldering and in ruins, the black smoke rising high in air and hanging like a pall over the ruined city. Away off in the distance, on the McDonough road was the rear of Howard's column, the gun barrels glistening in the sun, the white topped wagons stretching away to the south, and right before us, the fourteenth corps marching steadily and rapidly, with a cheery look and swinging pace that made light of the thousand miles that lay between us and Richmond. Some band by accident caught up the anthem of 'John Brown's Soul Goes Marching On.' The men caught up the strain and never before, or since, have I heard the chorus of 'Glory, Glory, Hallelujah,' done with more spirit, or in better harmony of time and place. Then we turned our horses' heads to the east; Atlanta was soon lost behind the screen of trees and became a thing of the past. Around it clings many a thought of desperate battle, of hope and fear, that now seems like the memory of a dream, and I have never seen the place since. The day was extremely beautiful. Clear sun light, with bracing air and an unusual feeling of exhil-

eration seemed to pervade all minds, a feeling of something
to come, vague and undefined, still full of venture and intense
interest. Even the common soldiers caught the inspiration
and many a group called to me as I worked my way past them
'Uncle Billy, I guess Grant is waiting for us at Richmond.'
Indeed the general sentiment was that we were marching to
Richmond, and that there we should end the war, but how
and when they seemed to care not, nor did they measure the
distance or count the cost in life, or bother their brains
about the great rivers to be crossed and the food required for
man and beast that had to be gathered by the way."

The army was now on the march destined to turn up
some where on the sea coast.

On the 22nd of October Hood had broken up his camp at
Gadsden, Alabama, and with twenty days' rations in wagons
and haversacks, and all useless baggage discarded, marched
upon Guntersville, on the Tennessee River, which he crossed
at Florence, and on the 31st of October entered Tuscumbia,
remaining here till about the middle of November when he began his march for the conquest of Tennessee and Kentucky,
his immediate objective being an attack upon Schofield, who
held the strategic points covering Nashville and East and
Middle Tennessee.

We will not now follow him to his defeat at Franklin and
Nashville, and will have no further notice to take of him till
we reach the Carolinas, where he will be incidentally mentioned. He is moving north, we to the south. The two goals
are wide apart. He seeks to scale the mountains that cross

his path, and camp upon the Cumberland River; we, to cross the rivers of Southern Georgia, and camp under the live oaks by the sea.

Our right wing, under Howard, on leaving Atlanta, pursued its march by two principal roads towards Macon and McDonough, and reached the Ocmulgee at Planter's Ferry and crossed over by pontoon on the 18th and 19th of November; thence the 17th corps marched toward and through Monticello toward Gordon. The 15th corps and the cavalry wrecked the railroads. Some fighting occurred at Macon between General Smith's Georgia militia and a brigade of the 15th corps armed with Spencer rifles.

By the 23rd General Sherman had reached Milledgeville with his left wing and took up his headquarters in the executive mansion of Governor Brown, who, with the state officers and Legislature, was hurrying to safer quarters further south.

The two wings of the army—the right at Macon, the left at Milledgeville—were now in close communication and the first stage of the march to the sea successfully accomplished in seventeen days.

An idea of the consternation produced in the South when it became known that our columns were moving to the southern boundary may be had by reference to the frantic appeals of the General commanding the department, from his headquarters at Corinth, for the possession of which we had struggled in 1862. He issued the following appeal:

"Corinth, Mississippi, November 18, 1864.

"To the People of Georgia:

"Arise for the defense of your native soil! Rally around your patriotic Governor and gallant soldiers! Obstruct and destroy all roads in Sherman's front, flank and rear, and his army will soon starve in your midst. Be confident. Be resolute. Trust in an overwhelming Providence, and success will soon crown your efforts. I hasten to join you in defense of your homes and firesides.

"P. G. T. BEAUREGARD."

To starve out Sherman's army would have been a herculean task. After the fall of Atlanta, Governor Brown had recalled Smith's militia from the front, that they might go home and gather their corn and sorghum and store it for the winter. This they had done, as if on purpose to feed us. They were now fleeing from Macon before detachments of the 15th corps to "Rally around their patriotic Governor," himself a fugitive. By the 27th the right wing had again struck the railroad, on renewing the march from Macon, at a point six miles from Sandersville (Tenille Station). Here the 17th corps took up the work of destroying the railroad, while the left wing was moving in the direction of Millen, hoping to release our prisoners there. It was while at Tenille that an officer inquired of a negro if he had seen any Yankees about there, and what they were doing. He replied, describing what he had seen in his own way. First there came along some cavalry and they burned the depot. Then came along some infantrymen and they burnt up the railroad, and just

Capt. S. S. Stricklin, Co. G.

before he had left they had "sot" fire to the well, after completing the destruction of the railroad. The 17th corps continued its march toward Millen, where we arrived on the 3rd of December. As before stated the Federal Prisoners had been taken South.

The Confederate generals had now became aware of our objective points and Hardee was interposing between us and points to the South, supported by Wheeler's cavalry and the Georgia militia. The Fourteenth corps was ten miles away on the Augusta road, while General Howard was south of the Ogeechee with the 15th corps. Generals Bragg and Wade Hampton had been summoned to the defense of Augusta, whither we did not expect to go. On the 4th of December the entire army was in motion upon several roads leading directly to Savannah, now fifty miles distant. The 17th corps moved along the railroad to Ogeechee church, where we found McLane, with his division intrenched, but he withdrew without offering battle, retreating toward Savannah. We followed somewhat more briskly, for, as we neared the coast, provisions began to get scarce. By the 10th of December we reached the defenses of Savannah, and the 15th corps and 17th corps formed the extreme right; the 14th and 20th the left.

We were soon after located on a rice plantation near Cheeves rice mill, where General Howard established his signal station on the left bank of the Ogeechee. To the east of us lay the city of Savannah, screened by timber of semi-tropical growth, and completely covered by extensive intrench-

ments further east of us, Ft. McAllister. A co-operate fleet
under Admiral Dahlgreen, was supposed to be in Ossabaw
Sound to assist in the destruction of the forts and bring us
supplies by way of the Ogeechee. To accomplish this, it was
necessary to first reduce Fort McAllister. Between us and
the defensive works were large rice farms that could be
flooded with water by lifting the sluice gates, which was done.
Some time was spent in constructing and experimenting with
portable bridges to cross the sluice channels. These were
to be carried as far as the men could wade, when, upon lo-
cating the ditch, they were to be placed across it, over which
the men were to be passed to storm the works. The water
was too deep and broad. Several were drowned and the
scheme was abandoned.

While waiting supplies from the fleet, the men of our
regiment subsisted for several days upon rice, which they
first separated from the straw and then pounded off the husks
from the grain in wooden mortars, which they obtained from
the negro quarters near by. Relief came soon on the 12th of
December. General Hazen got his division across the water
and stormed and took Fort McAllister with its garrison and
heavy guns. Generals Sherman and Howard witnessed the
assault from the signal station at the rice mill, and when the
firing ceased went in a skiff to the captured fort. The Commander-in-Chief proceeded in his skiff that night to the fleet
in Ossabaw Sound, where he met Admiral Dahlgreen on his
flagship, and the means of procuring rations for the army was
arranged between them.

Up to this time, two boats in the Savannah River had been captured, but, from some reason, the gunboats of the enemy in the river above had not appeared. The river and harbor were filled with torpedoes that were not removed till the entrance of our troops into Savannah.

On the 16th of December the position of the army was as follows: Slocum's left wing rested on the Savannah River, his right wing joining Howard at a canal. Howard extended to the right of Slocum, with his right wing down the Little Ogeechee. Preparations were now making for a siege by land, the defenses on the water side having proved impregnable against a naval attack in the earlier stages of the war. The strong forts guarding the city and harbor from the sea were Beaulieu, Rosedew, White Bluff, Bonaventura, Thunderbolt, Cansten's Bluff, Forts Tatnall and Boggs, besides others of lesser strength. By December the 17th matters relating to the reduction of Savannah had so far progressed that General Sherman, on that day, made a demand for the surrender of the city and the army defending it. General Hardee promptly declined and declared himself able to defend his position. Our heavy batteries were within three or four miles of the center of the city, which was, however, obscured by a dense forest, and the intervening space was covered with canals, ditches, bogs and swamps. No serious attack or fight occurred after the demand for surrender and General Sherman made a two days' visit to Ossabaw Sound to confer with Admiral Dahlgreen and General Foster about future operations. General Sherman was delayed by wind and low tides, and, upon his return, found that Generals Slocum and Howard had moved their headquarters into the city of Savannah. Hardee crossed the Savannah River into South Carolina, and Savannah became a prize of war as a result of the storming of Fort McAllister and the establishment of communication with the navy. Our regiment soon after went into camp near the suburbs of the city and some established friendly relation with the inhabitants, exchanging flour and bacon and greenbacks with its people for pies, nicknacks and other things which they had to offer. The city contained twenty to twenty-five thousand inhabitants. The houses were old, substantial and comfortable. There were good streets, broad pavements and beautiful promenades, shaded by live oaks and skirted with ornamental trees and shrubbery.

We visited some historic places—Pulaski's monument, and the old stoneware house on Thunderbolt Bay, in which the British used to incarcerate our grandfathers—soldiers of the revolution. A sort of unique reprisal happened to the British while we were in Savannah. A blockade runner, bringing supplies for our enemies with speed and flowing sail, entered the harbor, expecting to find her late friends, and was seized and sent to the prize court of New York as a lawful maritime capture. Sherman's army, if opportunity had offered, would have utterly destroyed the navy yard where she was built. There was no "Anglomania" in that army.

Here ended the march to the sea that consummated the ruin of Georgia. Horses, mules and cattle by the thousands had been appropriated and consumed. Millions of dollars would be required to rebuild the railroads and other public property destroyed, to say nothing of the vast amount of corn, hogs and potatoes that had fed an army of sixty thousand men and five thousand camp followers for forty days. Within the forts, arsenals and warehouses at Savannah were stored two hundred and fifty sea coast or siege guns and other munitions of war, and thirty-one thousand bales of cotton, which was turned over by General Sherman to the agents of the government. The ram Savannah was sunk in the river and numerous other water craft destroyed. General Sherman's field order No. 6 contained a complete summary of events within his military division since the close of the Atlanta campaign and will afford additional interest to this chapter:

(Special Field Order No. 6.)

Headquarters Military Division of the Mississippi in the Field, Savannah, Ga., Jan. 8, 1865.

"The General commanding announces to the troops composing the Military Division of the Mississippi that he has received from the President of the United States, and from Lieutenant-General Grant, letters containing their high sense and appreciation of the campaign just closed, resulting in the capture of Savannah and the defeat of Hood's army in Tennessee. In order that all may understand the importance of events it is proper to revert to the situation of affairs in September last. We held Atlanta, a city of little value to us, but so important to the enemy that Mr. Davis, the head of the rebellious faction in the South, visited his army near Palmetto and commanded it to regain the place and also to ruin and destroy it by a series of measures which he thought would be effectual. That army, by a rapid march, gained our railroad near Big Shanty, and afterward about Dalton. We pursued it, but it moved so rapidly that we could not over-take it, and General Hood led his army successfully far over toward the Mississippi in hope to decoy us out of Georgia. But we were not thus to be led away by him, and preferred to lead and control events ourselves. Generals Thomas and Schofield, commanding the departments to our rear, returned to their posts and prepared to decoy General Hood into their meshes, while we came on to complete the original journey. We quietly and deliberately destroyed Atlanta and all the railroads which the enemy had used to carry on war against us, occupied his state capital and then captured his commer-cial capital, which had been so strongly fortified from the sea as to defy approach from that quarter. Almost at the very moment of our victorious entry into Savannah came the wel-come and expected news that our comrades in Tennessee had also fulfilled nobly and well their part, had decoyed General Hood to Nashville and then turned on him, defeating his army thoroughly, capturing all his artillery and great numbers of prisoners, and were still pursuing the fragments down in Alabama. So complete a success in military opera-tions, extending over half a continent, is an achievement that entitles it to a place in the military history of the world. The armies serving in Georgia and Tennessee, as the local

garrisons of Decatur, Bridgeport, Chattanooga and Murfrees-
boro, are all alike entitled to the common honors, and such
regiments may inscribe on their colors, at pleasure, the word
"Savannah" or "Nashville." The General commanding, em-
braces in the same general success the operations of the cavalry, under Generals Stoneman, Burbridge and Gillem, that
penetrated into Southwest Virginia and paralyzed the efforts
of the enemy to disturb the peace and safety of East Tennessee. Instead of being put on the defensive we have at all
points assumed the bold offensive and have completely
thwarted the designs of the enemies of our country."

By Order of

MAJOR-GENERAL WILLIAM T. SHERMAN.

S. M. DAYTON, Aide-de-Camp.

Chapter IX.

 T has been said in a former chapter that the march to the sea was only a means to an end, the establishment of a new base of supply for further campaigning, the ultimate objective being the capture of Richmond, the destruction and dispersion of the hostile armies opposing the Federal Union, and the close of the drama of war to be brought about by conquering a peace, based upon the continuance of the Union and the integrity of contiguous states.

Supplies of food, clothing and ammunition having been accumulated at Savannah, Hilton Head, Beaufort and other points along the sea coast, the command of Savannah was turned over to General Foster, commanding the department of the South, and the order of General Sherman for the Carolina march was given on the 19th day of January, A. D., 1865. The 17th corps had already been dispatched to Beaufort Island where it had arrived about the 10th of January, quite a number of the regiments, our own among them, having taken

passage on Admiral Dahlgreen's flag ship, The Harvest Moon,
With the greater portion of Howard's wing, we had crossed
the pontoon from the Island of Beaufort to the main land,
and at the time the order for the forward movement began,
the greater portion of this wing was grouped together among
the live oaks near and around Pocotaligo, having taken and
captured the strong works at that point as they were hastily
abandoned on our approach. In the march through South
Carolina, the relative position of the two wings of the army
were the same as in the march from Atlanta; the right wing
under Howard, the left under Slocum.

General Slocum's wing crossed the Savannah River and
entered South Carolina in the latter part of January, but
owing to heavy and continuous rains, the real movement
northward was not actually begun till about the 1st of February.

As is usually the case in military operations, so in this.
It was the object of the commander to mislead his antagonists so that stories were widely circulated of intended movements against Charleston and Augusta, by this army or detachments from it, but in this there was not the slightest semblance of truth. On the contrary, another big swath was to
be cut through South and North Carolina, the railroads to
be broken up and destroyed, the supplies of the coast cities
and defenses were to be cut off, and the garrisons and inhabitants left to shift for themselves, in which event want and
privation would work their ruin and render them powerless

for mischief. Their batteries frowning upon the sea would
be rendered useless and the gunners become fugitives or
prisoners. It was not so much a shooting them out of these
defensive works as it was the eating them out of all the
means of defense. This done, they must quit or starve. Such
are the abominable and inhuman consequences of war, but it
is less inhuman than the slaughter of the men in battle.
Property losses may be repaired, but the dead upon the battlefield are not restored to life.

Our first real objective then was Goldsboro, where an
intermediate base of supply might be established for the
furnishing of munitions and material necessary to the final
march upon Lee's army at Richmond.

The first point of real resistance was known to be the
line of the Salkichatchie, at the place where the Charleston
railroad crossed. Behind this stream and its swamps, tribu-
taries and dense forests, General Hardee, under whose tactics
we had not only been drilled in camp, but in which we had
had experience and instruction in battle, had collected all the
available forces of his department, supported by the indefatigable cavalry of Wheeler and Wade Hampton, and was
entrenched and ready to dispute the passage northward. For
some time, Mower's division of the seventeenth corps feigned
an attempt at crossing in the direction of Charleston.

On the 4th of February Generals Giles A. Smith and General Mower conducted their division through the swamps, the
men wading to their arm pits, crossed over by Rivers bridge,
getting in the rear of the enemy's works, and, driving them

out, captured the position. The rest of the right wing followed and crossed over. The result was that the enemy abandoned the entire line of the Salkichatchie, and by the 7th Howard was upon the railroad at several points, thus severing communications with Augusta and Charleston. From the moment this was done these cities, and the garrisons defending them, were doomed. The seventeenth corps remained on the railroad till the 9th, having made a complete wreck of it by destroying the trestles, burning the ties and heating and twisting the rails so that they were totally worthless till sent to the foundries and straightened out.

The enemy was now concentrating his forces. Some detachments of Hood's old army had reached Augusta under the command of General Dick Taylor, a son of the old hero of Buena Vista. The garrison of Charleston had also united with Hardee.

Our columns were now directed upon Columbia, the capital of South Carolina, while strong demonstrations of cavalry and infantry were made in the direction of Augusta. The seventeenth corps moved by way of Orangeburg, on the North Edisto River, and on the complete destruction of the railroad, this corps was to turn directly toward Columbia which was but weakly defended by Wade Hampton's cavalry, who, it will be seen in the sequel, was abandoned to his fate, it being then the impression of his chiefs that Branchville or Augusta, perhaps, each of them, would be the points of attack. We crossed the South Edisto on the 11th of February, while the columns to our left, after crossing, halted till we

should have occupied Orangeburg. General Sherman, though
a most accurate and able writer, is mistaken in his statement,
Page 275, vol. II, of his Memoirs, that this place was first oc
cupied by the skirmishers of either Giles A. Smith's or Mow
er's division. The facts are, it was taken by the skirmishers
of our brigade, most of them from the 31st Illinois and the
12th Wisconsin regiments. The writer was in command of
these skirmishers.

Orangeburg is situated on some smart hills north of the
Edisto, which, at that time, was flooded with water, the entire
river bottom being overflowed. These skirmishers, after being in the water nearly all night, approached the broken
bridge across the Edisto shortly after daylight, and as soon
as it was repaired, we were instructed that the enemy occupied some lunettes at the foot of the hills at the water's edge.
We then received orders from the brigade commander to
sling knapsacks and swing our cartridge boxes around our
necks, to cross the bridge and deploy in the water, to close in
on these lunettes, but not to fire till within a rod of the enemy.
These orders were carried out. We mounted the hill overlooking the little town of Orangeburg that lay north of some
breastworks between us and the town. While in this position the skirmishers opened fire and we could plainly see persons running about in confusion in the town and about the
breastworks and hear a considerable screaming of steam
whistles.

Then the aid-de-camp brought us orders to raise the yell
and go over the works, which was done in handsome style, the

JOHN W. STEWART, CAPTAIN CO. K.

entire brigade following close upon our heels. On entering
the town, we formed column and marched at double quick
along the principal street toward the depot, deployed into
line, and opened fire on a train of cars loaded with reinforcements. The engineer reversed his engine and was soon out of
range. A few prisoners and wounded were picked up. The
men then plundered the depot which was filled with peanuts,
each soldier stuffing his haversack.

The captors of Orangeburg became the sentries for the
night and occupied a pine forest a mile and a half east of the
town. Their reserve made a barricade of rails at the edge
of the timber on the high road—precaution against cavalry—
and ate peanuts with great zeal and animation and then
rested on pine boughs and blankets from the fatigues of the
day.

Orangeburg, though a small town, is not without ce-
lebrity. It was here that Generals Nathaniel Green and
Francis Marion and their associates formed the plan of their
attack upon Lord Cornwallis at Eutaw Springs, during the
war for Independence, and the country round about is the
scene of bloody foray and reprisals between the Tories and
Marions' men, in the days of our Revolutionary struggle.

The work of demolition along the railroad was again resumed, the familiar piles of burning ties and twisted rails
again meeting the eye as far as could be seen along the railroad track. The poultry, swine, cattle and corn round about
was eaten up, the railroad ruined to the point where it
crosses the Santee, when our head column again turned to-

ward Columbia, to which point the other marching columns were converging. By the 14th of February the fifteenth corps was on the Congaree River, six or eight miles below Columbia. The columns of General Howard were to cross the Saluda and Broad Rivers near their mouths, occupy Columbia and destroy the railroads and public buildings and to march thence to Winsboro, completing the destruction of roads and bridges en route. By the 17th of February General Howard's head of column was at the river, opposite Columbia, and was rebuilding the bridge for the purpose of passing it. A portion of the fifteenth corps had been ferried over. About 10 o'clock the mayor of the city came out and surrendered the city to General Howard. Our regiment crossed to the Columbia side near night fall and bivouaced in sight of the depot and the spires of churches and other buildings in the city. Nearly all were oblivious to passing events, for, notwithstanding we could see the smoke of the burning cotton about the depot and small burning flakes carried by the wind toward the city, few, if any of us, expected that morning would find the City of Columbia in ashes.

Most of our men passed the night in sleep, but some of the more hardy entered the city and were with Generals Howard and Logan in their fruitless attempts to extinguish the flames and save the city. Some of the more reckless entered the liquor houses and added to the confusion by becoming intoxicated. These men, of various regiments were picked up during the night and corralled. We marched past them on the day after, and they presented rath-

er a sorry spectacle under guard and suffering as they were
for want of rest. General Sherman says the seventeenth
army corps did not enter the City of Columbia at all. Whether this means as organized, I do not know, but I do know that
the 31st Illinois did march directly through the central part
of the city, the morning after the fire, and I am not aware
that we had been detached from the rest of the brigades and
divisions of that corps.

At Columbia, we were joined by some of our men who had
been prisoners at Charleston, and, here also, were found the
foundries and factories for the manufacture of Confederate
money. All were destroyed, but much of the money, in various stages of manufacture, was taken by the soldiers and
sent north as mementoes of the destruction of the capital of
South Carolina. The shells, cannon and other munitions of
war found at Columbia were dumped into the Saluda River,
and the heads of column turned in the direction of Winsboro,
through which we passed on the 22d of February, having been
preceded by General Slocum with the left wing. The Confederate leaders began concentrating at Charlotte, but were
again misled, while we pushed on to Fayetteville via Cheraw
The Catawba River flowed across our path at flood tide, and,
after the greater portion of the army had crossed it, the
bridges were washed away, leaving an army corps on the
south side, and causing a halt till the accident could be repaired. The invasion of South Carolina was now yielding fruit.
Wilmington had experienced the fate of Charleston, and had
surrendered on the 22d, while Hardee was now hastening to

the defense of Cheraw which was entered by our foragers about the 1st or 2d of March. The enemy mistaking these foragers for the vanguard, and expecting an immediate attack, burned the bridges across the Pedee and struck out for Fayetteville. Stores and munitions had been sent to Cheraw from Charleston and other coast cities. These fell into our hands. As soon as pontoons could be laid, the right wing under Howard, crossed over and moved directly upon Fayetteville, the seventeenth corps having the extreme right, and the most direct road. Most of Hardee's troops were scattered to our left and rear or grouped about Charlotte. The march upon Fayetteville was a repetition of the horrors of the Salkiehatchie. Water had to be waded, roads corduroyed, streams bridged, and obstructions eliminated or turned, but the troops never slacked in their ardor, but kept right on. At times, they struck up a song that rolled down the column from front to rear, or, when some ludicrous scene was passing, they started a cheer that traversed the entire length of the column, before it died out.

Kilpatrick's cavalry and the foragers had some severe fighting with Wade Hampton's cavalry, but beyond this there was no serious fighting and the army closed in on Fayetteville on the 11th of March, establishing connection with General Terry at Wilmington by way of the Cape Fear River. A steamboat came up on the 12th and brought tidings of the outside world, from which it was learned that the Confederacy was going to pieces all around us.

The army was now well established on the soil of North Carolina and arrangement was made for the next stage of the march which must virtually end the war. To this end Goldsboro was to be occupied and the railroads repaired from Wilmington and Newburn, also to the end that the soldiers, now badly in need of shoes and clothing, could be supplied preparatory to the final move upon Richmond. It was now necessary, however, that future movements be conducted with celerity and caution. Our old antagonist, Joseph E. Johnston, had again found favor at Richmond and was now in command of all the troops of the Confederacy destined to oppose the progress of this army. A magnificent state arsenal with twenty-five cannon and thirty-six hundred barrels of powder had been destroyed at Cheraw, forty-three cannon had been dumped into the river at Columbia. At Fayetteville were twenty guns and a fine United States arsenal. All were utterly destroyed. Refugees and negroes, by the thousands, who had followed our march, were sent from Fayettville to Wilmington and other coast towns and cities, and, again stripped as for a foot race, the army crossed the Cape Fear River, and began a cautious march toward Raleigh and Goldsboro, the seventeenth corps still on the right flank. At the same time, Generals Schofield, at Newburn, and Terry at Wilmington, also directed their commands to Goldsboro. General Slocum's column moved along Cape Fear River toward Raleigh, and on the 16th of March encountered Hardee with a strong column at Averysboro, where a sharp battle occurred between him and the twentieth corps, supported by Kilpatrick's cavalry. Hardee fell back in the direction of Bentonville. From Averysboro the left wing turned east towards Goldsboro, but on the 18th it ran up against the now concentrated and well posted enemy near Bentonville. The right wing was now turned to the west to form a junction with Slocum and the time was spent in deployments and skirmishing, till the 21st of March, in order that Generals Terry and Schofield might reach Goldsboro with needed supplies. On that day, in dark and drizzling rain, we moved upon Johnston with Mower's division, the greater portion of which broke through the enemy's line and had nearly reached his communications with the rear, when it was recalled by General Sherman, who by reason of the murky weather and obscure position of the enemy, did not fully comprehend the peril of Johnston's army. The position of our regiment during the day was on the left of Mower, on the skirmish line, and in the mud trenches.

The aggregate loss of our army was one thousand, six hundred and four men and officers. That of the enemy, two thousand, three hundred and forty-three. This was the last battle in which the regiment and Sherman's army were engaged. We have purposely omitted the details of this sanguinary engagement, the brunt of which was borne by the fourteenth and twentieth corps of the left wing, and also because the story has been well told by commanding officers of both armies, the most important graphic writer on the subject being Wade Hampton, of the Confederate cavalry, and who, on the day of the battle, held an important command.

The stories of these generals are published in the "War Series" of the Century Magazine, and the technical soldier will find pleasure and profit in their careful perusal. Johnston's attack upon our left wing at Bentonville was bold, daring and discreet, but he had a miscellaneous army collected from Hoke, Bragg, Hardee, Lee and remnants of his and Hood's old veterans. Had the army under him been composed of Hood's veteran battalions that fought at Atlanta on the 22d of July, 1864, we may readily conjecture what might have been the fate of our exposed left flank at Bentonville. But these veterans were no more. Time and bullets, privation and death had thinned their ranks, and the forests around Atlanta and Jonesboro, the hills about Franklin and Nashville, the swamps of the Carolinas, Savannah and Georgia contained their bones. Their leaders were powerless to call them to arms, their crests no longer blaze in the battle front, their names were but the echoes of a lost cause.

From the battlefield of Bentonville, Sherman's army again marched toward Goldsboro, where General Terry had already arrived with the 10th corps, and railway communications were established with Newburn and Wilmington.

By the 24th of March the entire army was grouped about Goldsboro. We were now nearing the field of General Grant's operations, and with the accession of the commands of Schofield and Terry, now with us, and a few weeks' supplies which were being accumulated, Sherman's army would be able to whip Lee should he escape from his trenches and move southward from Richmond and attack us with the allied armies of himself and Johnston. This campaign was, in some respects, more remarkable than any recorded in history. A march of four hundred and twenty-five miles had been accomplished by an army of sixty thousand men in mid-winter in fifty days. Five great rivers, extensive pine forests, and numerous swamps had been traversed, hundreds of miles of corduroy had been made, roads cut through swamp and forest, while the soldiers had, in the main, subsisted off of the country. Arriving at Goldsboro, many of the soldiers were barefooted and ragged, with faces blackened by the smoke of the resinous camp fire, around which they had bivouaced. Much of the time they had been wet, cold and hungry, wading water, sometimes to their necks, sleeping on the ground or on wet pine boughs. They presented at the end of this long march a picture of hardy endurance and grim determination that had not been witnessed in modern civilization for fifty years, and never before on this continent, by so large a body of men. Animated by the nearing of the end, cheered by the hope of a reunited country, and the elimination of all cause of quarrel among a people of homogeneous pursuits, they endured the present suffering and caught assuring glimpses of the grandeur of the coming future, when the states of this Union should consecrate their efforts to the building of a lasting peace.

For a hundred years the civilized world had gazed with admiration upon the picture of Napoleon at the passage of the Alps, about which the venerable and gifted Sir Walter Scott has written that "no soldier except the French could

GROUP OF SOLDIERS, CO. G.

have endured such a march," and that "no general but Napoleon would have required it at their hands."

The march over Mount St. Bernard was truly a remarkable and dazzling military feat, but it was accomplished in a few hours, and the French army entered the plains of Italy, the most delightful climate in Europe where they soon forgot the few brief hours of the horrors that had been left behind. The privations of Sherman's army were endured for fifty days and only such constitutions as had become immune to suffering could long survive the strain of the appalling march through the Carolinas.

Johnston's army withdrew from Bentonville in good order for the defense of Raleigh, while that of Sherman sought needed rest and recuperation at Goldsboro. Here we were supplied with clothing, rations and all things needful for the final push against the last armies of the Confederacy.

While we were about Goldsboro, preparing for the last move on the military chess board, the following order was promulgated at Washington, which so well reflects the results of the movements of Sherman's army, that we give it in full:

GENERAL ORDER NO. 50.

War Department, Adjutant-General's Office.

Washington, D. C., March 27th, 1865.

Ordered—1. That at the hour of noon on the 14th day of April, 1865, Brevet Major-General Anderson will raise and plant upon the ruins of Fort Sumter, in Charleston Harbor, the same United States flag which floated over the battlements of that fort during the Confederate assault, and which was lowered and saluted by him and the small force of his command when the works were evacuated on the 14th day of April, 1861.

2. That the flag when raised, be saluted by one hundred guns from Fort Sumter, and by a national salute from every fort and Confederate battery that fire upon Fort Sumter.

3. That suitable ceremonies be had upon the occasion, under the direction of Major-General William T. Sherman, whose military operations compelled the Confederates to evacuate Charleston, or in his absence, under the charge of Major-General O. A. Gilmore, commanding the department. Among the ceremonies will be the delivery of a public address by the Rev. Henry Ward Beecher.

4. That the naval forces at Charleston, and their commander on that station, be invited to participate in the ceremonies of the occasion.

By order of the President of the United States.

EDWARD M. STANTON, Secretary of War.

While this order was being written General Sherman was at City Point in conference with General Grant, arranging plans for the final capture or dispersion of Lee's and Johnston's armies. The ceremonies, however, were carried out on April 14th, while General Sherman who cared nothing for display or ceremony was at Raleigh, N. C., dictating orders for the movements of his army. The 14th was celebrated throughout the United States and General Anderson's old flag went up over the ruins of Sumter amid the plaudits of the Nation.

On April 5th General Sherman had communicated to his army commanders his orders for the next march to begin April 10th, the objective point being the Ronoake River with Norfolk as the new base of supply. But on the same day information reached the general from General Grant at Richmond that General Lee was apparently on the move for Danville. General Sherman immediately directed his columns to fall upon General Johnston wherever he might go or wherever he might be found, and so the whole army began its march upon Raleigh, distant about fifty miles. From his headquarters at Smithfield en route to Raleigh, General Sherman communicated the following order:

SPECIAL FIELD ORDER NO. 54.

Headquarters Military Division of the Mississippi.

In the field, Smithfield, North Carolina, April 12, 1865.

The general commanding announces to the army that he has official notice from General Grant that General Lee surrendered to him his entire army on the 9th instant at Appomattax Court House, Virginia. Glory to God and our country, and all honor to our comrades in arms toward whom we are marching.

A little more labor, a little more toil on our part, the great race is won, and our Government stands regenerated after four long years of war.

W. T. SHERMAN, Major-General Commanding.

By the 14th of April the army had closed in and around Raleigh with Johnston's army a few miles off. On the same day he sent to General Sherman a flag of truce looking to a meeting between the two generals, to arange terms of surrender. They met between the two armies, each with his staff, at the house of Mr. Bennett, and General Sherman informed General Johnston of the assassination of President Lincoln, on the evening of April 14th, the fact having been concealed by him from his officers and the army. On his way back to Raleigh General Sherman showed the dispatch announcing the death of Mr. Lincoln to General Logan, and precautionary measures were taken to prevent lawless acts of violence and vandalism that the general feared might follow the announcement of the terrible crime.

It is not our purpose to enter into a review of the negotiations that took place between Generals Johnston and Sherman, the bitter acrimony of the public press that followed, the unjust assault upon General Sherman and the ill feeling and estrangement between him and the great war secretary. The result of it all was the surrender of all the troops under General Johnston's control on the 26th day of April, 1865. Of this number there were present with General Johnston 36,817, and in other portions of his department 52,453, an aggregate of 89,270.

To General Schofield, with headquarters at Raleigh, was confided the duty of carrying out the terms of surrender. He was also made military governor of North Carolina, and with this winding up of the ball, the war was over. The scene will now be shifted. We will pass from the field of bloodshed and destruction to the peaceful and orderly homeward march,

LOUIS McKANEY, CORPORAL Co. C.

pausing long enough at Petersburg, Richmond and Fredricksburg to note the havoc that war had made, thence across the
Potomac and to the grand triumphal review at Washington
and the final muster out in the prairie state, which must be
the last chapter of our task.

Chapter X.

T the conclusion of the events mentioned in the last chapter General Sherman left Raleigh for Moorehead City and the army marched by easy stages toward Richmond, no flankers being thrown out to guard against surprise. The foraging ceased while the columns were confined to the principal highways, lined in many places by the paroled prisoners, and officers of Lee's and Johnston's armies between whom and our own soldiers friendly greetings were exchanged. In the early part of May the army crossed the Ronoake River, marched to Petersburg and lingered long enough to gaze upon the elaborate system of fortifications and ditches that had so long barred the entrance to Richmond. At Manchester on the west side of the James River, we camped for a few days and in the interval of renewing the march many of the men visited the capital, Libby Prison, Castle Thunder and other noted places. Standing on the steps of the capitol, and looking at the bronze statuary placed there in past bellum times, and that had been the pride of the old Union, a thousand memories rushed upon the mind. Yonder stands the heroic figure of Patrick Henry, scroll in hand, on which was printed his famous words "Give me liberty or give me death," and close by him the bronze Andrew Jackson that recalled his immortal declaration "By the eternal, the Union must and shall be preserved," so that the looker on reverently rejoiced that the historic oath of the old heroes had been kept, and that out of the chaos of disturbed relations the nation was now moving toward a more durable union and broader freedom.

On the 11th of May the left wing, under Slocum, crossed the pontoon bridge over the James, and was followed by the right wing, army of the Tennessee, under General Logan, now commanding, since the assignment of General Howard to take charge of the freedman's bureau.

By the 12th the march of the right wing began in earnest on the most direct route to Washington via Fredricksburg.

The route was one continuous scene of the wreck and havoc of four years of war and devastation, long lines of earthworks stretched in every direction, over hill and valley, while the low lands were traversed in every conceivable direction by the inevitable corduroy road. Farms were fenceless and for want of cultivation, foul and uninviting. The camps where thousands had congregated were filled with stench and malaria. Small and sluggish streams were polluted with deadly offal by the bodies of dead animals, in some were the remains of men.

Fredricksburg presented a ghastly and sickening appearance. Suggestive of ghosts it was a city of chimneys without houses. The beginning of Burnside's battle had raged through the streets of the town, the crossing of the Rappahannock by his advance was effected in open boats and barges. Barksdale's brigade, of Mississippi, sharp shooters, were in the houses, behind brick walls, in secluded alleys behind curb stones and in walled gardens. They fired from every direction. Fredricksburg became a slaughter pen, but in spite of this the Federal troops effected the crossing, passed through the town and were hurled to destruction against Marye's Heights. These heights were defended by stone fences, and against these stone walls the brigades of Burnside were powerless. Repeated assaults were followed by repeated repulses. It became necessary for Burnside to recross the river, while the Confederate cannon added to their discomfiture. Fredricksburg was in the line of fire, spared by neither friend nor foe. The houses were battered down, the garden walls were levelled, the very side walks were seamed and ripped with shot and shell, great bombs exploded in the streets, making ugly holes, others crashed through the walls of houses, smashing everything.

Such were our impressions of Fredricksburg. It was here that George Washington studied the military art. Here the story was started that he was the only Virginian that could throw a stone across the Rappahannock. From here he marched during the French and Indian war with General

Braddock on that illfated expedition that died with its general on the battlefield of the Monongahela.

Many recollections cluster around Fredericksburg, but we must resume our march through Alexandria, where we camped on the 19th of May.

Then came the order for the grand review of the army of the Potomac, and the armies under General Sherman to occur on the 23d and 24th of May.

The army of the Potomac passed through the principal streets of the city on the 23d, and during the afternoon and night of the same day, the fifteenth, seventeenth and twentieth corps crossed the Potomac to the long bridge and bivouaced in the suburbs of the city, the troops in the rear closing up to the bridge ready to cross on the 24th.

The 24th of May was not only superb because of the delightful weather, but it was magnificent in accessaries of military and spectacular scenery. It looked as if the great republic was on dress parade, the house tops, the windows, the doors and balconies, all available space, around, below, above was packed with men, women and children. They were well clothed. The nation had put on its best. Ten thousand boquets made settings for the picture. Cannon boomed from the forts along the Potomac.

Generals Sherman and Howard, with their staffs, preceded the column down Pennsylvania Avenue, followed by General John A. Logan at the head of his old corps, the fifteenth, seventeenth, twentieth and fourteenth corps following behind in the order named, the regiments in column by company. For six hours and a half, regiment after regiment, brigade after brigade and division after division passed the reviewing stand of the President and his cabinet, then out to the camps newly assigned them on the north side of the Potomac.

After this splendid pageant had vanished men no longer wondered at the effectiveness of this remarkable organization of sixty-five thousand men, that after a march of two thousand miles, and having experienced every variety of suffering and anxiety known to war, had now at the end traversed the principal thoroughfares of the capital city, moving with the exactness of well regulated machinery, and had retired to camp as if unwearied with toil.

We occupied camps near the city of Washington in and about the old redoubts of General Jubal Early (who so closely menaced Washington at one time), and remained there till June 6, 1865, when we took the cars via Baltimore for Parkersburg, West Virginia, thence to Louisville, Ky., where we remained till final muster rolls and discharges were prepared. Then we were transported by rail to Camp Douglas, Illinois, and there received final pay and discharge from service. All that had not fallen by the way gladly sought their homes in the land they loved the best.

General Sherman visited his troops at Louisville, Ky., for the last time, July 4, 1865. He had, however, promulgated his order ending his connection with the war on May 30th, 1865, as follows:

SPECIAL FIELD ORDER NO. 76.

Headquarters Military Division of the Mississippi.

In the Field, Washington, D. C., May 30, 1865.

The general commanding announces to the armies of the Tennessee and Georgia that the time has come for us to part. Our work is done and armed enemies no longer defy us. Some of you will go to your homes and others will be retained in the service till further orders.

And now that we are about to separate, to mingle with the civil world, it becomes a pleasing duty to call to mind the situation of affairs, when, but little more than a year ago, we were gathered about the cliffs of Lookout Mountain and all the future was wrapped in doubt and uncertainty.

Three armies had come together from distant fields with separate histories, yet bound by one common cause, the union of our country and the perpetuation of the Union of our inheritance. There is no need to recall to your memories Tunnell Hill, with Rock Face Mountain and Buzzard Roost Gap, the ugly forts of Dalton behind.

We were in earnest and paused not for danger and difficulty, but dashed through Snake Creek Gap and fell on Resacca, then on to the Etawah, Dallas, Kenesaw, and the heats of the summer found us on the banks of the Chattahoochie, far from home and dependent on a single road for supplies. Again we were not to be held back by any obstacle and crossed over and fought four hard battles for the possession of the citadel of Atlanta. That was the crisis of our history. A doubt still clouded our future, but we solved the problem, destroyed Atlanta, struck boldly across the State of Georgia, severed all the main arteries of life to our enemy, and Christmas found us at Savannah.

Waiting there only long enough to fill our wagons, we again began a march, which for peril, labor and results, will compare with any ever made by an organized army. The floods of the Savannah, the swamps of Combahee and Edisto, the "high hills" and rocks of the Santee, the flat qagmires of the Pedee and Cape Fear Rivers, were all passed in mid-winter, with its floods and rains, in the face of an accumulating enemy, and after the battles of Averysboro and Bentonville, we once more came out of the wilderness to meet our friends at Goldsboro. Even then we paused only long enough to get new clothing, to reload our wagons, and again pushed on to Raleigh and beyond, until we met our enemy sueing for peace, instead of war and offering to submit to the injured laws of his and our country. As long as that enemy was defiant, no mountains, nor rivers, nor swamps, nor hunger, nor cold, had checked us, but when he who had fought us so hard and so persistently, offered submission, your general thought it wrong to pursue him further and negotiations followed which you all know resulted in his surrender.

How far the operations of this army contributed to the final overthrow of the Confederacy and the peace which now dawns upon us, must be judged by others and not by us, but that you have done all that men could do has been admitted by those in authority, and we have the right to join in the universal joy that fills our land because the war is over, and our government stands vindicated before the world by the joint actions of the volunteer armies and navy of the United States.

To such as remain in the service your general need only remind you that success in the past was due to hard work and discipline, and that the same work and discipline are equally important in the future. To such as go home he will only say that our favored country is so grand, so extensive, so diversified in soil and climate and productions, that every man may find a home and occupation suited to his taste. None should yield to the natural impatience sure to result from our past life of excitement and adventure. You will be invited to seek new adventures abroad. Do not yield to temptation, for it will lead only to death and disappointment.

Your general now bids you farewell, with the full belief that, as in war you have been good soldiers, so in peace you will make good citizens, and if unfortunately a new war should arise in our country "Sherman's Army" will be the first to buckle on its old armor and come forth to defend the Government of our inheritance.

By Order of Major-General W. T. Sherman.

L. M. Day, Assistant Adjutant-General.

The colonel who had organized this peerless regiment, now Major-General John A. Logan, had in obedience to orders from the War Department, while at Louisville, Ky., promulgated his final order severing his connection with the army of the Tennessee. It is fitting that it be published in this book as follows:

Headquarters Army of the Tennessee.

Louisville, Ky., July 13, 1865.

The profound gratification I feel in being authorized to release you from the onerous obligations of the camp and return you laden with laurels to homes where warm hearts wait to welcome you, is somewhat embittered by the painful reflection that I am sundering the ties that trials have made true, time made tender, suffering made sacred, perils made proud, heroism made honorable, and fame made forever fearless of the future. It is no common occasion that demands the disbandment of a military organization, before the resistless power of which mountains bristling with bayonets have bowed, cities surrendered and millions of brave men been conquered.

Although I have been but a short period your commander, we are not strangers. Affections have sprung up between us during the long years of doubt, gloom and carnage, which we have passed through together, nurtured by common perils, suffering and sacrifices and rivetted by the memories of gallant comrades whose bones repose beneath the sod of a hundred battlefields, nor times nor distance will weaken or efface. The many marches you have made, the dangers you have despised, the haughtiness you have humbled, the duties you have discharged, the glory you have gained, the destiny you have discovered for the country in whose cause you have conquered, all recur at this moment in all the vividness that marked the scenes through which we have just passed. From the pens of the ablest historians of the land, daily drifting out upon the current of time, page upon page, volume upon volume of your heroic deeds, and floating down to future generations will inspire the student of history with admiration, the patriot American with veneration for his ancestors, and the love of Republican liberty with gratitude for those, who in a fresh baptism of blood, reconstructed the powers and energies of the Republic to the cause of constitutional freedom. Long may it be the happy fortune for each and every one of you to live in the full fruition of the boundless blessings you have secured to the human race. Only he whose heart has been thrilled with admiration of your impetuous and unyielding valor in the thickest of the fight can appreciate with what pride I recount the brilliant achievements which immortalize you and enrich the pages of our national history. Passing by the earlier, but no less signal trials of the war in which you participated and inscribed upon your banner such victories as Donelson and Shiloh, I recur to campaigns, sieges and victories that challenge the world and elicit the unwilling applause of all Europe. Turning your backs upon the blood-bathed heights of Vicksburg you launched into a region swarming with enemies, fighting your way and marching without adequate supplies to answer the cries for succor that came to you from the noble but beleaguered army at Chattanooga. Your steel next flashed among the mountains of the Tennessee and your weary limbs found rest before the embattled heights of Mission Ridge and there, with dauntless courage, you breasted against the enemies destructive fire and shared with your comrades of the army of the Cumberland the glories of a victory than which no soldier can boast a prouder.

In that unexampled campaign of vigilant and vigorous warfare from Chattanooga to Atlanta you freshened your laurels at Resacca, grapling with the enemy behind his works, hurling him back dismayed and broken. Pursuing him from thence, marking your path by the graves of fallen comrades, you again triumphed over superior numbers at Dallas, fighting your way from there to Kenesaw Mountain, and under the murderous artillery that frowned from its rugged heights, with a tenacity and constancy that finds few parallels, you labored, fought and suffered through the broiling rays of a southern midsummer sun until at last you planted your colors upon the topmost heights. Again on the 22nd of July, 1864, rendered memorable through all time for the terrible struggle you so heroically maintained under discouraging disasters, and that, saddest of all reflections, the loss of that exemplary soldier and popular leader, the lamented McPherson, your matchless courage turned defeat into a glorious victory. Ezra Chapel and Jonesboro added new laurels to a radiant record, the latter unbarring to you the proud Gate City of the South.

The daring of a desperate foe in thrusting his legions northward, exposed the country in your front, and though rivers, swamps and enemies opposed, you boldly surmounted every obstacle, beat down all opposition and marched onward to the sea. Without any act to dim the brightness of your historic page the world rang plaudits when your labors and

ner" waved once more over the walls of one of our proudest
cities of the seaboard. Scarce a breathing spell had passed
when your colors faded from the coast and your columns
plunged into the swamps of the Carolinas. The suffering you
endured, the labors you performed, and the success you
achieved in these morasses, deemed impassable, forms a creditable episode in the history of the war. Pocotaligo, Salke-
hatchie, Edisto, Ranchville, Orangeburg, Columbia, Bentonville, Charleston and Raliegh are names that will ever be
suggestive of the resistless sweep of your columns through
the territory that cradled and nurtured and from whence was
sent forth on its mission of crime, misery and blood, the dis-
turbing and disorganizing spirit of secession and rebellion
The work for which you pledged your brave hearts and
brawny arms to the government of your fathers you nobly
performed. You are seen in the past gathering through the
gloom that enveloped the land rallying as guardians of men's
proudest heritage, forgetting the thread unwoven in the
loom, quitting the anvil and abandoning the work-shop to
vindicate the supremacy of the laws and the authority of the
constitution. Four years have you struggled in the bloodiest
and most destructive war that ever drenched the earth with
human gore. Step by step you have borne our standard until
to-day, over every fortress and arsenal that rebellion had
wrenched from us, and over every city, town and hamlet, from
the lakes to the gulf and from ocean to ocean, proudly floats
the starry emblem of our national unity and strength. Your
rewards, my comrades, are the welcoming plaudits of a grate-

ful people. The consciousness that in saving the Republic
you have won for your country renewed respect and power
at home and abroad; that in the unexampled era of growth
and prosperity that dawns with peace there attaches mightier
wealth of power and glory than ever before to that loved
boast.

"I am an American citizen." In relinquishing the implements of war for those of peace let your conduct be ever
that of warriors in times of peace. Let not the lustre of
that bright name you have won as soldiers be dimmed by
any improper acts as citizens, but as time rolls on let your
record grow brighter and brighter still.

JOHN A. LOGAN, Major-General.

ROSTER

THIRTY-FIRST INFANTRY REGIMENT

❧ ❧ ❧ ❧ Three Years' Service ❧ ❧ ❧ ❧

FIELD AND STAFF

NAME AND RANK	RESIDENCE	Date of rank or enlistment	Date of Muster	REMARKS
COLONELS				
John A. Logan	Carbondale	Aug. 10, 1861	Sept. 18, 1861	Pro. Brig. Gen. Mar. 21, 1862
Lindorf Osborn	Murphysboro	April 1, 1862		Resigned Feb. 24, 1863
Edwin S. McCook	Pekin	Feb. 24, 1863	Apr. 9, 1863	Resigned Sept. 26, 1864. Breveted Brig. Gen. 1865
Robert N. Pearson	Springfield	April 3, 1865		Pro. Bvt. Br. Gen., 1865. M. O. July 19, '65 as Lt. Col.
LIEUTENANT-COLONELS				
John H. White	Marion	Sept. 8, 1861	Sept. 18, 1861	Killed at Fort Donelson, Feb. 15, 1862
Edwin S. McCook	Pekin	Feb. 16, 1862		Promoted Colonel
John D. Reese	Denmark	Feb. 24, 1863	Apr. 9, 1863	Died of wounds, July 1, 1863
Robert N. Pearson	Springfield	July 1, 1863	Aug. 15, 1863	Promoted Colonel
William B. Short	Kankakee	July 11, 1865	Not Mustered	M. O. July 19, 1865, as Major.
MAJORS				
Andrew J. Kuykendall	Vienna	Sept. 8, 1861	Sept. 18, 1861	Resigned May 1, 1862
John D. Reese	Denmark	May 1, 1862		Promoted Lieut. Colonel
Robert N. Pearson	Springfield	Feb. 24, 1863	Apr. 9, 1863	" "
Martin V. B. Murphy	Anna	July 1, 1863		Died Aug. 15, 1863
Harry Almon	Pinckneyville	Aug. 15, 1863	Oct. 1, 1863	Resigned July 27, 1864
William B. Short	Kankakee	April 20, 1865	May 23, 1865	Promoted Lieut. Colonel
ADJUTANTS				
Charles H. Capehart	Washington, D. C	Sept. 17, 1861	Sept. 18, 1861	Resigned May 16, 1862
Robert N. Pearson	Springfield	May 16, 1862	May 17, 1862	Promoted Major
Joseph B. Kuykendall	Vienna	Feb. 24, 1863	Apr. 9, 1863	Resigned June 8, 1864
Monroe J. Potts	Harrisburg	June 8, 1864	Dec. 18, 1864	Promoted Captain Co. G
James W. Seaman	St. Louis, Mo	Nov. 10, 1864	Not Mustered	Declined. Com. canceled
Francis B. Thacker	Vienna	April 29, 1865	May 13, 1865	Mustered out July 19, 1865
QUARTERMASTERS				
Lindorf Osborn	Murphysboro	Sept. 8, 1861	Sept. 18, 1861	Promoted Colonel
Michael F. Swortzcope	"	April 2, 1862		Mustered out Apr. 6, 1865
Joshua B. Davis	Pinckneyville	June 20, 1865	June 26, 1865	Mustered out July 19, 1865
SURGEONS				
Emery A. Merrifield		Mar. 1, 1863		Commission canceled
David T. Whitnell	Vienna	Jan. 16, 1863	Mar. 26, 1863	Resigned June 10, 1864
Gustave Suhfras	Collinsville	Dec. 17, 1864	Jan. 1, 1865	Mustered out July 19, 1865
FIRST ASS'T SURGEONS				
David T. Whitnell	Vienna	Sept. 8, 1864	Sept. 18, 1861	Promoted Surgeon
Ebenezer VanDyke		Aug. 10, 1863	Aug. 27, 1863	Resigned Aug. 27, 1864
David M. Dunn	Bethalto	Aug. 27, 1864		M. O. June 1, '65, as H. Stew.
CHAPLAIN				
Jacob Cole	DuQuoin	Sept. 18, 1861	{ Sept. 18, '61 Sept. 18, '64 }	Mustered out July 19, 1865

Non-Commissioned Staff

NAME AND RANK	RESIDENCE	Date of rank or enlistment	Date of muster	REMARKS
SERGEANT MAJORS				
Harry Almon	Pinckneyville		Sept. 18, 1861	Promoted Captain Co. I
Joseph R. Kuykendall	Vienna			Promoted 1st Lieut. Co. B
John B. Raymond	Peru			Promoted 2d Lieut. Co. E
Newton Mount	Vienna	Jan. 5, 1864	Jan. 5, 1864	Promoted 1st Lieut. Co. D
Samuel P. Steele	Mound City	"	"	Mustered out July 19, 1865
COMMISSARY SERG'NTS				
Jasper Johnson	Vienna		Sept. 18, 1861	Promoted 2d Lieut. Co. D
Robert N. Pearson	Centralia	Sept. 18, 1861	"	Reduced at his request Trans. to Co. K.
Robert L. Carpenter	Patoka	Feb. 24, 1864	Mar. 15, 1864	Reduced at his request. Trans. to Co. K.
Albert Swortzcope	Jackson co	Feb. 7, 1864	Mar. 6, 1864	Mustered out July 19, 1865
Q. M. SERGEANTS				
John S. Hoover	New Castle, Ind		Sept. 18, 1861	Promoted 1st Lieut. Co. K
Michael F. Swortzcope	Murphysboro			Promoted Regimental Q. M
Joshua B. Davis	Pinckneyville	Dec. 17, 1863	Dec. 17, 1863	Promoted 1st Lieut. Co. H
Zachariah B. Allen	Hamilton co	Dec. 18, 1863	Dec. 18, 1863	Mustered out July 19, 1865
HOSPITAL STEWARDS				
Robert Moore	Anna			Promoted 2d Lieut. Co. E
David M. Dunn	Bethalto	June 1, 1862	June 1, 1862	Mustered out May 31, 1865
PRINCIPAL MUSICIANS				
Orson Nichols	Galesburg			Mustered out
Samuel D. Billings	Centralia			"
John J. Fuller	Pekin	Jan. 5, 1864	Jan. 5, 1864	Mustered out July 19, 1865
Samuel P. Steele	Mound City			Reduced. Trans to Co. E
John Turrell	Pekin			Mustered out Sept.—, 1864

COMPANY A

CAPTAINS.				
John D. Reese	Denmark	Sept. 8, 1861	Sept. 18, 1861	Promoted Major
William B. Short	Pinckneyville	May 1, 1862		"
Daniel Quillman	"	June 20, 1865	June 26, 1865	Mustered out June 26, 1865
FIRST LIEUTENANTS				
John Campbell	Pinckneyville	Sept. 8, 1861	Sept. 18, 1861	Died Apr. 18, 1862
Davidson C. Moore	"	April 18, 1862	July 15, 1862	Resigned July 3d, 1864
Daniel Quillman	"	July 3, 1864	Apr. 2, 1865	Promoted
James R. Tyler	Cairo	June 20, 1865	June 26, 1865	Mustered out July 19, 1865
SECOND LIEUTENANTS				
Davidson C. Moore	Pinckneyville	Sept. 8, 1861	Sept. 18, 1861	Promoted
Isham E. Willis	"	May 1, 1862		Mustered out Jan. 4, 1865
John M. Brown	"	July 18, 1865	Not Mustered	M. O. July 19, '65, as Serg't
FIRST SERGEANT				
William H. Kinzey	Pinckneyville	Aug. 15, 1861	Sept. 18, 1861	
SERGEANTS.				
Andrew Campbell	Pinckneyville	Aug. 15, 1861	Sept. 18, 1861	Died May 24, 1862
Stephen J. Taylor	"	"	"	Disch. Aug. 16, 1862
William B. Short	"	"	"	Promoted Captain
Thomas J. Short	"	"	"	Died Feb. 13, 1862

NAME AND RANK	RESIDENCE	Date of rank or enlistment	Date of muster	REMARKS
CORPORALS				
James Crain	Pinckneyville	Aug. 15, 1861	Sept. 18, 1861	Disch. July 23, 1862; disabil....
Noah Guymon	"	"	"	Trans. to Invalid Corps ....
Thomas B. Green	"	"	"	Re-enlisted as Veteran ....
William J. Walker	"	Aug. 22, 1861	"	Wounded. Disch. Dec. 27, '61
John M. Brown	"	Aug. 15, 1861	"	Re-enlisted as Veteran..........
James W. Logan	"	"	"	" " ....
John C. Milligan	"	"	"	Killed at Fort Donelson, Feb. 15, 1862........
Aquilla B. Hamilton	Perry co	Aug. 22. 1861	"	Wounded. Disch. July 23, '62
MUSICIANS				
Robert F. Johnson	Pinckneyville	Aug. 15, 1861	Sept. 18, 1861	....
Michael F. Swortzcope	Murphysboro	Sept. 8, 1861	"	Promoted Q. M. Sergeant .....
WAGONER				
Matthew M. Edgar	Denmark	Aug. 15, 1861	Sept. 18, 1861	....
PRIVATES				
Almon, Harry	Pinckneyville	Aug. 15, 1861	Sept. 18, 1861	Promoted Sergeant Major .....
Ayers, Thomas	Perry co	"	"	Died Feb. 28, 1862 ....
Armstrong, Thomas A	"	"	"	
Black, John	"	"	"	Re-enlisted as Veteran ....
Brown, William M	Pinckneyville	"	"	Died Nov. 10, 1861; wounds....
Brown, Samuel	Perry co	"	"	Died Feb. 7, 1864 ....
Baker, Frederick	Pinckneyville	"	"	Re-enlisted as Veteran ....
Brown, William G		"	"	Disch. Apr. 21, 1862; disabil....
Campbell, William E	Steel's Mills	"	"	Disch. Aug. 15, 1862; disabil ...
Chappell, Benjamin	Pinckneyville	"	"	Disch. Oct. 15, 1862; disabil! ...
Carpenter, Warren	"	"	"	Re-enlisted as Veteran............
Davis, Joshua B	"	"	"	" "
Davis, Harmon	"	Aug. 30, 1861	"	Disch. Apr. 21, 1862; disabil....
Evans, William H	"	Aug. 15, 1861	"	Died Nov. 18, 1861; wounds ....
Exam, Andrew J	"	"	"	Disch. May 21, 1862; wounds
Eaton, William	"	Aug. 22, 1861	"	Trans. to 1st Ill Battery ....
Fannin, Benjamin	Perry co	Aug. 15, 1861	"	Died Oct. 16, 1863 ....
Foster, Samuel H	Pinckneyville	"	"	....
Gladson, James	"	"	"	....
Gray, Richard	"	"	"	....
Gamble, Robert	"	"	"	Re-enlisted as Veteran............
Gamble, John	"	"	"	
Greyer, Andrew T	Tamaroa	"	"	Died Jan. 1, 1862; wounds ....
Gunn, John A	"	Aug. 22, 1861	"	Re-enlisted as Veteran ....
Huey, John A	Pinckneyville	Aug. 21, 1861	"	Died Mar. 1, 1862; wounds .....
Heath, Oliver S	"	Aug. 15, 1861	"	Died Oct. 14, 1861 ....
Holcomb, Oliver K	"	"	"	Mustered out Sept. 24, 1864....
Hamilton, William	"	Aug. 21, 1861	"	Disch. May 26, 1862; disabil ...
Harmon, John	"	Aug. 22, 1861	"	....
Hale, Isaac N	"	Aug. 21, 1861	"	
Heape, Thomas	"	Aug. 27, 1861	"	Disch. Apr. 1, 1862; wounds ....
Henry, Hamilton	"		"	....
King, Samuel		Aug. 15, 1861	"	Died at Boliver, Tenn., Nov. 9, 1862
Knox, Charles	Pinckneyville	Aug. 22, 1861	"	Died at St. Louis ....
Lipe, Gabriel	"	Aug. 15, 1861	"	Disch. May 27, 1862; disabil.....
Leslie, John	"	Aug. 22, 1861	"	Killed at Belmont, Mo., Nov. 7, 1861 ...
Marlow, Richard	"	Aug. 21, 1861	"	Died near Vicksburg, May 31, 1863........
Miller, William F	"	Aug. 30, 1861	"	Deserted Sept. 30, 1861..... ....
McCullough, L. M	"	Aug. 15, 1861	"	Died Apr. 4, 1864.... ....
McClurkin, Thos. V	"	Aug. 21, 1861	"	Died May 26, 1862; wounds....
Moore, William T	"	Aug. 22, 1861	"	Died at Jackson, Tenn., July 6, 1862
Murry, George W	Tamaroa	"	"	Died Mar. 27, 1862........ ....
Murry, Merritt	"	Aug. 27, 1821	"	Died Dec. 8, 1861............ ....
McQuade, Wilson	Pinckneyville	Aug. 21, 1821	"	Killed at Belmont, Mo., Nov. 7, 1861 ....
North, William	"	Aug. 15, 1861	"	Mustered out Sept. 20, 1864....
North, Jasper	"	"	"	Died Mar. 1, 1862.............
Norht, Levi	"	"	"	Dishc. May 21, 1862; wounds

Name and Rank	Residence	Date of rank or enlistment	Date of muster	Remarks
Opper, Michael	Pinckneyville	Aug. 15, 1861	Sept. 18, 1861	
Pittsford, William H	"	"	"	
Presswood, Levi	"	Aug. 22, 1861	"	Re-enlisted as Veteran..
Pyle, William	"	"	"	" "
Potter, Sylvester	Tamaroa	"	"	Disch. Apr. 21, 1862; wounds...
Potter, Nelson	Pinckneyville	"	"	Died Memphis, Feb. 14, 1863...
Quillman, Daniel	"	Aug. 15, 1861	"	Re-enlisted as Veteran
Quillman, John R	"	"	"	
Rhine, David A	"	Aug. 22, 1861	"	Killed at Fort Donelson, Feb. 15, 1862
Ragland, Hawkins	"	Aug. 21, 1861	"	Died at home June 3, 1862
Ramsey, Robert L	"	Aug. 22, 1861	"	Killed at Fort Donelson, Feb. 15, 1862
Rollins, Thomas	"	Aug. 27, 1861	"	Re-enlisted as Veteran
Robinson, William T	"	"	"	" "
Spear, Thomas	"	Aug. 15, 1861	"	
Swallow, Isaac N	"	"	"	Killed at Fort Donelson, Feb. 15, 1862
Stewart, William	"	"	"	Killed at Fort Donelson, Feb. 15, 1862
Stout, Aaron	"	Aug. 22, 1861	"	
Tucker, Abram	"	Aug. 15, 1861	"	Re-enlisted as Veteran
Tyler, James R	Cairo	Sept. 11, 1861	"	Re-enlisted as Veteran, Promoted to Corp'l
Vancil, Thomas M	Pinckneyville	Aug. 15, 1861	"	Re-enlisted as Veteran
Watkins, Samuel	"	"	"	Killed at Fort Donelson Feb. 15, 1862
Wheeler, Levi	"	"	"	Killed at Fort Donelson, Feb. 15, 1862
Wilson, William G	"	"	"	
Winters, Edmund H	Tamaroa	Aug. 22, 1861	"	Disch. Apr. 21, 1862; wounds...
Wallace, Thomas J	Pinckneyville	Aug. 27, 1861	"	Disch. Apr. 21, 1862; disabil...
Willis, Isham E	"	Aug. 15, 1861	"	Promoted 2d Lieutenant
Young, William	"	Aug. 27, 1861	"	Mustered out Sept. 17, 1864

RECRUITS

Name and Rank	Residence	Date of rank or enlistment	Date of muster	Remarks
Allen, William I	Pinckneyville	Jan. 17, 1864	Jan. 17, 1864	Mustered out July 19, 1865
Bastian, Joseph	Murphysboro	Aug. 30, 1862	Sept. 23, 1862	M. O. May 31, 1864; leg amp...
Bowers, Jacob	"	Oct. 6, 1862	Oct. 25, 1862	
Boles, Cornelius	"	Aug. 30, 1862	Sept. 23, 1862	Deserted Feb. 9, 1863
Bonney, Philip C		Oct. 10, 1862	Sept. 25, 1862	
Bolly, Peter	Murphysboro	Aug. 30, 1862	Oct. 28, 1863	
Brown, George M		Sept. 26, 1862	Nov. 4, 1862	Absent. Wounded at M. O. of Regiment
Black, Daniel	Pinckneyville	Jan. 1, 1864	Jan. 1, 1864	Died Nov. 6, 1864
Bingham, John H	DuQuoin	Feb. 1, 1864	Feb. 1, 1864	Killed near Atlanta, Ga., July 22, 1864
Clardy, James H	Pinckneyville	Sept. 23, 1861		Died at DuQuoin, Ill., Sept. 2, 1863
Crawford, James		Dec. 1, 1861		Died Aug. 9, 1862
Connor, John	Grand Cote Pra	Jan. 13, 1862	Jan. 18, 1862	Disch. July 23, 1862; wounds...
Childers, Martin S	Murphysboro	Aug. 30, 1862	Sept. 23, 1862	Disch. May 16, 1863; disabil...
Craig, Andrew P	Raleigh	Feb. 11, 1864	Apr. 11, 1864	Mustered out June 10, 1865
Craig, John W	Lost Prairie	Mar. 24, 1865	Mar. 26, 1865	Mustered out July 19, 1865
Collins, John A	DuQuoin	Feb. 5, 1864	Feb. 5, 1864	Pris. war. No Disch. given...
Davis, Abel C	Murphysboro	Aug. 30, 1662	Sept. 23, 1862	Disch. Sept. 18, 1861; disabil...
Davis, Philip L	"	"	"	Mustered out July 19, 1865
Dixon, Andrew	Lost Prairie	Mar. 24, 1865	Mar. 26, 1865	" "
Dixon, James	"	"	Mar. 24, 1862	" "
Evans, John M	DuQuoin	Feb. 1, 1864	Feb. 1, 1864	Killed near Kenesaw Mt., June 27, 1864
Foster, William P	Pinckneyville	Apr. 1, 1862	Apr. 1, 1862	Re-enlisted as Veteran
Glover, Joshua V	"		Sept. 18, 1861	Deserted Jan. 25, 1863
Goodwin, William	"	Sept. 28, 1861		Tr. to Inv. Corps, Oct. 27, '63
Gordon, Aaron	"			
Greyman, John	"	Apr. 1, 1862	Apr. 1, 1862	Disch. Sept. 8, 1862; disabil.....
Huey, Samuel M	Anna	Jan. 17, 1864	Jan. 17, 1864	Mustered out July 19, 1865
Hodge, Walter C	Lost Prairie	Mar. 24, 1865	Mar. 24, 1865	
Hoaglin, John N	DuQuoin	Feb. 5, 1864	Feb. 5, 1864	Died, Rome, Ga., Sept. 2, 1864
Jones, Jacob L		Aug. 17, 1863	Aug. 17, 1863	Trans. to 10th Mo. Cav
Keeler, Thomas H	Pinckneyville	Mar. 8, 1864		Mustered out July 19, 1865
Montgomery, Samuel	Pinckneyville	Dec. 1, 1861		
Marshal, Thomas	Murphysboro	Aug. 30, 1862	Sept. 23, 1862	Mustered out May 31, 1865
Mitchell, Eichering T	Pinckneyville	Jan. 17, 1864	Jan. 17, 1864	Mustered out July 19, 1865

Name and Rank	Residence	Date of rank or enlistment	Date of muster	Remarks
McCoy, William H	Carlinville	Apr. 29, 1864	Apr. 29, 1864	Mustered out July 19, 1865......
Maxwell, Enoch	Lost Prairie	Mar. 24, 1865	Mar. 24, 1865	" " " ......
McKinstry, John	"	"	"	" " "
North, Levi	Anna	Jan. 17, 1864	Jan. 17, 1864	M. O. July 19, 1865, as Corp'l
North, Robert	"	"	"	Mustered out July 19, 1865......
Nangle, George W. D.....	Cairo	Dec. 14, 1863	Dec. 16, 1863	" " " ......
Osborne, Henry	Pinckneyville	Dec. 1, 1861	....	Re-enlisted as Veteran ... .
Reynolds, Marcus G.......	Murphysboro	Oct. 6, 1862	Oct. 25, 1862	Deserted Feb. 9, 1863 ....
Reynolds, David M.........	"	"	"	
Reed, Joseph K				Mustered out July 19, 1865......
Steele, Robert	Pinckneyville		Sept. 18, 1861	Discharged July 23, 1862........
Short, Jacob A	Limestone	Feb. 9, 1865	Feb. 9, 1861	Mustered out July 19, 1865 ......
Swortzcope, A. R	DeSoto	Feb. 29, 1864	Feb. 29, 1865	Prom. Commissary Serg't......
Thompson, Lewis S.........	Pinckneyville		Sept. 18, 1861	Died at Paducah, Ky., Mar. 10, 1862.
Thompson, Edwin S.........	Ch'y Valley, N. Y.	Aug. 30, 1862	Aug. 30, 1862	Discharged Feb. 19, 1863 ......
Tippi, Alonzo		Aug. 23, 1862	Nov. 5, 1862	Mustered out June 20, 1865......
Weatherford, Char. N......	Murphysboro	Aug. 30, 1862	Sept. 23, 1862	Deserted Feb. 9, 1863 ....
White, William	Carbondale	Oct. 22, 1862	Oct. 25, 1862	Deserted Nov. 10, 1862 ....
Welch, Talbert................	Benton................	Jan. 16, 1862	Jan. 16, 1862	Died Mar. 4, 1862; wounds......

VETERANS

Name and Rank	Residence	Date of rank or enlistment	Date of muster	Remarks
Black, John....................	Pinckneyville	Jan. 5, 1864	Jan. 5, 1864	Died, Andersonville prison, July 30, 1864. Gr. 4315......
Brown, John M................	"	Jan. 5, 1864	Jan. 5, 1864	M. O. July 19, 1865, as Serg't
Baker, Frederick.............	"	"	"	" " " "
Carpenter, Warren	"	"	"	M. O. July 19, 1865, as Corp'l
Davis, Joshua B	"	Dec. 17, 1863	Dec. 17, 1863	Promoted Q. M. Sergeant......
Fuller, John J	"	Jan. 5, 1864	....	Trans. to non-com. staff ....
Green, Thomas B	"	"	Jan. 5, 1864	M. O. July 19, 1865, as Corp'l
Gamble, Robert	"	"	"	Mustered out July 19, 1865......
Gunn, John A..................	"	"	"	" " " ......
Glover, Joshua V	"	"	"	" " " ......
Logan, James W..............	"	"	"	" " " ......
Osborne, Henry	"	"	"	Killed near Canton, Miss. Feb. 28, 1864
Preswood, Levi	"	"	"	M. O. July 19, 1865, as Corp'l
Pyle, William ....-.........	"	"	"	Mustered out July 19, 1865......
Quillman, Daniel..........	"	"	"	Prom. 1st Serg't, 1st Lieut. and Captain ....
Rollins, Thomas R	"	"	"	Mustered out May 30, 1865......
Robinson, William T.........	"	"	"	Killed at Louisville, Ky., July 2, 1865 ....
Speers, Thomas	"	"	"	M. O. July 19, 1865, as Corp'l
Tyler, James R	"	"	"	Prom. Serg't and 1st Lieut......
Tucker, Abraham	"	"	"	Mustered out July 19, 1865......
Vancil, Thomas M	"	"	"	Captured; reported died at Andersonville ....

DRAFT'D AND SUBSTITUTE RECRUITS

Name and Rank	Residence	Date of rank or enlistment	Date of muster	Remarks
Anderson, Henry	Nebraska	Oct. 14, 1864	Oct. 14, 1864	Sub. M. O. June 19, 1865......
Adams, Samuel		Sept. 28, 1864	Sept. 28, 1864	Sub. M. O. May 31, 1865 ......
Andrews, William	Millbrook	Sept. 27, 1864	Sept. 27, 1864	Mustered out May 31, 1865......
Andrews, William H.........	Princeville	"	"	" " " ......
Buck, Alonzo W.............	Chandlerville.......	Oct. 13, 1864	Oct. 13, 1864	Sub. M. O. July 19, 1865 ......
Burke, Michael..............		....	Dec. 16, 1864	" " " ......
Blum, August	Rednow	Sept. 27, 1864	Sept. 27, 1864	Mustered out May 31, 1865......
Chandler, Eber	Eldorado	Oct. 26, 1864	Oct. 26, 1864	Sub. M. O. July 19, 1865......
Courtney, Richard..	Banner...............	Oct. 4, 1864	Oct. 4, 1864	Drafted. M. O. July 19, 1865..
Campbell, David R		....	Dec. 16, 1864	Sub. M. O. July 19, 1865 ......
Carroll, James R. V.........				Drafted. M. O. July 19, 1865..
Cox, Edward	Lake	Sept. 28, 1861	Sept. 28, 1864	Mustered out May 31, 1865......
Dixon, Thomas..............		....	Oct. 16, 1864	Sub. M. O. July 19, 1865......
Eames, William..............				Mustered out May 31, 1865 ......
Finney, William				Mustered out June 17, 1865 ......
Lovelady, Samuel D	Jefferson	Oct. 12, 1864	Oct. 12, 1864	Drafted. Absent, sick at muster-out of Reg't.......
Leer, Charles		....	Dec. 17, 1864	Sub. M. O. July 19, 1865 ......
Laire, Geo. H	Princeville	Sept. 27, 1864	Sept. 27, 1864	Mustered out May 31, 1865......
Mitchell, Isaac..............		Sept. 21, 1864	Oct. 1, 1864	Sub. M. O. July 19, 1865......
McKinnan, John	Limestone............	Dec. 15, 1864	Dec. 15, 1864	Mustered out July 19, 1865......
Mahoney, Michael............	Harlem................	Dec. 16, 1864	Dec. 21, 1864	" " " ......
McCurdy, John	Akron................	Sept. 27, 1864	Sept. 27, 1864	Mustered out May 31, 1865......

Name and Rank	Residence	Date of rank or en- listment	Date of muster	Remarks
McKinley, John	Serena	Sept. 29, 1864	Sept. 29, 1864	Mustered out May 31, 1865
Rogers, Joseph P.	Cass	Oct. 4, 1864	Oct. 4, 1864	Drafted. M. O. July 19, 1865
Reed, Samuel		Sept. 21, 1864	Sept. 21, 1864	Sub. M. O. May 31, 1865
Soaper, Samuel	Orion	Oct. 4, 1864	Oct. 4, 1864	Drafted. M. O. July 19, 1865
Snyder, Louis A		Dec. 8, 1864	Dec. 8, 1864	" "
Savage, William C	Akron	Sept. 27, 1864	Sept. 27, 1864	Mustered out May 31, 1865
Slygh, Charles C.	Millbrook	Sept. 29, 1864	Sept. 29, 1864	" "
Soaper, John	Akron	Sept. 27, 1864	Sept. 27, 1864	" "
Shephard, William J	Buckeye	Dec. 19, 1864	Dec. 17, 1864	Sub. Deserted June 29, 1865
Williams, Joseph J.	Orion	Oct. 4, 1864	Oct. 4, 1864	Drafted. M. O. July 19, 1865
Wages, Isaac	Banner	"	"	" " "
Wheeler, John	Princeville	Sept. 27, 1864	Sept. 27, 1864	Mustered out May 31, 1865
Ward, Boswell	Akron	"	"	" "

COMPANY B

CAPTAINS

Thomas J. Cain	Harrisburg	Sept. 8, 1861	Sept. 18, 1861	Resigned Sept. 3, 1862
Sterne W. Forgy	"	Sept. 3, 1862	Apr. 6, 1863	Resigned Aug. 8, 1863
William W. Largent	"	Aug. 8, 1863	Apr. 6, 1865	Mustered out July 19, 1865

FIRST LIEUTENANTS

Cressa K. Davis		Sept. 8, 1861		Prom. Co. F, 6th Ill. Cav
Sterne W. Forgy	Harrisburg	Sept. 23, 1861		Promoted
Robert Lewis	Stonefort	Sept. 3, 1862	Not mustered	Resign'd Mar. 17, '63, as 2d Lt.
Joseph B. Kuykendall	Vienna	"		Promoted Adjutant
William W. Largent	Harrisburg	Feb. 24, 1863	June 22, 1863	Promoted
William L. Dillard	"	Aug. 8, 1863	Apr. 2, 1865	Mustered out July 19, 1865

SECOND LIEUTENANTS

Sterne W. Forgy	Harrisburg	Sept. 8, 1861	Sept. 18, 1861	Promoted
Geo. W. Youngblood	Stonefort	Sept. 23, 1861		Died Feb. 26, 1862, of wounds rec'd at Ft. Donelson
Robert Lewis	"	Feb. 26, 1862		Promoted
William W. Largent	Harrisburg	Mar. 17, 1863	May 17, 1863	"
William Gaskins	"	Feb. 24, 1863	June 22, 1863	Resigned June 8, 1864
John J. Dunn	Bankston	July 18, 1865	Not mustered	M. O. July 19, 1865, as Serg't

FIRST SERGEANT

Robert Lewis	Stonefort	Aug. 10, 1861	Sept. 18, 1861	Promoted

SERGEANTS

Jacob S. Stucker	Stonefort	Aug. 10, 1861	Sept. 18, 1861	Disch. Apr. 20, 1862; disabil
Samuel Stiff	Harrisburg	"	"	Disch. Jan. 13, 1863; wounds
Geo. W. Youngblood	Stonefort	"	"	Promoted 2d Lieutenant
Elijah Pierson	Harrisburg	"	"	Disch. Aug. 25, 1862; disabil

CORPORALS

Augustus E. Drayer	Sarahsville	Aug. 10, 1861	Sept. 18, 1861	Mustered out Sept. 21, 1864
James H. Dunn	Mitchellsville	"	"	
Geo. W. Cain	Harrisburg	"	"	Died Feb. 17, 1862; wounds
William Allen	Sarahsville	"	"	Disch. order Gen. Halleck, May 30, 1862
William W. Largent	Harrisburg	"	"	Pro. 1st Serg't, then 2d Lieut.
David M. Farthing	Stonefort	"	"	Re-enlisted as Veteran
John S. Harris	Harrisburg	"	"	Disch. Nov. 9, 1861; disabil
Isaac E. Gatewood	"	"	"	Transferred to Co. I

MUSICIANS

R. H. Huddleston	Harrisburg	Aug. 20, 1861	Sept. 18, 1861	Disch. order Gen. Halleck May, 80. 1862
Thomas J. Lynch	Stonefort	Aug. 10, 1861	"	Deserted Feb. 20, 1863

WAGONER

William Woods	Harrisburg	Aug. 10, 1861	Sept. 18, 1861	

Name and Rank	Residence	Date of rank or enlistment	Date of muster	Remarks
PRIVATES				
Allen, William H	Marion	Aug. 8, 1861	Sept. 18, 1861	
Abney, Harmon	South America	Aug. 10, 1861	"	Killed at Fort Donelson, Feb. 15, 1862
Armstrong, Dempsey	Harrisburg	"	"	Disch. Apr. 20, 1862; disabil
Brown, Benjamin H	Stonefort	"	"	Died Nov. 9, 1862
Blackman, Bennett L	Harrisburg	Aug. 20, 1861	"	Disch. for long absence, May 30, 1862
Barnett. Edward F	Bankston	"	"	Died Feb. 17, 1862; wounds
Barnett, Edmund	"	"	"	Re-enlisted as Veteran
Crank, Calvin P	Harrisburg	"	"	Died June 14, 1862
Camden, Shelton W	Stonefort	"	"	Disch. Apr. 2, 1862; disabil
Choat, John D	"	"	"	Re-enlisted as Veteran
Cocherhan, Jonathan C	"	"	"	Died Nov. 4, 1862
Carrier, John	"	"	"	Died Mar. 29, 1862
Cassels, James	"	"	"	Died Jan. 13, 1862
Duncan, Stephen	Harrisburg	Aug. 10, 1861	"	Deserted Feb. 20, 1863
Dillard, William L	"	Aug. 20, 1861	"	Re-enlisted as Veteran
Dunn, Alfred	Bankston	"	"	Disch. Apr. 20, 1862; disabil
Duncan, John	Mitchellsville	"	"	
Dunn, John J	Bankston	"	"	Re-enlisted as Veteran
Dodds, William J	"	"	"	Died, Memphis, Mar. 22, 1863.
Elam, John	Mitchellsville	Aug. 10, 1861	"	Re-enlisted as Veteran
Emery, Christopher	"	"	"	Re-enlisted as Veteran
Farmer, Daniel	Harrisburg	"	"	
Fitts, John W	"	"	"	Disch. Apr. 20, 1862; disabil
Glascow, Lemuel	Mitchellsville	"	"	Died Sept. 5, 1861
Gaskins, William	Harrisburg	Aug. 20, 1861	"	Promoted
Harvey, Thomas G	Bankston	Aug. 10, 1861	"	
Hill, Esau	Mitchellsville	"	"	
Hall, Isaac W	Stonefort	"	"	Disch. May 2, 1862; wounds
Hutson, John	Harrisburg	Aug. 20, 1861	"	Disch. Sept. 27, 1862; wounds.
Kirby, William E	Stonefort	"	"	Disch. Apr. 20, 1862; disabil
Kline, Frank	Carbondale	Aug. 10, 1861	"	Re-enlisted as Veteran
Lemmons, William	Mitchellsville	"	"	Discharged Sept. 11, 1863.
Lebow, William	Rock Creek	"	"	Mustered out Sept. 16, 1864
Lewis, Lawson F.	Stonefort	"	"	Re-enlisted as Veteran
Lewis, Benjamin D	"	"	"	
Lynch, Thomas L	Marion	Aug. 10, 1861	Sept. 18, 1861	Transferred to Co. F.
Middleton, Joseph C	Harrisburg	"	"	Re-enlisted as Veteran
Moore, George W	Mitchellsville	"	"	
Mick, James Monroe	"	"	"	Disch. Apr. 20, 1862; disabil
Mick, Charles	Independence	"	"	Disch. Dec. 23, 1861; disabil
Mick, Leonard W	Mitchellsville	"	"	Re-enlisted as Veteran
Marcum, James W	Bankston	"	"	Mustered out Feb. 22, 1865
Norman, Jacob A.	Harrisburg	"	"	Re-enlisted as Veteran
Norman, Thomas B	"	"	"	" "
Neal, James	Bankston	"	"	
Ozment, Richard	"	"	"	
Ozment, James	"	"	"	Died June 30, 1964
Pierson, Richard	Harrisburg	"	"	Re-enlisted as Veteran
Pankey, Irby	Stonefort	"	"	Died at Lake Providence, La., Mar. 5, 1863
Purnell, John	"	"	"	Re-enlisted as Veteran
Pickering, James M	Harrisburg	"	"	Killed at Vicksburg, May 23, 1863
Parks, John Harvey	Marion	"	"	Deserted Dec. 31, 1862
Roper, James M.	Bankston	"	"	Died June 7, 1864
Reed, Alfred T	Mitchellsville	"	"	Killed at Fort Donelson, Feb. 15, 1862
Rushing, James H	Stonefort	"	"	Disch. May 6, 1862; wounds
Robinson, Isaac	"	"	"	Re-enlisted as Veteran
Rose, Thomas M	Bankston	"	"	" "
Randolph, James M.	Mitchellsville	"	"	Died Nov. 3, 1862
Randolph, Francis M.	"	"	"	Disch. Apr. 30, 1862; disabil
Russell, John E	Harrisburg	"	"	Disch. May 10, 1862; wounds
Simonds, John	"	"	"	Disch. July 23, 1862; wounds
Simonds, James R	"	"	"	Died Apr. 15, 1864
Stiff, George W	"	"	"	Disch. May 10, 1862; disabil
Stiff, Lewis.	"	"	"	
Sisk, Jasper	Stonefort	"	"	Re-enlisted as Veteran
Smith, Asa Davis	Marion	"	"	" "
Tolbert, Riley	Stonefort	"	"	Disch. Apr. 20, 1862; disabil
Williams, James M. G	Mitchellsville	"	"	Disch. Oct. 15, 1861; disabil

Name and Rank	Residence	Date of rank or enlistment	Date of muster	Remarks
Williams, Miles W............	Mitchellsville	Aug. 10, 1861	Sept. 18, 1861	Re-enlisted as Veteran............ ......
Willis, Eli....	Harrisburg...........		"	Died Feb. 22, 1862; wounds .....
Weld, Lewis H............	Stonefort.............	Sept. 18, 1861	"	Disch. July 23, 1862; disabil.....
Yates, John B..............	Bankston	Aug. 10, 1861	"	Killed, Belmont, Nov. 7, 1861...
Young, Benjamin S............	Stonefort.............	"	"	Disch. Apr. 20, 1862; wounds...

VETERANS.

Name and Rank	Residence	Date of rank or enlistment	Date of muster	Remarks
Barnett, Edmund................	Bankston	Jan. 5, 1864	Jan. 5, 1864	Mustered out July 19, 1865......
Choat, John......................	Stonefort.............	"	"	M. O. July 19, 1865, as Corp'l
Dunn, John J..........	Bankston	"	"	M. O. July 19, 1865, as Serg't
Dillard, William L	Harrisburg............	"	"	Promoted 1st Lieutenant
Dodds, Thomas J...............	"	"	"	Mustered out July 19, 1865......
Ealem, John W.................	Mitchellsville	"	"	
Emery, Chistopher............	"	"	"	Killed, Atlanta, July 22, 1864...
Farthing, David M............	Stonefort.........,...	"	"	Killed, Atlanta, July 21, 1864...
Kline, Frank......................	"	"	"	Mustered out July 19, 1865......
Lewis, Lawson F	"	"	"	" " ......
Mandril, Alfred D.............	Bankston	"	"	
Mick, Leonard W..............	Mitchellsville	"	"	M. O. July 19, '65, as 1st Serg.
Middleton, Joseph C...........	Harrisburg.........	"	"	Mustered out July 19, 1865......
Norman, Thomas B............	"	"	"	M. O. July 19, 1865, as Serg't
Norman, Jacob A	"	Feb. 26, 1864	Feb. 26, 1864	Mustered out July 19, 1865......
Pierson, Richard	"	Jan. 5, 1864	Jan. 5, 1864	Captured near Wateree River, Feb. 25, 1865............ ....
Purnell, John W..............	"	Feb. 26, 1864	Feb. 26, 1864	M. O. Oct. 19, 1865, as Serg't
Robinson, Isaac	Stonefort.............	Jan. 5, 1864	Jan. 5, 1864	M. O. July 19, 1865, as Corp'l
Rose, Thomas M...............	Bankston	"	"	" "
Sisk, Jasper......................	Stonefort.............	"	"	Mustered out July 19, 1865.....
Smith, Asa D	Marion....	"	"	" "
Stiff, George W	Harrisburg............	"	"	M. O. July 19, 1865, as Corp'l
William, Miles W..............	Mitchellsville	"	"	M. O. July 19, 1865, as Serg't

RECRUITS.

Name and Rank	Residence	Date of rank or enlistment	Date of muster	Remarks
Anglin, William H	Bankston	Nov. 24, 1861		Absent, wounded, at M. O......
Anglin, James S	Saline Co	Sept. 1, 1862	Oct. 17, 1862	Mustered out July 19, 1865 .....
Burgess, Lewis J...............	Harrisburg...........	Mar. 30, 1864	Mar. 30, 1864	" "
Choat, James	Cross Roads	Oct. 27, 1861	....	Disch. July 23, 1862; wounds...
Cain, Abraham	Bankston...........	Sept. 1, 1862	Oct. 17, 1862	M. O. July 19, 1965; as Corp'l
Cook, John M	Saline Co	"	"	Mustered out July 19, 1865.... .
Carrier, Edmund W.........	Harrisburg............	Mar. 30, 1864	Mar. 30, 1864	
Dodds, Thomas J............	"	Nov. 24, 1861		Re-enlisted as Veteran. ....
Dorris, John	Saline Co	Sept. 1, 1862	Oct. 17, 1862	Died Dec. 16, 1862; disease
Dorris, Willis....................	"	"		Abst., detached at M. O. Reg.
Dunn, Alfred J	Mitchellsville	Feb. 22, 1864	Mar. 16, 1864	Mustered out July 19, 1865 .....
Eaton, Andrew J	Sarahville	Oct. 12, 1861	....	Disch. for long absence, May 30, 1862
Evans, James L	Harrisburg............	Mar. 30, 1864	Mar 30, 1894	Mustered out July 19, 1865......
Feazel, Noah..	"	Sept. 1, 1862	Oct. 17, 1862	" "
Farthing, Edwin R	Saline Co	"	"	Discharged Feb. 19, 1863........
Ferguson, George W	Harrisburg...........	Mar. 30, 1864	Mar. 30, 1864	Mustered out July 19, 1865.....
Goldsboro, Henry J...........	Mitchellsville	Nov. 21, 1861	....	Died Apr. 15, 1864 ....
Gaskins, James	Saline Co	Sept. 1, 1862	Oct. "	Discharged Jan. 29, 1863.. ......
Gwinn, Francis M............	"	"	"	Captured Feb. 23, 1865.........
Hamilton, George W	"	"	"	M. O. July 19, 1865, as Corp'l
Lewis, Thomas B.......... ..	....	Apr. 11, 1864	Apr. 11, 1864	Mustered out July 19, 1865......
Lewis, Samuel E	"	"	"	" "
Medlin, Joshua..	Bankston	Nov. 16, 1861		Died Mar. 1, 1862; wounds......
Mandril, Alfred D.............	"	Nov. 24, 1861		Re-enlisted as Veteran............
McNew, Thomas F	Saline Co	Sept. 1, 1861	Oct. 17, 1861	Died July 23, 1864; wounds......
Morton, James W	Raleigh	Apr. 11, 1864	Apr. 11, 1861	Mustered out July 19, 1865 .....
Parks, Joseph N	Sarahville....	Nov. 27, 1861	Nov. 27, 1861	Mustered out June 9, 1865......
Pickering, Lycurgus F......	Harrisburg..........	Mar. 30, 1864	Mar. 30, 1864	Mustered out July 19, 1865......
Rude, Harvey M...............	"	Aug. 10, 1861	Sept. 18, 1861	Died Nov. 8, 1861.................
Raney, John A	Stonefort.............	Sept. 1, 1862	Oct. 17, 1862	Died Nov. 19, 1863...............
Randolph, Oliver G..........	Saline Co	"	"	Died Aug. 11, 1864; wounds ....
Rogers, George W	Harrisburg...........	Mar. 30, 1864	Mar. 30, 1864	Mustered out July 19, 1965......
Stucker, George M	Stonefort............	Sept. 20, 1861		Died Feb. 14, 1863 ....
Stiff, George W	Saline Co	Sept. 1, 1862	Oct. 17, 1862	Re-enlisted as Veteran............
Spears, John W	"	"	"	M. O. July 19, 1865, as Corp'l
Spears, James K		Nov. 15, 1863	Nov. 15, 1863	Killed before Atlanta, July 22, 1864 ....
Smith, Joseph W	....	....	....	Died June 7, 1864.................
Turner, Lewis J	Bankston	Sept. 23, 1861	....	

Name and Rank	Residence	Date of rank or enlistment	Date of muster	Remarks
Tate, Lorenzo	Saline Co	Sept. 1, 1862	Oct. 17, 1862	
Willis, Alexander R	Stonefort	Sept. 19, 1861		Disch. May 10, 1862; disabil
Willis, Sammel T	"	"		Died Feb. 22, 1862; wounds
Williford, James H. F	Marion	Sept. 24, 1861		Disch. Apr. 20, 1862; disabil
Williford, Joseph W	"	"		
Walker, William J	Bankston	Nov. 24, 1861		Discharged July 4, 1862
Webb, John	Marion	Dec. 2, 1861		Died Mar. 2, 1862
Webb, Jonathan	"	"		Disch. Oct. 14, 1862; disabil
Wilkins, John	Harrisburg	Feb. 22, 1864	Mar. 16. 1864	Mustered out July 12, 1865
Walker, William A	"	Mar. 30, 1864	Mar. 30, 1864	" "

DRAFTED AND SUBSTITUTE RECRUITS.

Boots, Joseph	Kingston	Oct. 18, 1864	Oct. 18, 1864	Sub. M. O. July 19, 1865
Bush, Thomas R	Jefferson	Oct. 13, 1864	Oct. 13, 1864	Mustered out July 19, 1865
Ballard, William A		Oct. 21, 1864	Oct. 21, 1864	Sub. M. O. July 19, 1865
Breene, Michael	Litchfield	Dec. 17, 1864	Dec. 17, 1964	Discharged June 29, 1865
Clemins, Andrew	Jefferson	Oct. 19, 1864	Oct. 19, 1864	Sub. M. O. July 19, 1965
Campbell, Benjamin	Quincy	Dec. 14, 1864	Dec. 17, 1864	Sub. Never reported to Co
Campbell, Javes	Kingston	Oct. 21, 1864	Oct. 21, 1864	Sub. M. O. July 19, 1865
Davis, Hudson B	Lamoille	Dec. 13, 1864	Dec. 15, 1864	Sub. Never reported to Co
Darnell, Sylvester	Jefferson	Oct. 12, 1864	Oct. 12, 1864	Mustered out July 19, 1865
Everson, Thomas F		Dec. 17, 1864	Dec. 17, 1864	Sub. M. O. June 9, 1865
Gamble, Oscar	Ohio	Oct. 10, 1864	Oct. 11, 1864	Sub. M. O. July 19, 1865
Hodge, Riley C	Jefferson	Oct. 13, 1864	Oct. 13, 1864	Mustered out July 19, 1865
Hughes, Patrick		Dec. 20, 1864	Dec. 20, 1864	Sub. M. O. July 19, 1865
Hand, George H			Nov. 28, 1864	Deserted July 13, 1865
Knapp, Charles			Sept. 29, 1864	Discharged May 31, 1865
Loman, James	Jefferson	Oct. 12, 1864	Oct. 12, 1864	Mustered out July 19, 1865
Loman, Elias	"	Oct. 14, 1864	Oct. 14, 1864	" "
Mills, Robert R	Peoria	Oct. 13, 1864	Oct. 13, 1864	Sub. M. O. July 19, 1865
Millis, William			Dec. 14, 1864	Never reported to Co
Moore, William B	Jefferson	Oct. 13, 1864	Oct. 13, 1864	Mustered out July 19, 1865
Mehan, Thomas	Felix	Dec. 14, 1864	Dec. 14, 1864	Sub. Never reported to Co
Morris, John			Dec. 20, 1864	Mustered out July 19, 1865
McCarty, John	Felix	Dec. 14, 1864	Dec. 14, 1864	Sub. M. O. July 19, 1865
McMaster, John	Utica	"	"	Sub. Never reported to Co
O'Brien, John	Chicago	Oct. 14, 1864	Oct. 14, 1864	Mustered out July 19, 1865
Porter, Newton C	LaHarpe	Dec. 14, 1864	Dec. 14, 1764	Sub. Never reported to Co
Rodges, Henry		Oct. 13, 1864	Oct. 13, 1864	Mustered out July 19, 1865
Robertson, Albert	Jefferson	Oct. 12, 1864	Oct. 12, 1864	" "
Rians, Charles E	Copley	Oct. 11, 1864	Oct. 11, 1864	Sub. M. O. July 20, 1865
Ross, John	Eden	Oct. 13, 1864	Oct. 13, 1864	Sub. Never reported to Co
Tyning, Patrick	Orone	Dec. 20, 1864	Dec. 20, 1864	Sub. M. O. July 6, 1865
Vannordstrand, Jas	Belleplaine	Oct. 15, 1864	Oct. 15, 1864	Sub. M. O. July 19, 1865
Wright, John	Kingston	Oct. 21, 1864	Oct. 21, 1864	" "
Wings, Nathan	Jefferson	Oct. 13, 1864	Oct. 13, 1864	Mustered out July 19, 1865
Wilson, John	Felix	Dec. 14, 1864	Dec. 14, 1864	Sub. Never reported to Co
Watson, Levi	Jefferson	Oct. 18, 1864	Oct. 18, 1864	Mustered out May 24, 1865
Young, Samuel	Cotton	Oct. 15, 1864	Oct. 15, 1864	Sub. M. O. July 19, 1865

COMPANY C

CAPTAINS.

William A. Looney	Sarahville	Sept. 8, 1861	Sept. 18, 1861	Resigned June 3, 1862
George W. Goddard	Marion	June 26, 1862		Discharged Oct. 19, 1864
S. C. Mooneyham	"	Oct. 19, 1864	Apr. 3, 1865	Mustered out July 19, 1865

FIRST LIEUTENANTS.

Daniel R. Pulley	Marion	Sept. 8, 1861	Sept. 18, 1861	Resigned Apr. 19, 1862
Philander Jones	"	April 18, 1862		Resigned Aug. 13, 1863
Fred'k B. Merriman	Peru	Aug. 13, 1863		Mustered out Aug. 13, 1863
William S. Morris	Marion	"	Apr. 2, 1865	Mustered out July 19, 1865

NAME AND RANK	RESIDENCE	Date of rank or en-listment	Date of muster	REMARKS
SECOND LIEUTENANTS.				
John H. White	Marion	Sept. 8, 1861		Promoted Lieut. Colonel
James M. Askew	"	Sept. 9, 1861		Resigned Dec. 18, 1862
S. C. Mooneyham	"	Dec. 18, 1862	Apr. 7, 1863	Promoted
Allen H. Wilson	"	July 18, 1865	Not Mustered	M. O. July 19, '65, as Serg't
FIRST SERGEANT.				
S. C. Mooneyham	Marion	Aug. 19, 1861	Sept. 18, 1861	Promoted
SERGEANTS.				
William P. Jones	Marion	Aug. 19, 1861	Sept. 18, 1861	
James F. Corder	"	"	"	Died Mar. 20, 1862
Alfred Hendrickson	"	"	"	Re-enlisted as Veteran
Daniel Richey	"	"	"	Tr. to Inv. Corps Nov. 2, '63
CORPORALS.				
James M. Jewell	Marion	Aug. 19, 1861	Sept. 18, 1861	
John F. Carter	"	"	"	Died Dec. 17, 1863
Joseph L. Franklin	"	"	"	Re-enlisted as Veteran
Allen W. Wilson	"	"	"	" "
John H. Davis	"	"	"	" "
John W. Chitty	"	"	"	" "
Thomas F. O'Neal	"	"	"	Killed, Atlanta, July 21, '64
Sneed H. Fulk	"	"	"	Died, Mar. 25, '62; wounds
MUSICIANS.				
William Rex	Marion	Aug. 19, 1861	Sept. 18, 1861	
John West		"	"	Disch. May 16, 1865; sentence of G. C. M.
WAGONER.				
James T. Saunders	Marion	Aug. 19, 1861	Sept. 18, 1861	Disch. Nov. 2, 1863
PRIVATES				
Abner, William W	Marion	Aug. 19, 1861	Sept. 18, 1861	Died, Memphis, Feb. 4, '63
Abner, Paul	"	"	"	Died, Apr. 8, 1862
Askew, Elisha H	"	"	"	Disch. Apr. 19, '62; disabil
Askew, James M	"	"	"	Promoted 2d Lieutenant
Arnold, Samuel	"	"	"	Disch. June 7, 1862; order of Gen. Halleck
Burns, Elisha W	"	"	"	
Burns, William W	"	"	"	Re-enlisted as Veteran
Bailey, Isaac	"	"	"	
Baker, Milo	"	"	"	Died Aug. 16, 1862
Bentley, Francis A	"	"	"	Transferred to Co. E
Cripps, James	"	"	"	Killed at Fort Donelson, Feb. 15, 1862
Crutrell, Charles W	"	"	"	Disch. Dec. 9, 1862
Corder, John	"	"	"	Re-enlisted as Veteran
Corder, Willis	"	"	"	" "
Colboth, George W.	"	"	"	" "
Chitty, James	"	"	"	" "
Davis, Elisha H	"	"	"	
Davis, Oliver	"	"	"	
Dufer, James L	"	"	"	Mustered out Sept. 21, 1864
Edwards, William H	"	"	"	Re-enlisted as Veteran
Edwards, Charles A	"	"	"	" "
Ferrell, William W	"	"	"	" "
Gasaway, Thomas M	"	"	"	
Gasaway. John	"	"	"	Died Mar, 21, 1862
Gunter, Nathan	"	"	"	Re-enlisted as Veteran
Gill, Martin V	"	"	"	Died Mar. 21, 1862
Gill, Stephen T	"	"	"	Re-enlisted as Veteran
Gill, Archie B	"	"	"	Died Mar. 15, 1863
Gill, William T	"	"	"	
Groves, Levi	"	"	"	
Huett, Robert T	"	"	"	Disch. June 7, 1862
Henson, George W	"	"	"	Re-enlisted as Veteran
Henson, James L	"	"	"	Trans. to 1st. Ill. Battery

Name and Rank	Residence	Date of rank or enlistment	Date of muster	Remarks
Hendrickson, And'w B	Marion	Aug. 19, 1861	Sept. 18, 1861	Re-enlisted as Veteran
Hendrickson, Hillery	"	"	"	"
Hill, James W	"	"	"	Deserted Sept. 14, 1863
Houston, Richard	"	"	"	Died Apr. 22, 1862
Houston, John W	"	"	"	Disch. Nov. 3, '62; disabil.
Jenkins, Joseph	Williamson co	"	"	Died June 26, 1862
Lewis, Guilford T	Marion	"	"	Re-enlisted as Veteran
Marks, Abner	"	"	"	Died Feb. 25, 1862
McDonald, James R	"	"	"	Transferred to Co. H
McCormick, Geo. W	"	"	"	
Moseley, John H	"	"	"	Captured at Belmont, Mo
Meskil, John	"	"	"	Re-enlisted as Veteran
McGowen, Silas H	"	"	"	Died, Memphis, May 16, '63
McGowen, Alfred	"	"	"	Re-enlisted as Veteran
Morris, William S	"	"	"	Died Oct. 27, 1861
McCoy, Milton B	"	"	"	Re-enlisted as Veteran
Owens, David N	Marion	"	"	Killed at Fort Donelson, Feb. 15, 1862
Owens, Thomas F	"	"	"	Re-enlisted as Veteran
Odum, Martin	"	"	"	Killed at Fort Donelson, Feb. 15, 1862
Odum, Edward	"	"	"	
O'Neal, Rolley S	"	"	"	Disch. Apr. 19, '62; wounds
Palmer, William	"	"	"	Disch. Nov. 7, '62; disabil
Pulley, Anderson G	"	"	"	
Pulley, William C	"	"	"	
Patterson, George W	"	"	"	Disch. June 7, 1862; order of Gen. Halleck
Perry, Oliver H	"	"	"	Disch. June 7, 1862; order of Gen. Halleck
Polston, Thomas J	"	"	"	Mustered out Sept. 29, 1864
Parsons, Charles	"	"	"	Disch. Oct. 19, '62; disabil
Rex, John	"	"	"	
Shrieve, Thos. M. R	"	"	"	Disch. Sept. 7, '62; disabil
Schafer, William	"	"	"	Re-enlisted as Veteran
Schafer, Lewis F	"	"	"	Died, Memphis, Feb. 4, '63
Simms, John J	"	"	"	Re-enlisted as Veteran
Stanley, Elias	"	"	"	
Stanley, Mark	"	"	"	Disch. May 16, 1865; sentence of G. C. M.
Simpson, John B	"	"	"	Re-enlisted as Veteran
Scott, Martin V	"	"	"	" "
Staton, George A	"	"	"	
Simmons, Wm. A. J	"	"	"	Disch. June 7, 1862; order of Gen. Halleck
Stone, William R	"	"	"	
Teal, William	"	"	"	Died Jan. 2, 1862
Teal, John	"	"	"	Died Jan. 8, 1862
Turner, William L	"	"	"	Disch. June 7, 1862; order of Gen. Halleck
Uselton, John W	"	"	"	Re-enlisted as Veteran
Violet, Seldon A	"	"	"	Killed at Fort Donelson, Feb. 15, 1862
Wilkins, James Y	"	"	"	
White, George W	"	"	"	Re-enlisted as Veteran
White, James	"	"	"	
Williamson, Henry	"	"	"	Died May 12, 1863
Whitaker, William	"	"	"	Re-enlisted as Veteran
VETERANS				
Burns, William	"	Jan. 5, 1864	Jan. 5, 1864	Deserted twice
Colboth, George W	"	"	"	Mustered out July 19, 1865
Chitty, James	"	"	"	
Corder, John	"	"	"	Killed, Atlanta, July 21, 1864
Corder, Willis	"	"	"	Mustered out July 19, 1865
Davis, John H	"	"	"	" "
Edwards, William H	"	"	"	M. O. July 19, '65, as Corp'l
Edwards, Charles A	"	"	"	
Ferrell, William W	"	"	"	Killed, Atlanta, July 21, '64
Franklin, Joseph L	"	"	"	Mustered out July 19, 1865
Gill, Stephens T	"	"	"	" "
Gunter, Nathan	"	"	"	
Henson, George W	"	"	"	Died Andersonville, Aug. 22, 1864. Gr. 6489

NAME AND RANK	RESIDENCE	Date of rank or enlistment	Date of muster	REMARKS
Hendrickson, And'w B	Marion	Jan. 5, 1864	Jan. 5, 1864	Mustered out July 19, 1865 .... .
Hendrickson, B	"	"	"	" " ......
Hendrickson, Hillery	"	"	"	" " ......
Marks, Abner	"	"	"	" " ......
McGowen, Silas H	"	"	"	" " ......
Morris, William S	"	"	"	Pro. Serg., then 1st Lieut......
Owen, David N	"	"	"	Mustered out July 19, 1865......
Odum, Martin	"	"	"	M. O. July 19, 1865, as Serg't
Schafer, William	"	"	"	M. O. July 19, 1865, as Corp'l
Simpson, John B	"	"	"	Deserted Aug. 31, 1864...........
Sims, John	"	"	"	Killed, Atlanta, July 21, 1864...
Scott, Martin V	"	"	"	" " ......
Uselton, John W	"	"	"	M. O. July 19, 1865, as Corp'l
White, George W	"	"	"	M. O. July 19, 1865, as Serg't
Wilson, Allen	"	"	"	" " ......
Whitaker, William	"	"	"	Mustered out July 19, 1865 ....

RECRUITS.

NAME AND RANK	RESIDENCE	Date of rank or enlistment	Date of muster	REMARKS
Burns, Robert S	Williamson co	Aug. 30, 1862	Oct. 17, 1862	Died at Oxford, Miss., Dec. 14, 1862 ....
Brown, James W	Marion	Mar. 1, 1864	Mar. 1, 1864	Mustered out July 19, 1865......
Corder, John H	Williamson co	Jan. 20, 1862	Jan. 20, 1862	Discharged June 7, 1862; order Gen. Halleck............
Corum, Wilson A	Marion	Aug. 30, 1862	Oct. 17, 1862	Mustered out July 19, 1865......
Caplinger, Leonard T	"	"	"	
Chitty, Alfred P	Grassy Creek	Nov. 17, 1863	Nov. 17, 1863	Mustered out July 19, 1865......
Chitty, Andrew J	"	"	"	" " ......
Dodds, Richards P	Marion	Aug. 30, 1862	Oct. 17, 1862	" " ......
Dodds, Joseph B	"	"	"	Deserted Feb. 6, 1863 ....
Eoff, William J	"	"	"	Died at Lagrange, Tenn., Dec. 2, 1862 ....
Edwards, James P	"	Apr. 1, 1864	April 1, 1864	Mustered out July 19, 1865......
Gasaway, William R	Carbondale	Feb. 20, 1864	Feb. 20, 1864	
Gregory, John	Marion	Apr. 1, 1864	Apr. 1, 1864	" " ......
Gunn, Alexander Ellis	"	Mar. 1, 1865	Mar. 1, 1865	
Henson, Oliver P	Williamson co	Mar. 25, 1862	Mar. 25, 1862	Corp'l. M. O. Apr. 6, 1865....
Hendrickson, Frederick H.	"	Jan. 1, 1862	Jan. 1, 1862	Re-enlisted as Veteran...........
Hendrickson, A. G. W	Marion	Aug. 30, 1862	Oct. 17, 1862	Mustered out July 19, 1865......
Harrison, Christopher J	"	"	"	" " ......
Hendrickson, Holladay	"	Apr. 1, 1864	Apr. 1, 1864	" " ......
Higgins, Ichabod	Raleigh	Apr. 11, 1864	Apr. 11, 1864	" " ......
Henson, William	Illinois	Jan. 30, 1864	Jan. 30, 1864	" " ......
Jewell, George W. C	Northern	Sept. 6, 1864	Sept. 6, 1864	Mustered out June 26, 1865......
Jones, William P	Marion	April 1, 1864	Apr. 1, 1864	Killed near Atlanta, Ga., July 22, 1864 .
Keaster, Wm. F	Crab Orchard	Jan. 9, 1862	Jan. 9, 1862	Killed at Fort Donelson, Feb. 15, 1862.
King, John	Marion	Aug. 30, 1862	Oct. 17, 1862	Deserted July 10, 1865 ....
King, James	"	"	"	Mustered out July 19, 1865 ......
King, William R	"	"	"	Deserted Mar. 30, 1863............
King, Robert	Carbondale	Feb. 20, 1864	Feb. 20, 1864	Mustered out July 19, 1865 ...
McHaney, Louis J	Illinois	Jan. 28, 1864	Jan. 28, 1864	M. O. July 19, 1865, as Corp'l
McHaney, Richard H	Carbondale	Feb. 29, 1864	Feb. 29, 1864	Mustered out July 19, 1865......
Mathis, William	Marion	April 1, 1864	Apr. 1, 1864	Killed. Atlanta, July 21, 1864...
O'Neal, William	Cairo	Dec. 13, 1861		
Rich, Thomas C	Marion	Aug. 19, 1861	Sept. 8, 1861	Died Memphis. Aug. 3, 1863....
Rice, Joseph	Harrisburg	Mar. 5, 1864	Mar. 5, 1864	Mustered out July 19, 1865......
Russel, Ellias M	Carbondale	Feb. 16, 1864	Feb. 16, 1864	" " ......
Scott, George W	Marion	Aug. 30, 1862	Oct. 17, 1862	Died at Lagrange, Tenn., Nov. 18, 1862 ....
Spiller, John B	Williamson co	"	"	Died at Young's Pt., La., Aug. 3, 1863 ....
Squires, Omer D	Marion	Jan. 28, 1864	Jan. 28, 1864	Mustered out July 19, 1865......
Sanders, John T	"	April 1, 1864	April 1, 1864	" " ......
Sanders, Cyrus W	"	"	"	Mustered out July 16, 1865......
Vineyard, Young	Harrisburg	Mar. 4, 1864	May 4, 1864	Mustered out June 24, 1865......
Williamson, Thomas	Cairo	Nov. 28, 1861		Died Feb. 10, 1862 ....
White, Amzie F	Marion	Feb. 10, 1864	Feb. 10, 1864	Mustered out July 19, 1865......

DRAFTED AND SUBSTITUTE RECRUITS

NAME AND RANK	RESIDENCE	Date of rank or enlistment	Date of muster	REMARKS
Auerback, Solomon		Sept, 21, 1864	Sept. 21, 1864	Sub. M. O. June 3, 1865........
Belir, Justice		Nov. 3, 1864	Nov. 3, 1864	Sub. M. O. July 19, 1865 ......

NAME AND RANK	RESIDENCE	Date of rank or enlistment	Date of muster	REMARKS
Bernhard, Jacob	Spring Grove		Aug. 25, 1864	Never reported to Co
Baker, William		Dec. 23, 1864	Dec. 23, 1864	Sub. Deserted Feb. 21, 1865
Clancy, Thomas		Dec. 9, 1864	Dec. 10, 1864	Sub. Never reported to Co
Cook, George	Appanoose	Dec. 24, 1864	Dec. 24, 1864	" "
Devin, John	Clyde		Dec. 23, 1864	Sub. M. O. July 19, 1865
Delaney, William			Dec. 14, 1864	Sub. Never reported to Co
Decatur, James		Dec. 15, 1864	Dec. 15, 1864	" " "
Fink, Henry			Aug. 11, 1864	" "
Farley, Frederick	Belle Prairie	Sept. 30, 1864	Sept. 30, 1864	Sub. M. O. May 29, 1865
Farmer, John		Dec. 20, 1864	Dec. 20, 1864	Sub. Deserted July 1, 1865
Henn, Andrew			Dec. 22, 1864	Deserted Feb. 21, 1865
Lunderkin, William	Springfield	Dec. 22, 1864	Dec. 22, 1864	Sub. M. O. July 19, 1865
Lee, John	Jefferson	Oct. 20, 1864	Oct. 20, 1864	Drafted. M. O. July 19, 1865
Lawson, William W	"	Oct. 13, 1864	Oct. 13, 1864	" " "
Lunsford, William L	"	"	"	" " "
Malone, Thomas	"	"	"	" " "
Milam, Thomas W		Dec. 1, 1864	Dec. 9, 1864	Sub. M. O. July 19, 1865
McFarland, Alexander	Walker	Oct. 19, 1864	Oct. 21, 1864	Sub. Never reported to Co
Newland, Robert H	Chicago	Aug. 15, 1864	Aug. 15, 1864	Sub. M. O. June 3, 1865
Niles, Ambrose B	Rock Creek	Dec. 26, 1864	Dec. 28, 1864	Mustered out May 29, 1865
Robinson, Calvin W		Dec. 12, 1864	Dec. 12, 1864	Drafted. Died Jan. 28, 1865
Shultz, Frank	Chicago	Oct. 14, 1855	Oct. 14, 1865	Sub. M. O. July 19, 1865
Smith, William	Marrowbone	Sept. 27, 1864	Sept. 27, 1864	Sub. Never reported to Co
Taylor, William		Dec. 15, 1864	Dec. 15, 1864	" " "
Weist, Christopher		Dec. 12, 1864	Dec. 12, 1864	Drafted. M O. July 19, 1865
Wolf, Henry		Dec. 15, 1864	Dec. 15, 1864	Sub. Never reported to Co

COMPANY D

NAME AND RANK	RESIDENCE	Date of rank or enlistment	Date of muster	REMARKS
CAPTAINS				
James H. Williamson	Massac co	Sept. 8, 1861	Sept. 18, 1861	Killed at Fort Donelson, Feb. 15, 1862
Levi B. Casey	Vienna	Sept. 15, 1862		Killed at Fort Hill, Vicksburg, June 28, 1863
James P. Anderson	Allen Springs	June 29, 1863	Not Mustered	Resigned as 1st Lieut. Commission canceled
George W. Sanders	Vienna	"	Dec. 22, 1663	Resigned Jan. 5. 1865
John W. Toler	Odin	Jan. 5, 1865	Feb. 24, 1865	Mustered out July 19, 1865
FIRST LIEUTENANTS				
Robert C. Nelson	Crimea	Sept. 8, 1861	Sept. 18, 1861	Resigned Nov. 1, 1861
James P. Anderson	Allen Springs	Mar. 1, 1862		Resigned Aug. 1, 1863
George W. Sanders	Vienna	June 29, 1863	Aug. 6, 1863	Promoted
Newton Mount	"	Jan. 5, 1864	Apr. 9, 1864	Died June 22, '64; wounds
John W. Toler	Jonesboro	June 22, 1864	Feb. 23, 1865	Promoted
Howel Y. Mangrum	Vienna	Jan. 5, 1865	May 20, 1865	Mustered out July 19, 1865
SECOND LIEUTENANTS				
Levi B. Casey	Vienna	Sept. 8, 1861	Sept. 18, 1861	Promoted Captain
James J. Bridges	"	Feb. 15, 1862		Resigned May 15, 1862
Jasper Johnson	"	May 15, 1862	Aug. 16, 1862	App. Com. Subs., May 1, '62
George W. Sanders	"	Mar. 23, 1863	July 1, 1863	Promoted
William W. Mount	"	June 29, 1863	Not mustered	Mustered out as private
James M. Bridges	"	July 18, 1865	"	M. O. July 19, '65, as Sergt
FIRST SERGEANT				
James P. Anderson	Allen Springs	Aug. 17, 1861	Sept. 18, 1861	Promoted 1st Lieutenant
SERGEANTS				
James J. Bridges	Vienna	Aug. 22, 1861	Sept. 18, 1861	Promoted 2d Lieutenant
Lewallen Nelson	Allen Springs	Aug. 17, 1861	"	Mustered out Lept. 23, 1864
Adam W. Hill	"	"	"	Pro. in Col'd Regt Apr. 20, '63.
Isaac Bain	Vienna	Aug. 22, 1861	"	Died Mar. 2, '62; wounds

Roster

NAME AND RANK	RESIDENCE	Date of rank or enlistment	Date of muster	REMARKS
CORPORALS				
George W. Sanders	Vienna	Aug. 22, 1861	Sept. 18, 1861	Promoted 2d Lieutenant
Benj. F. Gilbert	Crimea	"	"	Re-enlisted as Veteran
Thomas L. Coleman	Vienna	"	"	
Guilford Etheridge	Allen Springs	Aug. 17, 1861	"	
Robert G. Stone	Vienna	Aug. 22, 1861	"	Died Nov. 11, '61; wounds
Tilmon Phelps	Allen Springs	Aug. 17, 1861	"	
Gideon M. Sanders	Vienna	Aug. 22, 1861	"	Died Oct. 17, 1861
John N. Roland	Allen Springs	"	"	
MUSICIAN				
Joseph P. Dunsworth	Vienna	Aug. 22, 1861	Sept. 18, 1861	Disch. Mar. 29, '62; wounds
WAGONER				
Frederick Wise	Vienna	Aug. 22, 1861	Sept. 18, 1861	
PRIVATES				
Abernathy, Wiley	Vienna	Aug. 22, 1861	Sept. 18, 1861	Missing in action July 22, '64
Adams, Joel K	Mt. Pleasant	Sept. 1, 1861	"	
Allen, Jesse	Crimea	Aug. 22, 1861	"	Killed at Fort Donelson Feb. 15, 1862
Bridges, James M	Vienna	Aug. 22, 1861	Sept. 18, 1861	Re-enlisted as Veteran
Bowman, Ezekiel A	Crimea	"	"	Died in Pope co., Ill
Breeden, Isaac	Allen Springs	Aug. 17, 1861	"	Died at Jackson, Tenn., Sept. 15, 1862; wounds
Bass, George	Crimea	Aug. 22, 1861	"	Deserted Feb. 22, 1863
Bass, John	Allen Springs	Aug. 17, 1861	"	Died Feb. 9, 1862
Barnett, Caswell		Aug. 22, 1861	"	Deserted May 19, 1863
Burns, Mathew J	Vienna	"	"	
Crum, John S	"	"	"	
Chapman, William	"	"	"	Killed at Fort Donelson, Feb 15, 1862
Chapman, Lafayette	"	"	"	Re-enlisted as Veteran
Crum, Aaron C	"	"	"	Prisoner of war
Corn, William A	Allen Springs	"	"	Deserted Feb. 22, 1863
Casey, William L	Anna	"	"	Discharged Nov. 1, 1863
Cheek, James	Vienna	"	"	
Cheaves, William	Crimea	Sept. 1, 1861	"	Died Apr. 15, 1862
Casteel, Lewis. J. M	Allen Springs	Sept. 17, 1861	"	Disch. Sept. 28, '62; disabil
Davis, Jasper N	Vienna	Aug. 22, 1861	"	Killed at Champion Hills, May 16, 1863
Etheridge, George	Allen Springs	Aug. 17, 1861	"	Died March 23, 1862
Fisher, John R	Vienna	Aug. 22, 1861	"	Disch. Mar. 29, '62; disabil
Farmer, James	"	"	"	Died Oct. 23, 1861
Finney, Samuel	Allen Springs	"	"	Died Oct. 17, 1861
Gilbert, Elias C	Crimea	"	"	Serg't, Killed July 16, 1864
Gilbert, Thomas	"	Sept. 1, 1861	"	
Gaunn, Newton	Allen Springs	"	"	
Harpending, Hiram G.	Vienna	Aug. 22, 1861	"	Discharged June 12, 1862
Hunt, Thomas A	Crimea	"	"	
Hester, Samuel W.	Vienna	"	"	Re-enlisted as Veteran
Hamilton, Hiram S	"	"	"	
Hazel, Samuel A	Allen Springs	Sept. 17, 1861	"	Re-enlisted as Veteran
House, William J	Vienna	Aug. 22, 1861	"	Taken prisoner at Belmont, Nov. 7, 1861
Harrel, James E	"	"	"	Died Sept. 7, '62; wounds
Hill, Keenan J	"	"	"	Died March 28, 1862
House, Allen	"	"	"	Disch. Dec. 25. '64; disabil
Hart, William	Louisville, Ky	Sept. 1, 1861	"	
Honner, William H	Vienna	Sept. 8, 1861	"	Discharged June 12, 1862
Irvin, George	"	Aug. 22, 1861	"	Died Feb. 17, 1862
Ireland, Milton L	"	"	"	
Jackson, Colby	"	"	"	Died at home, Jan. —, 1862
Johnson, Jasper	"	Aug. 29, 1861	"	
Kinslow, Robert N	"	Aug. 22, 1861	"	Re-enlisted as Veteran
Kinslow, John A	"	"	"	
Kinslow, William J	"	"	"	Killed, Belmont, Nov. 7, '61
Kuykendall, Joseph B	"	"	"	Prom. Sergeant Major
Lovelace, Boelan	"	"	"	Died March 30. 1862
Lasley, James M	"	"	"	Died Feb. 17, 1862

NAME AND RANK	RESIDENCE	Date of rank or enlistment	Date of Muster	REMARKS
Mabury, Robert	Vienna	Aug. 22, 1861	Sept. 18, 1861	Died Feb. 18, '62; wounds
Mangrum, Robert F.	"	"	"	
Mangrum, Andrew J.	"	"	"	
Mount, Newton	"	"	"	Re-enlisted as Veteran
McDonald, Henry H.	"	"	"	Discharged June 12, 1862
Mangrum, Thomas S.	"	"	"	Died in prison, Macon, Ga. June 19, 1862
Mangrum, Howel Y.	"	"	"	Re-enlisted as Veteran
Murray, Thomas J.	"	"	"	Killed, Belmont, Nov. 7, '61
McGowan, James	"	"	"	Re-enlisted as Veteran
Mount, William M	"	"	"	Discharged Sept. 8, 1863
Nelson, William C	Allen Springs	Aug. 17, 1861	"	Deserted Feb. 7, 1862
Newton, Jesse	Vienna	Aug. 22, 1861	"	Wounded Feb. 15, 1862. Never heard from since
Newton, Barney	"	"	"	Re-enlisted as Veteran
Niblock, William C.	"	Sept. 1, 1861	"	
Pate, Joseph N	"	Aug. 22, 1861	"	Died Nov. 28, 1861
Phelps, George	Allen Springs	Aug. 17, 1861	"	Killed near Atlanta, July 22, 1864
Perkins, Henry S.	Vienna	Aug. 22, 1861	"	
Pearce, Cullin T.	"	"	"	
Roe, John	Crimea	"	"	Disch. Mar. 16. '63; wounds
Rolan, James	Allen Springs	Aug. 17, 1861	"	Re-enlisted as Veteran
Slankard, David	"	"	"	Died April 8, 1862
Stewart, Calvin M	Vienna	Aug. 22, 1861	"	Died at Monterey, July, '62
Scott, William H	"	"	"	Killed at Fort Donelson, Feb. 15, 1862
Simmons, George H	Crimea	"	"	Died Oct. 22, 1861
Seidman, Isaac	Vienna	"	"	Re-enlisted as Veteran
Stewart, Thomas B.	"	"	"	Discharged June 12, 1862
Scarlet, Abraham	Golconda	"	"	Re-enlisted as Veteran
Stone, John	Vienna	Aug. 22, 1861	Sept. 18, 1861	Re-enlisted as Veteran
Toler, John W	Jonesboro	"	"	" "
Thacker, Francis B.	Vienna	"	"	" "
Vinson, William	Allen Springs	Aug. 17, 1861	"	Discharged June 12, 1862
Walker, Francis M	Vienna	Aug. 22, 1861	"	" "
Wise, Isaac	"	"	"	
Youbanks, Henry	Allen Springs	Aug. 17, 1861	"	Disch. Mar. 25, '62; disabil

VETERANS

Bridges, James M	Vienna	Dec 17, 1863	Dec. 17, 1863	M. O. July 19, '65, as Serg't
Bellemy, David W	"	"	"	" " "
Brummitt, Thomas J.	"	Jan. 5, 1864	Jan. 5, 1864	Died June 25, 1884
Chapman, Lafayette	"	"	"	Mustered out July 19, 1865
Gilbert, Benjamin F.	"	"	"	Died Oct. 18, 1864
Gurley, Hiram	Cairo	Feb. 1, 1864	Feb. 1, 1864	M. O. July 19, '65, as Serg't
Hazel, Samuel A	Allen Springs	Jan. 5, 1864	Jan. 5, 1864	Mustered out, July 19, 1865
Hester, Samuel W	Vienna	"	"	" "
Kinslow, Robert N	"	"	"	M. O. July 19, '65, as Corp'l
Lasley, Francis M.	"	Jan. 1, 1864	Jan. 1, 1864	M. O. July 19, '65, as Serg't
McGowan, James	"	Jan. 5, 1864	Jan. 5, 1864	Mustered out July 19, 1865
Mangrum, Howel Y.	"	"	"	Pro. Serg't, then 1st Lieut
Mount, Newton	"	"	"	Prom. Sergeant Major
Roland, James	Allen Springs	"	"	Disch. Mar. 28, '65; disabil
Ragan, Richard C	Vienna	"	"	M. O. July 19, '62, as Corp'l
Stone, John	"	"	"	Mustered out July 19, 1865
Scarlet, Abraham	"	"	"	Killed near Atlanta, Ga., July 21, 1864
Siebman, Isaac D	"	"	"	M O. July 19, '65, as Corp'l
Thacker, Francis B	"	"	"	Promoted Adjutant
Toler, John W.	"	"	"	Pro. Serg't, then 1st Lieut
Newton, Barney S.	"	"	"	M. O. July 19, '65, as Serg't

RECRUITS

Brummitt, Thomas J.	Johnson co	Nov. 11, 1861		Re-enlisted as Veteran
Bellemy, David W	Vienna	Nov. 23, 1861		" "
Criley, Amos	Raleigh	Apr. 11, 1864	Apr. 11, 1864	Mustered out July 19, 1865
Campbell, Nathan	Vienna	Apr. 4, 1864	Apr. 4, 1864	Died June 25, 1864
Donahue, Alexander	"	July 27, 1864	July 27, 1864	Never reported to Co
Denning, Josiah B.	Murphysboro		Oct. 9, 1862	Died, Andersonville prison, Sept. 1, '64. Gr. 7514
Elkins, Alvey H	Vienna	Feb. 7, 1864	Feb. 7, 1864	Mustered out July 19, 1865
Evans, Jarvis	Raleigh	Apr. 11, 1864	Apr. 11, 1864	Died Dec. 12, 1864

NAME AND RANK	RESIDENCE	Date of rank or enlistment	Date of muster	REMARKS
Elkins, Neezebert	Vienna	Apr. 1, 1864	Apr. 1, 1864	Missing in action, July 22, '64.
Gurley, Hiram	"	Nov. 12, 1861		Re-enlisted as Veteran
Gray, Samuel H	Murphysboro		Aug. 30, 1862	Mustered out July 19, 1865
Graff, Andrew	"		Oct. 7, 1862	M. O. July 19, '65, as Corp'l
Grantham, Allen J	Raleigh	Apr. 11, 1864	Apr. 11, 1862	Mustered out July 19, 1865
Gray, Eli	"	"	"	Mustered out June 22, 1865
Hill, James K. P.	Vienna	Nov. 23, 1861		
House, Elcana	"	Dec. 4, 1861		Disch. Mar. 11, '63; wounds
Hayes, William	"	Dec. 21, 1863	Dec. 21, 1863	Mustered out July 19, 1865
Imhoff, Ananias	Murphysboro		Aug. 30, 1862	
Imhoff, James	"	Aug. 30, 1862	"	Mustered out July 19, 1865
Kerreon, Henry		Aug. 5, 1864	Aug. 5, 1864	Never reported to Co
Lasley, Francis M	Vienna	Dec. 4, 1861		Re-enlisted as Veteran
Longworth, Morris		Aug. 12, 1864	Aug. 12, 1864	Mustered out May 29, 1865
Lestikar, Albert		Aug. 8, 1864	Aug. 18, 1864	Mustered out July 19, 1865
Mohler, Thomas J	Carbondale	Jan. 18, 1864	Jan. 18, 1864	M. O. July 19, '65, as Corp'l
Mead, David H	Vienna	Apr. 1, 1861	Apr. 1, 1864	Mustered out July 19, 1865
Martin, Monroe	Murphysboro		Aug. 30, 1862	Disch. Nov. 26, '62; disabil
Montroy, David	Anna	Mar. 9, 1864	Mar. 9, 1864	Discharged Oct. 21, 1864
McGhee, John	Vienna	Apr. 4, 1864	Apr. 4, 1864	Mustered out July 19, 1865
Oliver, John				
Owen, James D	Brownsville			Died Sept. 3, 1863
Pate, John	Murphysboro		Aug. 30, 1862	
Pate, Matthew			"	Died Feb. 5, 1863
Plemons, William	Allen Springs		Sept. 1, 1862	Mustered out May 31, 1865
Ragan, Samuel	Vienna	Feb. 22, 1864		Disch. Sept. 28, '63; disabil
Ragan, Samuel	"		Feb. 22, 1864	Mustered out July 19, 1865
Ragan, Richard C	"	Aug. 17, 1861	Sept. 18, 1861	Re-enlisted as Veteran
Riddle, James	"	Apr. 9, 1864	Apr. 9, 1864	Mustered out July 19, 1865
Simpson, James A	"			
Shamburg, Frederick	"	Mar. 7, 1864	Mar. 7, 1864	Mustered out July 19, 1865
Sanders, Ross H	"	Apr. 1, 1864	Apr. 1, 1864	Died June 3, 1864
Turley, William S	"	Apr. 4, 1864	Apr. 4, 1864	Mustered out July 19, 1865
Tyler, George	Chicago	Mar 15, 1864	Mar. 15, 1865	" "
Welch, Lewis	Murphysboro		Oct. 6, 1862	" "
Welch, Patrick				Never reported to Co
Waters, John H	Vienna	Apr. 11, 1864	Apr. 11, 1864	Died April 15, 1865
DRAFTED AND SUBSTITUTE RECRUITS				
Allen, Garrett	Bloomfield	Oct. 13, 1864	Oct. 14, 1864	Sub. M. O. June 21, 1865
Brown, James		Dec. 15, 1864	Dec. 15, 1864	Sub. Deserted Jan. 16, 1865
Coats, Seth K	LaHarpe	Oct. 24, 1864	Oct. 24, 1864	Sub. M. O. July 19, 1865
Challiss, Benj. F		"	"	" " "
Chase, Benj. F	Greenville	Oct. 21, 1864	Oct. 21, 1864	" " "
Carroll, Luke	Orland	Oct. 5, 1864	Oct. 5, 1864	" " "
Cooper, James			Dec. 14, 1864	Drafted. M. O. July 18, 1865
DeBoer, John	Ariena	Oct. 24, 1864	Oct. 24, 1864	Sub. M. O. July 19, 1865
Ducket, Frederick	Ellington	Oct. 3, 1864	Oct. 3, 1864	Sub. Disch, Jan. 21, 1865
Dixon, Elijah			Sept. 19, 1864	Mustered out May 21, 1865
Davis, William	Clover	Sept. 28, 1864	Sept. 28, 1864	Mustered out May 31, 1865
Eske, Charles		Sept. 22, 1864	Sept. 22, 1864	Sub. M. O. July 19, 1865
Eldridge, Daniel				Pro. Lieu. in 149th Ill. Inf.
Freitcher, Abraham	Osage	Oct. 7, 1864	Oct. 7, 1864	Mustered out July 19, 1865
Griffith, Benj. I	Magnolia	Oct. 19, 1864	Oct. 19, 1864	" "
Goodman, Socrates E.	Oxford	Sept. 28, 1864	Sept. 28, 1864	Drafted. M. O. June 13, 1865
Hendrix, Joseph A				Mustered out July 19, 1865
Hefferman, John F	Marine	Oct. 10, 1864	Oct. 10, 1864	Sub. M. O. July 19, 1865
Howard, Charles	Parton	Oct. 17, 1864	Oct. 17, 1864	" " "
Hazelip, Robert		Dec. 23, 1864	Dec. 23, 1864	Sub. Deserted June 28, 1865
Kelly, Thomas	Clover	Sept. 28, 1864	Sept. 18, 1864	Drafted. M. O. May 31, 1865
Littelle, William B			Oct. 14, 1864	Mustered out July 19, 1865
Murphy, Michael S			Dec. 16, 1864	
Marion, Jonathon			Nov. 14, 1864	Never reported to Co
Mundy, Linder			Dec. 13, 1864	
Mahoney, Francis O				Deserted Jan. 16, 1865
Oberly, Augustus	Atkinson	Sept. 28, 1864	Sept. 28, 1864	Drafted. M. O. May 31, 1865
Reed, John E		Dec. 22, 1864	Dec. 22, 1864	Sub. M. O. July 19, 1865
Stewart, Archibald R.		Dec. 16, 1864	"	" " "
Smith, Henry	Tubile	Sept. 26, 1864	Sept. 26, 1864	Drafted. M. O. May 31, 1865
Scudder, Edward	Alton	Sept. 22, 1864	Sept. 22, 1864	Sub. M. O. May 13, 1865
Taylor, Isaac P	Elmwood	Sept. 27, 1864	Sept. 27, 1864	Drafted. M. O. June 24, 1865
Thorpe, John	Clover	Sept. 28, 1864	Sept. 28, 1864	Died Dec. 8, 1864
Tapping, James M	Magnolia	Oct. 20, 1864	Oct. 20, 1864	Sub. M. O. May 11, 1865

Name and Rank	Residence	Date of rank or enlistment	Date of muster	Remarks
Watson. William	Peoria	Dec. 13, 1864	Dec. 13, 1864	Sub. M. O May 30, 1865
Work, Albert	Osage	Oct. 7, 1864	Oct. 7, 1864	Mustered out July 19, 1865
White, William		Dec. 3, 1864	Dec. 2, 1864	Sub. Never reported to Co
Williams, Thomas	Litchfield	Nov. 29, 1864	Nov. 29, 1864	" " "
Wells, Edward S	Palestine	Oct. 8, 1864	Oct. 8, 1864	Sub. Disch. Feb. 27, 1865
Wiesbrick, Charles				Died Feb. 1, 1865
Wright, Oliver		Dec. 22, 1864	Dec. 22, 1864	Sub. Died Apr. 23, 1865

COMPANY E

CAPTAINS

Irvin C. Batson	Anna	Sept. 8, 1861	Sept. 18, 1861	Resigned May 20, 1862
Martin V. B. Murphy	"	May 20, 1862		Promoted Major.
John B Raymond	Peru	July 1, 1863	Oct. 4, 1863	Mustered out Dec. 31, 1864
James M. Sanders	Marion	Dec. 31, 1864	Apr. 2, 1865	Mustered out July 19, 1865

FIRST LIEUTENANTS

Josephus C. Gilliland	Anna	Sept. 8, 1861	Sept. 18, 1861	Resigned Feb. 3, 1862
William Miller	"	Feb. 3, 1862		Resigned May 20, 1862
William V. Sanders	"	May 20, 1862		Resigned Sept. 2, 1862
Thomas M. Logan	Murphysboro	Sept. 2, 1862		Resigned Feb. 23, 1862
Surrey Steele		Feb. 28, 1863		Commission canceled
James N. Sanders	Marion	Feb. 23, 1863	June 15, 1863	Promoted
James Pinegar	Jonesboro	Dec. 31, 1864	Apr, 2, 1865	Mustered out July 19, 1865

SECOND LIEUTENANTS

Robert E. Elmore	Anna	Sept. 8, 1861	Sept. 18, 1861	Resigned Feb. 3, 1862
Martin V. B. Murphy	"	Feb. 3, 1862		Promoted Captain
Robert Moore	Saratoga	May 20, 1862		Dismissed Mar 23, 1863
John B Raymond	Peru	Mar. 23, 1863		Promoted Captain
Martin L. Coonce	Anna	July 18, 1865	Not Mustered	M. O. July 19, 1865, as Serg't

FIRST SERGEANT

William Miller	Anna	Aug. 26, 1861	Sept. 18, 1861	Promoted 1st Lieutenant

SERGEANTS

William V. Sanders	Anna	Aug. 26, 1861	Sept. 18, 1861	Promoted 1st Lieutenant
John S. Prickett	Carbondale	"	"	Killed at Fort Donelson, Feb. 15, 1862
Samuel B. Gower	"	"	"	Disch. July 4, 1862; disabil
Jesse Watson	Anna	"	"	Tr. to Iv. Corps Sept. 19, 1863

CORPORALS

Ily W. Oakes	Marion	Aug. 26, 1861	Sept. 18, 1861	Deserted Apr. 20, 1862
Jonathan A. Baker	"	"	"	
William J. Baker	"	"	"	
Jonathan U. Rodden	"	"	"	Re-enlisted as Veteran
John C. Emerson	Anna	"	"	Disch. Apr. 18, 1862; disabil
James N. Sanders	Marion	"	"	Promoted
William M. Dening	"	"	"	Discharged Dec. 27, 1861
Thomas J. Jolly	Anna	"	"	Re-enlisted as Veteran

MUSICIANS

James H Pinegar	Anna	Aug. 26, 1861	Sept. 18, 1861	Re-elisted as Veteran
Thomas G. Stafford	"	"	"	Died Mar. 14, 1862; wounds

WAGONER

Joab Treece	Anna	Aug. 26, 1861	Sept. 18, 1861	Discharged Nov. 15, 1863

PRIVATES

Bays, Francis M	Anna	Aug. 26, 1861	Sept. 18, 1861	Deserted Apr. 15, 1862
Bays, David M	"	"	"	
Bush, John W	Marion	"	"	Re-enlisted as Veteran

NAME AND RANK	RESIDENCE	Date of rank or enlistment	Date of muster	REMARKS
Batson, Abner A	Anna	Aug. 26, 1861	Sept. 18, 1861	Disch. Oct. 12, 1862; disabil ....
Batson, John C	"	"	"	Died at Cairo, Feb. 2, 1862 ......
Crowder, Asa W	"	"	"	Discharged Jan. 1, 1863...........
Crowder, Nathaniel G	"	"	"	
Culp, James R	"	"	"	Killed, Belmont, Nov. 7, 1861...
Craiglow, Daniel	"	"	"	
Clark, Henry W	"	"	"	
Collins, Ballard	"	"	"	Supposed taken prisoner at Fort Donelson ....
Coonce, Martin L	"	"	"	Re-enlisted as Veteran...........
Cox, Joshua	Marion	"	"	" " " ....
Cox, Hezekiah	Carbondale	"	"	
Cook, Asa	Marion	"	"	Re-enlisted as Veteran............
Caraker, Elijah	Anna	"	"	M. O. Sept. 28, 1864; as Corp'l
Cluts, George	"	"	"	
Cochran, Jeremiah	"	"	"	Re-enlisted as Veteran............
Dillow, Willis F	"	"	"	
Dillow, Daniel	"	"	"	Disch. Sept. 6, 1862; wounds...
Dillow, Ephriam	"	"	"	Re-enlisted as Veteran............
Dillow, Abram J	"	"	"	Disch. Feb. 19, 1862; wounds...
Dillow, Peter	"	"	"	Died Mar. 11, 1862 ....
Dixon, Reuben M	Marion	"	"	Disch. Aug. 4, 1864; disabil....
Dixon, William A	"	"	"	Re-enlisted as Veteran............
Dowell, William J	Anna	"	"	" " " ....
Davis, James	"	"	"	
Denning, Cyrus	Carbondale	"	"	Discharged Dec. 23, 1861........
Edwards, James	Anna	"	"	Deserted Apr. 15, 1862
Emerson, Richard J	"	"	"	Disch. Mar. 25, 1862; wounds...
Emerson, Samuel B	"	"	"	Died Oct. 28, 1861 ....
Fry, James	"	"	"	Died Nov. 28, 1861 ...
Gentry, Thomas G	Marion	"	"	Killed Belmont, Nov. 7, 1861...
Gentry, Alexander	Carbondale	"	"	Mustered out July 19, 1865 .....
Grammer, Isaac	Jonesboro	"	"	Disch. on account of wounds ..
Greer, James	"	"	"	Missing in act'n Sept. 5, 1862..
Hawk, Frank	Marion	"	"	Killed at Burnt Bridge, Tenn. Sept. 5, 1862 ..
Hare, John	Jonesboro	"	"	Mustered out Sept. 22, 1864.....
Hare, Wesley	"	"	"	Mustered out Sept. 28, 1864.....
Hiller, Jeremiah	Carbondale	"	"	Re-enlisted as Veteran ....
Hopkins, William G	Anna	"	"	Died Aug. 3, 1863................
Lumpkins, George W	"	"	"	Died Mar. 13, 1862 ....
Murphy, Martin V. B	"	"	"	
McCoy, William P	Marion	"	"	Disch. Apr. 2, 1862; disabil......
Mann, Albert G	"	"	"	
Montgomery, Andrew J	Anna	"	"	Re-enlisted as Veteran............
McMillan, Hamilton W	Marion	"	"	" " " ....
Miller, Silas H	Anna	"	"	Disch. May 11, 1862; disabil....
Manees, Isaac	"	"	"	
Oller, Hiram	"	"	"	
Parish, William J	"	"	"	Disch. Aug. 4, 1862; wounds.....
Pruitt, James H	"	"	"	Re-enlisted as Veteran............
Pruitt, James O	"	"	"	" " " ....
Perhamous, Thomas	Marion	"	"	Re-enlisted as Veteran............
Powell, John	Anna	"	"	
Perham, John H	"	"	"	
Rushing, James	Marion	"	"	Disch. Aug. 1, 1862; disabil.....
Rushing, Robert C	Anna	"	"	Re-enlisted as Veteran............
Recards, Philip	"	"	"	
Rodden, Upton A	"	"	"	Discharged Jan. 1, 1863..........
Reed, William R	Jonesboro	"	"	Re-enlisted as Veteran ....
Rice, Riley	"	"	"	Disch. July 4, 1862; disabil ....
Shamburg, Frederick	"	"	"	Disch. Sept. 2, 1862; disabil....
Swafford, Wesley C	"	"	"	
Sanders, Isaac J	"	"	"	Disch. Apr. 2, 1862; wounds.....
Simmerman, Winton	"	"	"	
Tope, Frederick	Marion	"	"	Disch. May 26, 1862; wounds...
Treece, Lewis	Anna	"	"	Disch Apr. 18, 1862; disabil....
Treece, Jacob	"	"	"	Discharged Jan. 1, 1863.........
Wall, Thompson	"	"	"	
Wall, William	"	"	"	Re-enlisted as Veteran ....
Wallace, Anselin	"	"	"	" " " ....
White, Thomas P	Marion	"	"	
West, William	Anna	"	"	Disch. Aug. 4, 1862; disabil .....
West, Andrew J	"	"	"	Re-enlisted as Veteran...........
Watson, James	"	"	"	Discharged Nov. 5, 1863 ....

NAME AND RANK	RESIDENCE	Date of rank or enlistment	Date of Muster	REMARKS
Watson, William	Anna	Aug. 26, 1861	Sept. 18, 1861	Disch. Apr. 2, 1862; disabil......
Walker, Hugh	Jonesboro	"	"	Died Oct. 11, 1861
Yates, Thomas	"	"	"	Re-enlisted as Veteran...........

VETERANS.

NAME AND RANK	RESIDENCE	Date of rank or enlistment	Date of Muster	REMARKS
Bush, John W	Marion	Jan. 5, 1864	Jan. 5, 1864	Mustered out July 19, 1865...
Brooks, Matthew C	Anna	"	"	" "
Cook, Asa	Marion	"	"	M. O. July 19, 1865, as Corp'l..
Coonce, Martin L	Anna	"	"	M. O. July 19, 1865, as Serg't
Cochran, Jeremiah	"	"	"	Abs't, sick, at M. O. of Reg....
Cox, Joshua	Marion	"	"	M. O. July 19, 1865, as Serg't.
Dillow, Ephraim	Anna	"	"	Killed near Kenesaw Mt., June 11, 1864
Dowell, William J	"	"	"	Mustered out July 19, 1865......
Dickson, William A	Marion	"	"	" " "
Hiller, Jeremiah	Carbondale	"	"	Killed near Atlanta, Ga., July 22, 1864 ....
Harvell, William	Alexander co.	Jan. 10, 1864	Jan. 10, 1864	M. O. July 19, 1865, as Corp'l
Jolley, Thomas J	Union co	Jan. 5, 1864	Jan. 5, 1864	Mustered out July 19, 1865......
McMillen, Hamilton W.	Marion	"	"	" " "
Montgomery, Andrew J	Anna	"	"	Killed near Kenesaw Mt., June 27, 1864
Pinegar, James H	"	"	"	Prom. Serg't, then 1st Lieut.....
Pruitt, James O	"	"	"	Mustered out July 19, 1865......
Pruitt, James H	"	"	"	" " "
Perhamons, Thos. J	Marion	"	"	" " "
Rodden, Jonathan U	Union co	"	"	Died Oct. 9, 1864 ....
Rushing, Robert C	Williamson co	"	"	Mustered out July 19, 1865......
Reed, William R	Jonesboro	"	"	" " "
Steele, Samuel	Pulaski co	"	"	Promoted Serg't Major...........
West, Andrew J.	Anna	"	"	Killed near Atlanta, Ga., July 22, 1864
Wallace, Anselin	"	"	"	M. O. July 19. 1865, as Serg't
Wall, William	"	Feb. 26, 1864	Feb. 26, 1864	Died July 29, 1864; wounds ....
Yates, Thomas	Jonesboro	Jan. 5, 1864	Jan. 5, 1864	Mustered out July 19, 1865......

RECRUITS

NAME AND RANK	RESIDENCE	Date of rank or enlistment	Date of Muster	REMARKS
Adkinson, James	Murphysboro	Aug. 30, 1862	Sept. 23, 1862	Died at home, Apr. 23, 1864 .....
Bentley, Francis A	Marion			Pro. 2d Lt. 9th La. Inf. A. D....
Brooks, Matthew C	Anna			Re-enlisted as Veteran..........
Brookman, John W.	Murphysboro	Aug. 30, 1862	Sept. 23, 1862	Discharged Apr. 6, 1863..........
Butler, Benjamin	Anna	Sept. 16, 1862	Oct. 17, 1862	Killed at Champion Hills, May 16, 1863
Craig, John J	Raleigh	Apr. 11, 1864	Apr. 11, 1864	Mustered out June 22, 1865......
Craig, Calvin	"		"	Mustered out June 30, 1865......
Davis, William H	Marion	Oct. 15, 1861		....
Dolan, Arthur	Murphysboro	Aug. 30, 1862	Sept. 23, 1862	Died Jan. 17, 1864
Harvill, William		Jan. 20, 1862		Re-enlisted as Veteran ....
Hagler, Levi R	Union co	Apr. 27, 1862		Died Oct. 10, 1862 ....
Haltwick, John	Murphysboro	Aug. 30, 1862	Sept. 23, 1862	Mustered out May 31, 1865... ..
Hileman, Alexander..	Anna		Oct. 17, 1862	Died June 27, 1864
Haire, Robert R.	"	Sept. 20, 1862	"	Mustered out June 22, 1865.....
Henly, Thomas J.	Murphysboro	Oct. 13, 1862	"	Died June 12, 1863 ....
Hughes, Thomas J	"	Oct. 9, 1862	"	
Hughes, Edward	"	"	"	Mustered out July 19, 1865
Johnson, Ezra G	"	Aug. 30, 1862	Sept. 23, 1862	Disch. May 14, 1864; disabil.....
Logan, Thomas M	"	"	"	Promoted 1st Lieutenant.........
Mann, William R	Marion			Killed at Fort Donelson, Feb. 15, 1862 ......
Moore, Robert	Anna	Sept. 19, 1861	....	Prom. Hospital Steward ....
Murphy, John M.	"	Aug. 30, 1862	Oct. 17, 1862	Died Jan. 8, 1863 ......
Maneese, John P	"	Sept. 15, 1862	"	Mustered out July 19, 1865 .....
Mathis, Daniel	South Pass	Feb. 17, 1864	Feb 17, 1864	Mustered out July 20, 1865......
Phifer, James	Murphysboro..	Aug. 30, 1862	Sept. 23, 1862	Mustered out May. 31, 1865 .....
Reynolds, Isaac W.	"	Oct. 3, 1862	Oct. 17, 1862	Deserted Feb. 20. 1863 ....
Pierce, Thomas J.	Raleigh	Apr. 11, 1894	Apr. 11, 1864	Mustered out July 19, 1865 .....
Sheets, Valentine B.	Murphysboro	Oct. 6, 1862	Oct. 17, 1862	Tr. to Inv. Corps Oct. 27, 1863
Thetford, Henry	"	Aug. 30, 1862	Sept. 23, 1862	Deserted Feb. 8, 1863 ....
Vandergraff, David	"		"	Mustered out May 81, 1865 .....
Wall, Hardin	Anna	Apr. 7, 1864	Apr. 7, 1864	Abs't, sick, at M. O. of Reg ....
Yates, Wesley	"	Sept. 20, 1862	Oct. 17, 1862	....

NAME AND RANK	RESIDENCE	Date of rank or enlistment	Date of muster	REMARKS
DRAFT'D AND SUBSTITUTE RECRUITS				
Archer, Eugene A			Sept. 29, 1864	Mustered out May 31, 1865
Barnes, James R			"	Drafted. Never reported to Co.
Burris, John H	Jefferson	Oct. 20, 1864	Oct. 20, 1864	Drafted. M. O. July 19, 1865
Bartley, Daniel	St. Clair co	Dec. 23, 1864	Dec. 23, 1864	Sub. M. O. July 19, 1865
Birdnow, John L		Dec. 6, 1864	Dec. 6, 1864	Drafted. M. O. July 10, 1865
Bowers, Henry	Richwood	Oct. 13, 1864	Oct. 13, 1864	Mustered out May 26, 1865
Bender, Peter	Lambville	Sept. 29, 1864	Sept. 29, 1864	Mustered out May 31, 1865
Curtis, Wilber F	Walnut Grove	Oct. 5, 1864	Oct. 5, 1864	Drafted. M. O. July 19, 1865
Croy, Jacob	Jefferson	Oct. 13, 1864	Oct. 13, 1864	" " "
Crowley, Patrick		Dec. 19, 1864	Dec. 19, 1864	Sub. M. O. July 19, 1865
Conners, John	Clarion	Dec. 21, 1864	Dec. 21, 1864	Sub. Absent, sick at M O. o Regiment
Carland, John				Sub. Never reported to Co
Clausin, William H	Columbia	Sept. 27, 1864	Sept. 27, 1864	Sub. M. O. May 31, 1865
Crooker, Joseph O	Mendota	Sept. 30, 1864	Sept. 30, 1864	Mustered out May 31, 1865
Davis, William S	Jefferson	Oct. 15, 1864	Oct. 15, 1864	Drafted. Disch. May 11, 1865; wounds
Englehart, John C	Walnut Grove	Oct. 5, 1864	Oct. 5, 1864	Drafted. M. O. July 19, 1865
Eichenlaub, George	Jefferson	Oct. 18, 1864	Oct. 18, 1864	" " "
Edmonson, Bertram	Chicago	Oct. 10, 1864	Oct. 10, 1864	Sub M. O. July 19, 1865
Frazier, John			Dec. 1, 1864	Drafted. M. O. July 19, 1865
Fisher, John O	Wilburton	Oct. 18, 1864	Oct. 18, 1864	Mustered out May 31, 1865
Gallup, John N	Mendota	Sept. 30, 1864	Sept 30, 1864	" " "
Hewitt, David	Hope	Oct. 3, 1864	Oct. 3, 1864	Drafted. M O. July 19, 1865
Higginson, Henry C			Mar. 11, 1864	Never reported to Co.
Herr. Frederick	Serena	Oct. 2, 1864	Oct. 2, 1864	Sub. M O. May 31, 1865
Hammond, Charles		Dec. 22, 1864	Dec. 22, 1864	Sub. Deserted Jan. 20, 1865
Jordan, William		Dec. 22, 1864	Dec. 22, 1864	Sub. Deserted Jan. 20, 1865
Kopp, Augustus		Sept. 28, 1864	Sept. 29, 1864	Drafted. Killed at Bentonville, Mar. 22, 1865
Lynch. Daniel	Cook co	Oct. 10, 1864	Oct. 10, 1864	Sub. M. O. July 19, 1865
Lynch, George		Dec. 21, 1864	Dec. 21, 1864	Sub. Never reported to Co
Lindenmire, Cipron	Westfield	Sept. 29, 1864	Sept. 29, 1864	Mustered out May 31, 1865
McGowen, James	Libertyville	Oct. 11, 1864	Oct. 11, 1864	Sub. M. O. July 19, 1865
McMullen, Cuthbert C	Manlius	Sept. 29, 1864	Sept. 29, 1864	Mustered out May 31, 1865
Persin, Frank		Dec. 7, 1864	Dec. 7, 1860	Drafted. M. O. July 19, 1865
Peckner. Frank			Dec. 21, 1864	Sub. Never reported to Co
Peters, Daniel	Wheatland	Oct. 18, 1864	Oct. 18, 1864	Drafted. M. O. July 19, 1865
Ryans, James W	Jefferson	Oct. 21, 1864	Oct. 21, 1864	Sub. M. O. July 19, 1865
Roberts, John H	Greenville	Oct. 10, 1864	Oct. 10, 1864	" " "
Ruggs, Benjamin F	Olis	Sept. 25, 1864	Sept. 25, 1864	Sub. Never reported to Co
Richards. Charles	Chicago	Aug. 1, 1864	Aug. 1, 1864	" " "
Snodsmith, John		Oct. 13, 1864	Oct. 13, 1864	Drafted. M. O. July 19, 1865
Stephens, Joseph D	Eagle	Sept. 27, 1864	Sept. 27, 1864	Drafted. Died May 16, 1865
Stange, John	Westfield	Sept. 29, 1864	Sept. 29, 1864	Died Jan. 9. 1863
Swabuland, Frederick	Pineville	"	"	Drafted. Died Mar. 24, 1865
Weber, John	Millboro	Oct. 31, 1864	Oct. 31, 1864	Abs't, sick, at M. O. of Reg't.
Wilkins, Jackson	Lambville	Oct. 11, 1864	Oct. 11, 1864	Sub. Absent, sick at muster-out of Regiment
Worman, Thomas	Ophil	"	"	Sub. M. O. July 19, 1865
White, John R	Floyd	Nov. 2, 1864	Nov. 2, 1864	Sub. Never reported to Co
Weatherford, John P	Jefferson	Oct. 15, 1864	Oct. 15, 1804	Mustered out May 26, 1865

COMPANY F.

NAME AND RANK	RESIDENCE	Date of rank or enlistment	Date of muster	REMARKS
CAPTAINS				
John W. Rigby	Caledonia	Sept. 8, 1861		Resigned Apr 18, 1863
Patrick H. Ayers	"	Apr. 18, 1863	May 28, 1863	Mustered out May 25, 1865
John P. Carnes		June 20, 1865	June 20, 1865	Mustered out July 19, 1865
FIRST LIEUTENANTS				
George W. Goddard	Marion	Sept. 8, 1861		Resigned Apr. 19, 1862
Patrick H. Ayers	Caledonia	Apr. 19, 1862		Promoted
Philip Sipple	Carlinville	Apr. 18, 1863	May 28, 1863	Discharged Dec. 10, 1864
John P. Carnes	Caledonia	Dec. 10, 1864	Apr. 8, 1865	Promoted
John H. Hunter	Vermont	June 20, 1865	June 26, 1865	Mustered out July 19, 1865

NAME AND RANK	RESIDENCE	Date of rank or enlistment	Date of muster	REMARKS
SECOND LIEUTENANTS				
James M. Hale..	Pulaski co............	Sept. 8, 1861	....	Died Feb. 15, 1862.............. ..
Philip Sipple......................	Caledonia	Feb. 15, 1862	....	Promoted ....
John P. Carnes	Pulaski co	Apr. 18, 1863	May 28, 1863	" ....
Lorenzo D. Hartwell..........	Williamson co......	July 18, 1865	Not mustered	M. O. July 19, '65, as Serg't...
FIRST SERGEANT				
James F. Richardson	Johnson co............	Aug. 30, 1861	Sept. 18, 1861	Disch. Apr. 19, '62; disabil......
SERGEANTS				
Philip Sipple..	Carlinville	Aug. 22, 1861	"	Promoted 2d Lieutenant ....
Samuel Graves................	Pulaski co	"	"	....
Harrison Burklow	"	"	"	
William L. Burtin	Johnson co............	Sept. 2, 1861	"	Disch. July 27, 1862; disabil.....
CORPORALS				
James Meadows	Johnson co	Aug. 29, 1861	Sept. 18, 1861	Missing in action July 22, '64...
Robinson King	Williamson co	Sept. 2, 1861	"	Killed at Fort Donelson, Feb. 15, 1862... ...
Moses, Youngblood..........	Pulaski co	Aug. 22, 1861	"	Disch. Apr. 19, 1862; disabil.....
Thomas M. Lyerly...... ----	"	"	"	
William Lambert	Johnson co	Aug. 31, 1861	"	....
James O. Hunt	Pulaski co	Aug. 22, 1861	"	Deserted April 28, 1863 ....
Andrew J. Grant	Williamson co	Sept. 2, 1861	"	Died May 31, 1862...................
Francis Brennan...........	Mound City	Aug. 22, 1861	"	....
MUSICIANS				
Samuel Steel, Jr...............	Mound City.........	Aug. 22, 1861	Sept. 18, 1861	Trans. to non-com. staff..........
Washington McCormick...	"	"	"	Re-enlisted as Veteran ....
WAGONER				
William J. Yokum	Pulaski co	Aug. 31, 1861	Sept. 18, 1861	Tr. to V. R. C. June 24, 1864...
PRIVATES				
Ayers, Patrick H...............	Caledonia	Aug. 31, 1861	"	Promoted 1st Lieutenant ....
Burch, Joseph	Vienna	Aug. 29, 1861	"	Died Mar. 12, 1862.................
Burton, Andrew G	Johnson co	Sept. 2, 1861	"	
Burton, James G..	"	"	"	Died Mar. 26, 1862.................
Bowyer, William R..........	"	Sept. 18, 1861	"	Re-enlisted as Veteran ....
Brown, James W	"	Sept. 2, 1861	"	Disch. Apr. 18, '62; disabil ......
Carns, John P.................	Pulaski co	Aug. 22, 1861	"	Promoted 2d Lieutenant ....
Carns, Daniel ---- ----	"	Sept. 1, 1861	"	
Campbell, Martin V.	Johnson co...........	Aug. 29, 1861	"	Died Jan. 12, 1862.. ....
Campbell, James T	"	"	"	Disch. Apr. 19, '62; disabil ......
Corder, Edward P	Williamson co	Sept. 2, 1861	"	Died Apr. 19, '62; wounds.. ......
Collins, Charles M............	Caledonia	Sept. 4, 1861	"	Killed at Fort Donelson, Feb. 15, 1862 ....
Dougherty, Stephen	Johnson co...........	Aug. 29, 1861	"	Discharged Feb. 2, 1863...........
Depolster, Hiram...............	"	"	"	Died July 10, 1862 ....
Ellenwood, John	Pulaski co	Sept. 4, 1861	"	Disch. May 17, '62; wounds.....
Franklin, Edward T..........	"	Aug. 22, 1861	"	Dropped, for long absence.....
Francis, Joel W	Johnson co...........	Aug. 30, 1861	"	Re-enlisted as Veteran ....
Grant, Thomas....	Williamson co	Sept. 2, 1861	"	Killed at Fort Donelson, Feb. 15, 1862.......... ....
Grap, Fielden M................	Johnson co	"	"	Missing in action. Reported dead ....
Hullett, Felix A.................	Pulaski co	Aug. 22, 1861	"	Died Feb. 17, 1862; wounds......
Hogg, Francis.................	Elizabeth...............	"	"	....
Horsley, Roland................	Johnson co	Aug. 19, 1861	"	Died Apr. 15, 1863 ....
Hobb, James H.................	"	Sept. 2, 1861	"	Disch. Aug. 25, 1862; disabil...
Hobb, Burgess J...............	"	"	"	Deserted May 1, 1863 ....
Hawkins, James M............	Williamson co	"	"	Mustered out Nov. 7, 1864 ......
Hartwell, Riley S	"	"	"	
Hartwell, Lorenzo D.........	"	"	"	Re-enlisted as Veteran ....
Hutson, George W	Vienna	Aug. 29, 1861	"	" " ....
Hogan, John....................	Pulaski co............	Sept. 4, 1861	"	Disch. Mar. 29, '62; disabil.....
Jenkins, Nathan...............	Johnson co............	Aug. 29, 1861	"	Disch. Mar. 12, 1862; disabil...
Kereiger, John.................	Pulaski co............	Aug. 22, 1861	"	....

Name and Rank	Residence	Date of rank or enlistment	Date of muster	Remarks
Lawrence, William	Johnson co	Aug. 29, 1861	Sept. 18, 1861	Killed, Belmont, Nov. 7, '61
Lewis, George W.	Williamson co	Sept. 2, 1861	"	Dropped for long absence
Lawliss, Benjamin H	Johnson co	Aug. 30, 1861	"	Died March 7, 1862
Lawless, Archibald B	"	"	"	Re-enlisted as Veteran
Moore, Richard	Caledonia	Aug. 22, 1861	"	Mustered out Nov. 10, 1864
Moore, Silden	"	Sept. 1, 1861	"	
Molohon, Joseph J	Johnson co	Aug. 30, 1861	"	Re-enlisted as Veteran
McGowen, William J	"	Aug. 29, 1861	"	Disch. Apr. 19, '62; disabil
May, Briant	"	Sept. 2, 1861	"	
May, George W	"	"	"	Re-enlisted as Veteran
May, Andrew J	"	"	"	
May, John		Aug. 31, 1861	"	
Miller, Thomas	Pulaski co	Aug. 22, 1861	"	Killed at Fort Donelson, Feb. 15, 1862
Newman, John	Williamson co	Sept. 2, 1861	"	Disch. Apr. 19, 1862; disabil
Newton, Isaac J	Johnson co	Aug. 31, 1861	"	Re-enlisted as Veteran
Nouman Amos	Williamson co	Sept. 2, 1861	"	Dropped for long absence
O'Daniel, Aaron	Johnson co	"	"	Disch. Apr. 19, 1862; disabil
Oliver, John M	"	Aug. 31, 1861	"	" " " "
Oglesby, George D	Williamson co	Sept. 2, 1861	"	Disch. July 27, 1862; disabil
Peirce, David G	Johnson co	Aug. 31, 1861	"	
Perry, Gilbert M	Williamson co	Sept. 2, 1861	"	
Price, Joshua	Johnson co	"	"	
Reed, Daniel	Pulaski co	Sept. 4, 1861	"	
Reed, John	"	"	"	Missing in action, July 22, '64.
Renner, Joseph A	Johnson co	Sept. 2, 1861	"	Deserted Feb. 21, 1863
Rose, William S	Williamson co	"	"	Died Mar 4, 1862; wounds
Steel, Samuel P	Mound City	Aug. 22, 1861	"	Disch. Aug. 1, 1862; disabil
Snider, Benoni	Johnson co	Aug. 31, 1861	"	Re-enlisted as Veteran
Simpson, Lewis G	"	"	"	
Simpson, James	"	Sept. 2, 1861	"	Died Feb. 24, 1862; wounds
Simpson, Stephen J	"	"	"	Re-enlisted as Veteran
Simmons, Wiley P	"	Aug. 31, 1861	"	Died Mar. 10, 1862
Saterfield, Jesse	"	Sept. 2, 1861	"	Died Feb. 16, 1863
Stovall, Miles A	Williamson co	"	"	Mustered out May 31, 1865
Terrell, Banister	Caledonia	Aug. 22, 1861	"	Deserted Feb. 21, 1863
Thomas, Josiah H	Johnson co	Sept. 2, 1861	"	Died Mar 22, 1862
Thomas, Henry H	"	Aug. 31, 1861	"	Re-enlisted as Veteran
Taylor, Miles A.	Jackson co	Sept. 2, 1861	"	Discharged Dec. 26, 1861; worthlessness
Underwood, Moses L	Johnson co	Aug. 31, 1861	"	Re-enlisted as Veteran
Vanderbilt, Van C. R.	Pulaski co	Aug. 22, 1861	"	
Vancleve, William R.	Johnson co	Aug. 31, 1861	"	Tr. to Inv. Corps, Oct. 27, 1863
Webb, Isaac M	"	"	"	
Wilhelm, Daniel	"	"	"	Dropped for long absence
West, Joseph	Williamson co	Sept. 2, 1861	"	Mustered out Dec. 31, 1864
Willeford, Joseph W.	"	"	"	Transferred to Co. B
Weaver, Jasper	Johnson co	Sept. 17, 1861	"	
Weaver, John	"	"	"	

VETERANS

Name and Rank	Residence	Date of rank or enlistment	Date of muster	Remarks
Bowyer, William R	Johnson co	Jan. 5, 1864	Jan. 5, 1864	Mustered out July 19, 1865
Calhoun, Joseph J.	"	"	"	" "
Francis, Joel W	"	"	"	M. O. July 19. '65, as Corp'l
Hutson, George W	"	Dec. 17, 1863	Dec. 17, 1863	M. O. July 19, '65, as Serg't
Hartwell, Lorenzo D	Williamson co	Jan. 5, 1864	Jan. 5, 1864	" " " "
Lawliss, Archibald B	Johnson co	"	"	Mustered out July 19, 1865
May, George W.	"	"	"	M. O. July 19, '65, as Serg't
McCormick, Washington	Pulaski co	"	"	M. O. July 19, '65, as Corp'l
Molohon, Joseph J	Chicago	Mar. 31, 1864	Mar. 31, 1864	Mustered out July 19, 1865
Newton, Isaac J	Johnson co	Jan. 5, 1864	Jan. 5, 1864	Killed before Atlanta, July 21, 1864
Simpson, Stephen J.	"	"	"	Deserted Aug. 18, 1864
Snider, Benoni	"	"	"	Mustered out July 19, 1865
Thomas, Henry H	"	"	"	" " "
Underwood, Moses L.	"	"	"	Abs., sick, at M. O. of Reg't

RECRUITS

Name and Rank	Residence	Date of rank or enlistment	Date of muster	Remarks
Branscome, Edmund	Vienna	Sept. 6, 1862	Sept. 6, 1862	Died Mar. 2, 1863
Boren, James G	Raleigh	Apr. 11, 1864	Apr. 11, 1864	Mustered out July 19, 1865
Calhoun, Joseph J.	Johnson co	Sept. 19, 1861		Re-enlisted as Veteran
Carritt, Thomas M	Vienna	Sept. 6, 1862	Sept. 6, 1862	Mustered out May 81, 1865
Clemson, Aaron B		Aug. 22, 1863	Aug. 22, 1868	M. O. July 19, '65, as Serg't

Name and Rank	Residence	Date of rank or enlistment	Date of muster	Remarks
Garner, Dallas	Benton	Apr. 9, 1862	Apr. 9, 1862	Mustered out Apr. 5, 1865.
Holmes, John	Johnson co.	Sept. 28, 1861		Disch. for long absence
Hartwell, Joseph W	Marion	Aug. 10, 1861	Sept. 23, 1862	Disch. Mar. 6, 1865; wounds...
Hageman, Henry T. V		Feb. 22, 1864	Mar. 1, 1864	Absent, sick, at M. O. of Reg,
Lemmons, Charles H	Vienna	Sept. 6, 1862	Sept. 6, 1862	M. O. May 31, 1865; as Corp'l.
Lynch, Thomas	Marion			Disch. Mar. 29, '62; disabil
Lynch, Thomas	"	July 20, 1862	July 20, 1862	Mustered out May 31, 1865
Leonard, Martin N		Sept. 28, 1863	Sept. 28, 1863	M. O. July 19, '65, as Corp'l...
Price, Peter	Murphysboro	Aug. 30, 1862	Sept. 23, 1862	Deserted Oct. 7, 1863
Price, Joseph T	"	"	"	Died April 5, 1863..
Reeves, John L. A	Nashville	Mar 1, 1862	Mar. 1, 1862	Deserted Jan. 7. 1863
Simmons, James W.	Johnson co.	Nov. 22, 1861		Deserted Feb. 21, 1863
Thomas, Joseph H	Vienna	May 1, 1864	May 1, 1864	Killed at Lovejoy Station, Sept. 4, 1864
Veach, Joseph K	Johnson co.	Sept. 19, 1861		Disch. Apr. 19, '62; disabil
Walker, David	Pulaski co	Sept. 27, 1861		Disch. July 28, 1862; disabil ...
Webb, James A	Carbondale	Feb. 6, 1864	Feb. 6, 1864	Deserted Jan., 1865; sentenced by G. C. M. to Dry Tortugas.

DRAFTED AND SUBSTITUTE RECRUITS

Name and Rank	Residence	Date of rank or enlistment	Date of muster	Remarks
Baugh, Erastus..		Oct. 14, 1864	Oct. 14, 1864	Drafted. M. O. June 22, '65...
Browning, William R.		Oct. 15, 1864	Oct. 15, 1864	Drafted. M. O. July 19. '65...
Byrne, James A.		Dec. 22, 1864	Dec. 22, 1864	Sub. Never reported to Co.
Baker, Martin		Dec. 1, 1864	Dec. 1, 1864	Drafted. Never reported to Co.
Burdick, Calvin		Oct. 21, 1864	Oct. 21, 1864	Sub. Died May 11, 1865.
Cruzen, Eli W	Jefferson	Oct. 15, 1864	Oct. 15, 1864	Drafted. M O. July 19, '65...
Colladay, Stephen M		Oct. 19, 1864	Oct. 19, 1864	Sub. M. O. July 19, 1865
Clesson, Derrick B..	Holland	"	"	Drafted. M. O. May 26, '65...
Cook, Benj. M	Jefferson.	Oct. 14, 1864	Oct. 14, 1864	Drafted. M. O. July 19, '65...
Combs, Henry B	"	"	"	Drafted. M. O. June 21, '65...
Clements William H				Sub. Died Jan. 9, 1865.
Davis, Newton J.	Jefferson	Oct. 15, 1864	Oct. 15, 1864	Drafted. M. O. July 19, '65...
Darnell, Marion	Holland	Oct. 19, 1864	Oct. 19, 1864	" " "
Duncan, John		"	"	Sub. M. O. May 29, 1865
Ford, Joseph F.	Jefferson	Oct. 15, 1864	Oct. 15, 1864	Drafted. M. O. July 19, '65...
Green, Robert H	"		"	" " "
Gooden, William		"	"	Sub. M. O. July 19, 1865
Hiltibidal, George W	Jefferson.	Oct. 14, 1864	Oct. 14, 1864	Drafted. M. O. July 19, '65...
Hays, John M		Oct. 15, 1864	Oct. 15, 1864	" " "
Henderson, Samuel P.			Oct. 17, 1864	" " "
Hunter, John H.		Oct. 13, 1864	Oct. 13, 1864	Promoted 1st Lieutenant
Huth, Conrad			Dec. 1, 1864	Drafted. M. O. July 19, '65...
Hoshels, Ludwick		Dec. 21, 1864	Dec. 21, 1864	Sub. M. O. July 19, 1865
Kyburty, John			Dec. 13, 1864	Drafted. M. O. July 19, '65...
Kinney, Thomas		Dec. '17, 1864	Dec. 17, 1864	Sub. M. O. July 27, 1865
Kane, John.		Dec. '14, 1864	Dec. 14, 1864	Sub. M. O. July 19, 1965
Lillie, Thomas		Dec. 28, 1864	Dec. 28, 1864	Sub. Never reported to Co....
McCann, Dallas	Jefferson	Oct. 14, 1864	Oct. 14, 1864	Drafted. M. O. July 19, '85...
McDonald, James		Dec. 23, 1864	Dec. 23, 1864	Sub. Never reported to Co....
Murphy, Michael			Dec. 13, 1864	Drafted. Never reported to Co.
Meyer, Jacob			Dec. 7, 1864	Drafted. M. O. July 19, '65...
McCraight, James	Lewistown	Oct. 11, 1864	Oct. 12, 1864	Sub. Died May 11, 1865.
Pittenger, Charles W		Oct. 18, 1864	Oct. 18, 1864	Sub. M. O. July 19, 1865
Putnam, Henry F		Sept. 30, 1864	Sept. 30, 1864	Sub. Never reported to Co....
Quim, George W.		Oct. 20, 1864	Oct. 20, 1864	Sub. M. O. July 19, 1865
Raugh, William	Jefferson.	Oct. 12, 1864	Oct. 12, 1864	Drafted. M. O. July 19, '65 ...
Ryans, Michael.		Oct. 27, 1864	Dec. 27, 1864	Sub Never reported to Co....
Shelton, Samuel P.		Oct. 15, 1864	Oct. 15, 1864	Drafted. M. O. July 19, '65...
Sanger, Henry P		Oct. 21, 1864	Oct. 21, 1864	Sub. M. O. July 19, 1865
Smith, John D		Oct. 13, 1864	Oct. 13, 1864	" " " "
Stephens, Matthew		Oct. 6, 1864	"	Sub. Never reported to Co....
Stine, Casper	Appanoose	Dec. 13, 1864	Dec. 13, 1864	Drafted. M. O. July 19, '65...
Schaffer, Charles..		Oct. 20, 1864	Oct. 20, 1864	Sub Never reported to Co ...
Smith, John		Dec. 22, 1864	Dec. 22, 1864	Sub. Deserted June 26, 1865.
Tunce, August			Dec. 6, 1864	Drafted. M. O. July 19, 1865..
Taylor, Drury M	Jefferson	Oct. 15, 1864	Oct. 15, 1864	Drafted. Deserted June 26, '65
Webster, John		Oct. 12, 1864	Oct. 12, 1864	Sub. M. O. July 19, 1865
Warty, Julius		Oct. 6, 1864	Oct. 2, 1864	Drafted. M. O. July 19, 1865...
Wilkins, William		Oct. 11, 1864	Oct. 12, 1864	Sub. Never reported to Co....
White, Daniel			Oct. 8, 1864	Drafted, Never reported to Co.
Woodruff, James (1)		Dec. 15, 1864	Dec. 15, 1864	Sub. Never reported to Co....
Woodruff, James (2)		Dec. 23, 1864	Dec. 23, 1864	
Worman, Thomas J.		Oct. 11, 1864	Oct. 11, 1864	Sub. Never reported to Co ...
Warner, John	Bruce	Oct. 21, 1864	Oct. 21, 1864	Sub. M. O. June 26, 1865......

NAME AND RANK	RESIDENCE	Date of rank or enlistment	Date of muster	REMARKS
Wyatt, Martin	Jefferson.............	Oct. 15, 1864	Oct. 15, 1864	Drafted. Deserted June 26, 1865
Yule, James C	....	Oct. 12, 1864	Oct. 12, 1864	Sub. M. O. July 19, 1865 .....

COMPANY G

CAPTAINS

Willis A. Stricklin	Harrisburg............	Sept. 8, 1861	Sept. 18, 1861	Resigned Mar. 14, 1863 ....
Simpson S. Stricklin.........	"	Mar. 14, 1863	May 17, 1863	Mustered out Nov. 10, 1864.....
Monroe J. Potts	"	Nov. 10, 1864	April 6, 1865	Mustered out July 19, 1865......

FIRST LIEUTENANTS

Larkin M. Riley	Harrisburg...........	Sept. 8, 1861	Sept. 18, 1861	Died Feb. 25, 1862 ....
Simpson S. Stricklin.........	"	Feb. 25, 1862	....	Promoted..
Monroe J. Potts	White co............	Mar. 14, 1863	May 17, 1863	Promoted Adjutant..................
William S. Blackman........	Stonefort	June 9, 1864	Dec. 17, 1964	Mustered out July 19, 1865......

SECOND LIEUTENANTS

Simpson S. Stricklin.........	Harrisburg	Sept. 8, 1861	Sept. 18, 1861	Promoted . ...
Benjamin Sisk	"	Feb. 25, 1862	....	Resigned Aug. 1, 1863 ...
John W. Stricklin	Saline co..............	July 18, 1865	Not Mustered	M. O. July 19, 1865, as Serg't

FIRST SERGEANT

William D. Cleary	Harrisburg...........	Sept. 2, 1861	Sept. 18, 1861	Discharged May 11, 1862...........

SERGEANTS.

Robert A. Johnson	Harrisburg...........	Sept. 2, 1861	Sept. 18, 1861	Died June 7, 1862................
LeRoy Dunn	"	"	"	Discharged Apr. 19, 1862 ....
Jeremiah Owen	"	"	"	Discharged May 26, 1862........
Andrew W. Horn	"	"	"	Discharged Aug. 18, 1862 ....

CORPORALS

John Dillinger	Jackson co..........	Sept. 4, 1861	Sept. 18, 1861	....
Monroe J. Potts	White co............	Sept. 2, 1861	"	Promoted 1st Lieutenant ....
James W. Smith..............	Jackson co..........	Sept. 4, 1861	"	....
Milton P. Young	Hamilton co	Sept. 2, 1861	"	Dropped from rolls ....
John B. Sewel	Jackson co..........	Sept. 4, 1861	"	Died Mar 14, 1863................
Hugh D. Wilson	Hamilton co	Sept. 2, 1861	"	Deserted Feb. 20, 1863............
Benjamin Sisk	Saline co.......	"	"	Promoted 2d Lieutenant..........
James W. Allen	Hamilton co	"	"	Died Feb. 21, '62; wounds........

MUSICIANS

Francis M. Allen..............	Hamilton co	Sept. 2, 1861	Sept. 18, 1861	Died Mar. 21, '62; wounds ......
Zachariah B. Allen	"	"	"	Re-enlisted as Veteran ....

WAGONER

Israel D. Lisk	Saline co..............	Sept. 2, 1861	Sept. 18, 1861	Discharged May 2, 1862...........

PRIVATES

Akin, Singleton........	Saline co............	Sept. 2, 1861	Sept. 18, 1861	....
Allen, William D..............	Hamilton co	"	"	Discharged May 2, 1862 ....
Allen, Moses P	"	"	"	Died Oct. 29, 1861 ....
Beal, Zachariah	Saline co.......	Sept. 14, 1861	"	Re-enlisted as Veteran ....
Baker, James	"	Sept. 2, 1861	"	Discharged May 10, 1862.........
Burch, Churchill	"	"	"	Re-enlisted as Veteran............
Bullington, Benj. S...........	"	"	"	Died Jan. 25, 1862 ....
Bridges, George W	"	"	"	Deserted Feb. 20, 1863 ....
Blackman, William S.......	"	"	"	Re-enlisted as Veteran
Blackman, David J	"	"	"	Discharged May 11, 1862.........
Baren, Reuben	Jackson co	Sept. 11, 1861	"	Discharged May 10, 1862.........
Brandon, William W	Saline co............	"	"	
Brandon, James M	"	"	"	....
Baren, William R..............	"	"	"	
Bolin, Andrew J	"	Sept. 2, 1861	"	Trans. to Co. D 18th Ill. Inf....

Name and Rank	Residence	Date of rank or enlistment	Date of Muster	Remarks
Burcham, William	"	Sept. 2, 1861	Sept. 18, 1861	Discharged May 23, 1863.........
Byron, Green H	"		"	Re-enlisted as Veteran ....
Dillon, Henry	"	Sept. 14, 1861	"	Died Feb. 16, 1863 ....
Dunn, John C	"	Sept. 2, 1861	"	Re-enlisted as Veteran ....
DeGrote, William H	"		"	" " ......
Dickson, James J	"		"	Died Nov. 3, 1861.. ....
Dickson, William E...........	"		"	Discharged Sept. 11, 1862.......
Estes, Chism J	"		"	Discharged April 20, 1862 ....
Estes, James H...............	"	Sept. 16, 1861	"	Wounded and died at Ft. Donelson................................
Ferrel, Henry W	"	Sept. 2, 1861		Died Sept. 11, 1862 ....
Furgerson, John W	"		"	Killed at Fort Donelson, Feb. 15, 1862.............................
Gholston, John W..........	Hamilton co	"	"	Re-enlisted as Veteran ....
Gholston, William J	Saline co.	"	"	Deserted Feb. 20, 1863 ....
Gholston, Thomas C	Hamilton co	Sept. 13, 1861	"	Died Jan 22, 1864 ....
Gates, John W	Saline co	Sept. 13, 1861	"	Discharged May 8, 1862 ....
Hewlet, William	"	Sept. 2, 1861	"	Died Jan. 13, 1862 ....
Howe, John	"		"	Re-enlisted as Veteran ....
Horton, William P...........	"		"	Died April 9, 1862.. ....
Hutchinson, Wm. C...........	Saline co...........	Sept. 2, 1861	"	Discharged Apr. 30, 1862 ....
Hill, Silas P	"	"	"	" " ....
Ingram, William A	"	"	"	Re-enlisted at Veteran ....
Jarvis, James M...............	Johnson co.........	Sept. 4, 1861	"	Killed at Champion Hills, May 16, 1863 ....
Johnson, Samuel	Saline co..............	Sept. 2, 1861	"	Deserted Feb. 20, 1863 ....
Jackson, Joseph G	"	"	"	Killed. Belmont, Nov. 7, '61....
Jennings, John B	"	"	"	Died May 23, 1862... ... .
Johnson, Ephraim	Hamilton co	Sept. 8, 1861	"	Died Oct. 17, 1861 ....
Jackson. William...........	Saline co...........	Sept. 14, 1861	"	Died, Mound City; wounds......
Keith, James E	"	Sept. 2, 1861	"	Died ....
Leftivitch, William G	Carbondale.........	Sept. 13, 1861	"	Re-enlisted as Veteran ....
Ladd, James..................	Saline co...........	Sept. 2, 1861	"	Deserted Nov. 7, 1861 ....
Mills, Alvis..................	"	"	"	Killed at Fort Donelson, Feb. 15, 1862 ....
McIlrath, James	"	"	"	....
Moore, Joab.................	"	Sept. 16, 1861	"	Re-enlisted as Veteran...........
Owen, Aaron............	"	Sept. 2, 1861	"	Discharged ....
Paterson, Timothy...........	"	"	"	Re-enlisted as Veteran ....
Porter, James A	Hamilton co	Sept. 13, 1861	"	Died Feb. 10, 1862 ....
Porter, Sanford..............	"	"	"	
Redman, William	Saline co..............	Sept. 2, 1861	"	Killed near Atlanta, July 22, 1864.......... ....
Roe, William J	"	"	"	
Stricklin, John W	"	"	"	Re-enlisted as Veteran............
Schrum, Jacob	"	"	"	" " ....
Sutton, James M	Hamilton co	Sept. 13, 1861	"	Deserted Dec. 3, 1862..........
Tuttle, Berry	Saline co.............	Sept. 2, 1861	"	Discharged Aug. 7, 1863 ....
Tuttle, Jessup	"	"	"	Re-enlisted as Veteran ....
Tanner, William..............	"	"	"	Died Dec. 12, 1862 ....
Tanner, Meredith.............	"	Sept. 11, 1861	"	Discharged Apr. 18, 1862.........
Thomas, William C...........	"	Sept. 2, 1861	"	Died Apr 28, 1862 ....
Thomas, John W.............	"	"	"	Re-enlisted as Veteran..... ....
Taylor, Robert M.............	"	"	"	" " ....
Taylor, Pleasant..............	"	"	"	....
Thompson, Richard...........	"	Sept. 11, 1861	"	Killed at Fort Donelson, Feb. 15, 1862 ....
Thompson, David H	"	"	"	Re-enlisted as Veteran..........
Vantriece, John W	Hamilton co	Sept. 13, 1861	"	" "
Vantriece, James E..	"	Sept. 2, 1861	"	Died Jan. 28, 1862 ....
Vineyard, Isaiah J..........	Saline co	"	"	Died Mar. 8, 1862..............
Watson, George M	"	"	"	Deserted Feb. 20, 1863 ....
Ward. William	"	"	"	" " ......
Winget, James	Jackson co..........	Sept. 11, 1861	"	Died Oct. 29, 1861 ....
Woodard, David	Union co	Sept. 2, 1861	"	Deserted Jan. 1, 1863.. ....
VETERANS				
Allen, Zachariah B	Hamilton co........	Dec. 18, 1863	Dec. 18, 1863	Transferred to N. C. Staff ......
Blackman, William S........	Williamson co... ...	"	"	Promoted 1st Lieutenant........
Burch, Churchill	Saline co..............	"	"	Mustered out July 19, 1865......
Beal, Zachariah	"	"	"	" " " ......
Byrom, Green H	"	"	"	
Dunn, John C	"	"	"	Mustered out May 30, 1865......
DeGrote, William H..........	"	"	"	Disch. June 27, '65; disabil......

Name and Rank	Residence	Date of rank or enlistment	Date of muster	Remarks
Gholston, John W	Hamilton co	Dec. 18, 1863	Dec. 18, 1863	Mustered out July 19, 1865......
Hays, William S	Saline co	"	"	"
How, John	"	"	"	Mustered out July 10, 1865 ....
Johnson, James T	"	"	"	M. O. July 19, '65; as Corp'l....
Jarvis, James M	Jackson co	"	"	Mustered out July 19, 1865 ...
Ladd, James	Saline co	"	"	"
Newman, Cyrus	Williamson co	"	"	Supposed killed at Atlanta, July 22, 1864
Owen, Aaron	Saline co	"	"	Killed, Atlanta, July 22, '64 ....
Porter, James A	Hamilton co	"	"	M. O. July 19, '65 as Corp'l ...
Schrum, Jacob	Saline co	"	"	
Stricklin, John W	"	"	"	M. O. July 10, '65, as 1st Sgt.
Tuttle, Jessup	"	"	"	Mustered out July 19, 1865
Thompson, David H	"	"	"	"
Thomas, John W	"	"	"	M O. July 19, '65; as Serg't...
Taylor, Robert M	"	"	"	Mustered out July 19, 1865
Taylor, Pleasant	"	"	"	Discharged July 15, 1865; arm amputated
Vantriece, John W	Hamilton co	"	"	M. O. July 19, '65, as Sergt.....
Wilkins, James Y	Jackson co	"	"	Mustered out July 19, 1865

RECRUITS

Name and Rank	Residence	Date of rank or enlistment	Date of muster	Remarks
Allen, William	Harrisburg	Feb. 6, 1864	Feb. 6, 1864	Detached at M. O. of Reg't.....
Brandon, John	"	Sept. 1, 1862	Oct. 17, 1862	Mustered out July 19, 1865......
Burcham, Levi	"	"	"	Discharged Feb. 26, 1863
Boren, James	"	"	"	Died Mar. 5, 1863
Brown, Nathan D	"	"	"	Mustered out July 19, 1865 ...
Bane, John R	"	"	"	Tr. to Inv. C'ps. Oct. 27, 1863..
Bell, John F		Feb. 29, 1864		Died March 26, 1865
Bronson, John N	Raleigh	Apr. 11, 1864	Apr. 1, 1864	Died May 26, 1864; wounds......
Campbell, Jacob C		Dec. 20, 1864		Dropped from rolls ..
Crider, John H	Harrisburg	Dec. 4, 1863	Dec. 4, 1863	Mustered out July 19, 1865
Cutril, Philip	Raleigh	Apr. 21, 1864	Apr. 24, 1864	" "
Dees, William H	Marion	Oct. 1, 1862	Oct. 17, 1862	Died May 26, 1865
Deen. Daniel				Deserted Feb. 20, 1863
Dial, Johnson				Deserted June 9, 1864 ...
Evarts, Thomas S		Feb. 29, 1864		Formerly of 128th Ill. Inf ......
Garris. Charles	Harrisburg	Sept. 1, 1862	Oct. 17, 1862	Died March 4, 1863
Groves, Richard H				Mustered out July 19, 1865 ....
Gulledge, Joseph R	Raleigh	Apr. 11, 1864	Apr. 11, 1864	" "
Hays, William S	Saline co	Oct. 14, 1862		Re-enlisted as Veteran ....
Hill, Gilum	Harrisburg	Sept. 1, 1862	Oct. 17, 1862	Disch. May 11, '65; wounds.....
Henderson, Daniel S	"	"	"	Killed at Raymond, Miss., May 12, 1863
Helms. William	Carbondale	Feb. 2, 1864	Feb. 2, 1864	Mustered out July 19, 1865......
Hutchinson, John H	Stonefort	Apr. 11, 1864	Apr. 11, 1864	" "
Henderson, Rueben M	Raleigh	"	"	Disch. May 31, '65; disabil......
Hutchinson, Jchn	"	"	"	Mustered out Aug. 22, 1865 .....
Howell, John				Discharged July 10, 1865......
Johnson, James T	Saline co	Dec. 1, 1861		Re-enlisted as Veteran ....
Johnson, William H		Aug. 15, 1863	Aug. 15, 1863	
McMurphy, John	Williamson co	Nov. 26, 1861		Died Sept. 2, 1863 ....
Morgan, Hezekiah	Franklin co	Dec. 2, 1861		Disch. May 1, 1862; wounds.....
Moore, Willis T	Harrisburg	Sept. 1, 1862	Oct. 17, 1862	
Mills. Burrell	Saline co	Sept. 17, 1861	Sept. 18, 1861	Died at Monterey, Tenn., June 10, 1862 ...
McIlrath, Robert J	"	Dec. 2, 1861		Discharged April 7, 1863
McCrasland, Wm. E	Raleigh	April 11, 1864	April 11, 1864	Mustered out July 19, 1865 ....
Newman, Cyrus	Williamson co	Nov. 20, 1861		Re-enlisted as Veteran ....
Owen, Francis M	"	Sept. 25, 1861		
Owen, Samuel	Harrisburg	Sept. 1, 1862	Oct. 17, 1862	Died Feb. 4, 1863 ..
Parks, Samuel M. D	Williamson co	Dec. 20, 1861		Discharged May 11, 1862
Phillips, Andrew B		Sept. 26, 1862	Nov. 4, 1862	Mustered out July 19, 1865......
Renfro Reuben	Harrisburg	Sept. 1, 1862	Oct. 17, 1862	Discharged Aug. 16, 1863......
Stricklin. Jasper N	"	"	"	
Scott John	"	"	"	Died Sept. 17, 1863 ....
Stricklin. Alsa		Sept. 26, 1862	Nov. 4, 1862	Mustered out July 19, 1865
Sandfer, William		Feb. 29, 1864		Trans from 128th Ill. M. O. May 19, 1865
Stucker, Green	Stonefort	Apr. 11, 1864	Apr. 11, 1864	Discharged Dec. 18, 1864 ......
Tanner, Thomas	Harrisburg	Sept. 1, 1862	Oct. 17, 1862	Mustered out July 19, 1864 ......
Tuttle. Harbard	"	Dec. 4, 1863	Dec. 4, 1863	Mustered out July 19, 1865......
Taylor, Isaac T	Raleigh	Feb. 15, 1864		" " "
Talbert, William S	McLeansboro	Apr. 11, 1864	Apr. 11, 1864	" " "

NAME AND RANK	RESIDENCE	Date of rank or enlistment	Date of muster	REMARKS
Whitehead, Charles	Williamson co	Nov. 26, 1861		Discharged Dec. 27, 1861
Webb, William P	Marion	Dec. 20, 1861		Mustered out July 19, 1865
Wilkins, James Y	Harrisburg	Aug. 19, 1861	Sept. 18, 1861	Re-enlisted as Veteran
Wilkins, James N	"	Sept. 1, 1862	Oct. 17, 1862	Died Feb. 28, 1863
Wiggs, John A				Absent sick, M. O. of Regim't
Warren, Thomas J	Raleigh	Apr. 11, 1864	Apr. 11, 1864	Tr. to V. R. C., April 25, 1865
White, Isaac J				Died July 22, 1864; wounds

DRAFTED AND SUBSTITUTE RECRUITS.

NAME AND RANK	RESIDENCE	Date of rank or enlistment	Date of muster	REMARKS
Allen, William H	Jefferson	Oct. 14, 1864	Oct. 14, 1864	Drafted. M. O. July 19, 1865
Ames, Joel	"	"	"	Sub. M. O. July 19, 1865
Adams, James H		Oct. 15, 1864	Oct. 15, 1864	Drafted. M. O. July 19, '65
Adams, John Q	Y. America	Sept. 28, 1864	Sept. 28, 1864	Drafted. M. O. July 19, '65
Armprest, Peter			Sept. 22, 1864	" " "
Brown, John		Dec. 24, 1864	Dec 24, 1864	Sub. Never reported to Co
Berry, Elias		Oct. 21, 1864	Oct. 21, 1864	Sub. M. O. July 19, 1865
Davenport, Lorenzo D	Jefferson	Oct. 12, 1864	Oct. 12, 1864	Drafted. M. O. July 19, '65
Dehler, Anton			Dec. 16, 1864	" " "
Fuller, Charles M		Oct. 14, 1864	Oct 14, 1864	Sub. M. O. July 19, 1865
Folks, Louis			Dec. 17, 1864	Drafted. M. O. July 19, '65
Greiner, Peter			"	" " "
Huff, William H	Jefferson	Oct. 15, 1864	Oct. 15, 1864	" " "
Hoffman, John			Dec. 10, 1864	" " "
Haverth, Powell			Dec. 14, 1864	Sub. M. O. July 19, 1865
Johnson, Henry		Dec. 24, 1864	Dec. 24, 1864	Sub Never reported to Co
Kreft, Frederick	Limestone	Oct. 19, 1864	Oct 19, 1864	Drafted. M. O. July 19, '65
Lybarger, Robert S		Oct. 18, 1864	Oct. 18, 1864	Sub. M. O. July 19, 1965
Lickens, Samuel	Alton	Oct. 13, 1864	Oct. 13, 1864	Drafted. Never reported to Co.
Melton, Isaac	Jefferson	Oct. 14, 1864	Oct. 14, 1864	Drafted. M. O. July 19, '65
Morton, Anton			Dec. 16, 1864	Sub. M. O. July 19, 1865
Mohor, Joseph			Dec. 22, 1864	Sub. Never reported to Co
Mathner, Amelias W			Dec. 24, 1864	" " "
Murray, Edward			"	" " "
McGill, A. H		Dec. 24, 1864	"	" " "
Reiss, Frank		Dec. 2, 1864	Dec. 2, 1864	Drafted. M. O. July 19, 1865
Roder, Max		"	"	Sub M. O. July 19, 1865
Riggs, Crisby D	Jefferson	Oct. 14, 1864	Oct. 14, 1864	Drafted. Deserted July 1, '65
Smith, Thomas H. A			Oct. 24, 1864	Drafted. M. O. July 19, 1865
Smith, Thomas J		Oct. 24, 1864	"	Sub. Never reported to Co
Schmuck, Joseph		Oct. 15, 1864	Oct. 15, 1864	Sub. M. O. July 13, 1865
Weber, Simond		Dec. 1, 1864	Dec. 1, 1864	Drafted. M. O. July 19, 1865
Wadkin, Eli	Jefferson	Oct. 14, 1864	Oct. 14, 1864	Drafted. Died May 29, 1865

COMPANY H

CAPTAINS.

NAME AND RANK	RESIDENCE	Date of rank or enlistment	Date of muster	REMARKS
Orsamus Greenlee	Cairo	Sept. 25, 1861	Sept. 18, 1861	Resigned May 10, 1862
Horace L. Bowyer	Carbondale	May 10, 1862		Died of wounds June 12, '63
Jesse Robberds	Union co	June 12, 1863	Aug. 7, 1863	Resigned Sept. 16, 1864
Augustus M. Jenkins	Jackson co	Sept. 16, 1864	Apr. 2, 1865	Mustered out July 19, 1865

FIRST LIEUTENANTS

NAME AND RANK	RESIDENCE	Date of rank or enlistment	Date of muster	REMARKS
Horace L. Bowyer	Union co	Sept. 25, 1861		Promoted
Jesse Robberds	"	May 10, 1862		"
David Culp	"	June 12, 1863	Aug. 6, 1863	Resigned Sept. 15, 1865
Joshua B. Davis	Pickneyville	Sept. 15, 1864	Feb. 23, 1865	Promoted Quartermaster
Samuel P. Steele	Mound City	July 13, 1865	Not mustered	M. O. July 19, '65, as Serg't Major

SECOND LIEUTENANTS

NAME AND RANK	RESIDENCE	Date of rank or enlistment	Date of muster	REMARKS
Jesse Robberds	Union co	Sept. 25, 1861		Promoted
William N. Miller	Pope co	May 10, 1862		Resigned June 10, 1863
David Culp	Union co	June 10, 1863	July 14, 1863	Promoted
John W. Cole	"	June 12, 1863	Not mustered	M. O. Sept. 1, '63, as Serg't
William A. York	Williamson co	July 18, 1865	"	M. O. July 19, '65, as Serg't

Name and Rank	Residence	Date of rank or enlistment	Date of muster	Remarks
FIRST SERGEANT				
William N. Miller	Pope co	Sept. 12, 1861	Sept. 25, 1861	Promoted 2d Lieutenant
SERGEANTS				
William P. Elmore	Union co	Sept. 1, 1861	Sept. 25, 1861	
Calvin A. Goodman	"	"	"	
David Culp	"	Sept. 10, 1861	"	Promoted 2d Lieutenant
Holden Brantley	Carbondale	Sept. 9, 1861	"	Discharged May 5, 1862
CORPORALS				
John V. Taylor		Sept. 10, 1861	Sept. 25, 1861	Re-elisted as Veteran
John Oliver	DuQuoin	Sept. 9, 1861	"	Killed at Fort Donelson, Feb. 15, 1862
James O. Hale	Union co	Sept. 1, 1861	"	
John Goodwin	"	Sept. 9, 1861	"	
Jasper B. Crane	"	Sept. 10, 1861	"	Killed at Fort Donelson, Feb. 15, 1862
Spencer M. Goodson	Jackson co	Sept. 9, 1861	"	
Thomas J. McCormick	Johnson co	Sept. 10, 1861	"	
John Lockey	Cairo	Sept. 9, 1861	"	
MUSICIANS				
James P. Thomas	Carbondale	Sept. 9, 1861	Sept. 25, 1861	
John H. Colp	"	"	"	Disch. April 30, 1864
WAGONER				
Axom Farmer	Williamson co	Sept. 29, 1861	Sept. 25, 1861	
PRIVATES				
Arnold, James M	Williamson co	Sept. 9, 1861	Sept. 25, 1861	
Adams, George W	Johnson co	Sept. 23, 1861	"	Discharged Dec. 22, 1861
Ashcraft, John	St. Johns	Sept. 9, 1861	"	
Busby, John	Carbondale	"	"	
Bowles, James W	Williamson co	Sept. 30, 1861	"	Died Nov. 11, 1862
Bramlet, Samuel	Pope co	Sept. 12, 1861	"	Re-enlisted as Veteran
Buckner, David B	Williamson co	"	"	" "
Black, George W	Union co	Sept. 15, 1861	"	
Burlison, John	"	Sept. 10, 1861	"	
Crane, Jasper N	Williamson co	Sept. 15, 1861	Sept. 25, 1861	Killed near Vicksburg, May 22, 1863
Cannon, Jasper N	"	Sept. 9, 1861	"	Disch. June 30, '62; disabil
Cook, George	Alexander co	Sept. 16, 1861	"	
Curtis, Daniel W	"	"	"	
Cole, William	Union co	Sept. 7, 1861	"	
Cole, John	"	"	"	Discharged Sept. 1, 1863
Crane, Elias	Williamson co	Sept. 15, 1861	"	Tr. to Inv. Corps, Oct. 27, '63
Croits, Michael	Will co	Oct. 2, 1861	"	Re-enlisted as Veteran
Donihoo, James H	Jackson co	Sept. 30, 1861	"	
DeWitt, John	Union co	Sept. 28, 1861	"	Deserted Oct. 21, 1863
Draper, William H	Jackson co	Sept. 9, 1861	"	
Deaton, George W	Williamson co	Sept. 12, 1861	"	Killed at Atlanta, Ga., July 22, 1864
Deaton, Joseph	"	"	"	Killed at Atlanta, Ga., July 22, 1864
Deaton, Dixon	"	"	"	Died April 6, 1862
Dent, William J	Pope co	"	"	Killed May 22, 1863
Dickson, Nathaniel R	Williamson co	Sept. 15, 1861	"	Deserted Oct. 31, 1863
Dunn, John	Union co	Sept. 23, 1861	"	Died Oct. 17, 1864
Dilday, Elias	"	Sept. 9, 1861	"	Died Mar. 9, 1862; wounds
Donne, William	Alexander co	Sept. 15, 1861	"	
Erwin, James M	Carbondale	Sept. 9, 1861	"	Died Feb. 8, 1862
Elkins, James G	Anna	Sept. 23, 1861	"	
Foster, William	Johnson co	Sept. 21, 1861	"	
Fields, Jesse	Union co	Sept. 20, 1861	"	Re-enlisted as Veteran
Fearo, Frederick	Alexander co	Oct. 12, 1861	"	Disch. June 10, '62; disabil
Gohram, Stephen	Jackson co	Sept. 9, 1861	"	
Grinnell, Benjamin	Cairo	Sept. 7, 1861	"	Discharged July 5, 1862
Hopkins, Joseph C	Pope co	Sept. 12, 1861	"	Died Jan. 19, 1862
Hickman, Phillip W	Alexander co	Sept. 7, 1861	"	Died Mar. 22, 1862; wounds

Name and Rank	Residence	Date of rank or enlistment	Date of muster	Remarks
Hannahan, Thomas D	St. Louis, Mo	Sept. 17, 1861	Sept. 25, 1861	Deserted Feb. 4, 1863
Henson, John	Chester	Sept. 7, 1861	"	Mustered out May 31, 1865
Harris, James	Union co.	Sept. 21, 1861	"	Deserted Feb. 20, 1863
Ingham, William	Jackson co.	Sept. 9, 1861	"	" "
Joyner, William L	Williamson co	Sept. 12, 1861	"	Disch. Dec. 27, '61; disabil
Jones, William	Johnson co	Sept. 10, 1861	"	Died July 27, '64; wonnds
Jones, Louis	Union co	"	"	
Jacobs, Luther F	"	Sept. 17, 1861	"	
Kelly, Giles J	Saline co	Sept. 12, 1861	"	
Keith, William H	Union co.	Sept. 9, 1861	"	Died Sept. 22, 1863
Kidd, Sylvester S	Jackson co.	Sept. 30, 1861	"	Died July 10, 1862
Lippsey, John W	"	Sept. 9, 1861	"	
Lacey, Bailey	Union co.	Sept. 21, 1861	"	Discharged Dec. 9, 1861
Lilley, James	"	Sept. 1, 1861	"	Deserted Oct 31, 1863
Lessley, John	"	"	"	Died Nov. 3, 1862
Latimore, Lessel B	"	Sept. 17, 1861	"	
Lamison, Peter L	Johnson co	"	"	
Lanter, Robert L	Union co	"	"	Died Mar. 26, 1862
McCarty, Michael	Jackson co	Sept. 9, 1861	"	Re-enlisted as Veteran
May, Charles	Alexander co	Sept. 7, 1861	"	Deserted May 16, 1863
Minton, Vardimin L	Jackson co.	Sept. 22, 1861	"	
McGinnis, Finnis F	Union co	Sept. 1, 1861	"	
McCormick, Geo. W	Marion	Oct. 1, 1861	"	Transferred from Co. C
Pierce, Hiram	Alexander co	Oct. 2, 1861	"	Died Mar. 30, '62; wounds
Parker, James A	"	Sept. 20, 1861	"	Missing in action, July 22, '64.
Parker, Tramel P	"	Sept. 7, 1861	"	
Parish, John J	Union co	Sept. 17, 1861	"	
Russell, Robert	Alexander co	Sept. 7, 1861	"	Disch. Apr. 19, '62; disabil
Robinson, Stephen	Williamson co	Sept. 18, 1861	"	
Stone, Michael	"	Sept. 9, 1861	"	Re-enlisted as Veteran
Skipworth, Joseph	Jackson co	"	"	" " "
Sheppard, James	Pulaski co	Sept. 8, 1861	"	
Tippi, Levi B	Williamson co.	Sept. 9, 1861	"	Re-enlisted as Veteran
Treece, Daniel B	Union co.	Sept. 1, 1861	"	" " "
Varnum, Ruffix B	Alexander co	Sept. 21, 1861	"	Died July 17, 1862
Wormack, Jesse	Johnson co	Sept. 10, 1861	"	Disch. Apr. 1, '62; disabil
Wright, Henry	Union co.	Sept. 16, 1861	"	
Waggle, William F.	"	Sept. 10, 1861	"	
Wiggs, Simpson	"	"	"	Disch. Apr. 1, '62; disabil.
Williams James	Williamson co.	Sept. 18, 1861	"	
York, William A	"	"	"	Re-enlisted as Veteran

VETERANS

Name and Rank	Residence	Date of rank or enlistment	Date of muster	Remarks
Bramlett, Samuel	Saline co	Jan. 5, 1864	Jan. 5, 1864	M. O. July 19, 1865, as Serg't
Buckner, David B	Williamson co	Dec. 18, 1863	Dec. 18, 1863	Mustered out July 19, 1865
Black, George W	Johnson co	Jan. 5, 1864	Jan. 5, 1864	Mustered out July 19, 1865
Croits, Michael	Union co	Dec. 18, 1863	Dec. 18, 1863	M. O. July 19, '65, as Corp'l
Fields, Jesse	"	"	"	
McCarty, Michael	Jackson co	Jan. 5, 1864	Jan. 5, 1864	Died Sept. 18, '64; wounds
Stone, Michael	Jackson co	Jan. 5, 1864	Jan. 5, 1864	Mustered out May 31, 1865
Skipworth, Joseph	Williamson co	"	"	" "
Taylor, John V.	Johnson co	"	"	M. O. July 19,'65, as 1st Serg't
Treece, Daniel B	Union co.	"	"	Died Nov. 6, 1864
Tipp, Levi B	Williamson co	"	"	M O. July 19. '65, as Corp'l
York, William A	"	"	"	M. O. July 19, '65, as Serg't

RECRUITS

Name and Rank	Residence	Date of rank or enlistment	Date of muster	Remarks
Atherton, James H	Alexander co	Jan. 26, 1862	Jan. 26, 1862	Mustered out Jan. 26, 1865
Butcher, William	Murphysboro	Aug. 30, 1862		Mustered out May 31, 1865
Brooks, Larkin H	Anna	Sept. 6, 1862		
Crain, Henry H	Williamson co.	Mar. 29, 1862	Mar. 29, 1862	Discharged
Crow, James	Raleigh	Apr. 11, 1864	Apr. 11, 1864	Mustered out July 19, 1865
Colp, Milton S		Sept. 25, 1862	Nov. 4, 1862	" "
Groda, Conrad	Cobden	Jan. 13, 1862	Jan. 13, 1862	
Gill, James J.	Murphysboro	Aug. 30, 1862		
Gill, John	"			Died Nov. 24, 1862
Goodman, Thomas		Jan. 25, 1864	Apr. 27, 1864	Mustered out July 19, 1865
Garrett, Robert	Carbondale	Apr. 20, 1864	Apr. 20, 1864	Abs't, sick, at M. O. of Reg
Gardiner, John	Anna	Jan. 5, 1864	Jan. 5, 1864	Mustered out June 16, 1865
Hart, Patrick	Union co.	Apr. 4, 1862	Apr. 4, 1862	Mustered out Apr. 4, 1865
Jenkins, Augustin M	Murphysboro	Aug. 30, 1862		Promoted Captain
Keel, John J	Raleigh	April 11, 1864	Apr. 11, 1864	Mustered out May 29, 1865
McCarver, William	Union co	Nov. 26, 1861		Refused by Surgeon

NAME AND RANK	RESIDENCE	Date of rank or enlistment	Date of muster	REMARKS
McCormack, James	Marion	Jan. 25, 1864	Jan. 25, 1864	Died Sept. 6, 1864
McNeal Samuel D		Feb. 29, 1864		Abs., sick, at M O. of Reg't
Phelmester, Thos. J		Aug. 15, 1862	Nov. 4, 1862	Mustered out July 19, 1865
Phelmester, William		Feb. 15, 1864		Killed near Atlanta, Ga., July 22, 1864
Roberts, John	Murphysboro	Aug. 30, 1862		
Reading, George	Dimick	Mar. 24, 1865	Mar. 24, 1865	Mustered out July 19, 1865
Tippey, William		Feb. 12, 1864		Abs't, sick, at M. O. of Reg't.
York, Edwin M	Anna	Feb. 22, 1864	Feb. 22, 1864	M. O. July 19, 1865, as Corp'l.

DRAFT'D AND SUBSTITUTE RECRUITS

NAME AND RANK	RESIDENCE	Date of rank or enlistment	Date of muster	REMARKS
Allen, Zachariah	Alton	Sept. 22, 1864	Sept. 22, 1864	Died Jan. 7, 1865
Blont, Daniel			Dec. 20, 1864	Never reported to Co
Brown, Patrick		Dec. 20, 1864	"	Sub. Never reported to Co
Brown, William J		Nov. 22, 1864	Sept. 22, 1864	Sub. M. O. May 31, 1865
Cannada, E. B		Oct. 12, 1864	Oct. 12, 1864	Sub. M. O. July 19, 1865
Carnier, William			Dec. 20, 1864	Sub. Never reported to Co
Conend, John				Never reported to Co.
Demint, Austin		Oct. 15, 1864	Oct. 15, 1864	Sub. M. O. July 19, 1865
Donohoo, James A	Jefferson	Oct. 24, 1864	Oct. 24, 1864	Drafted M O. July 19, 1865
Demint, Lewis		Oct. 15, 1864	Oct. 15, 1864	Sub. Died Apr. 14, 1865
Fields, Abram	Jefferson	Oct. 18, 1864	Oct. 18, 1864	Drafted. M O. July 19, '65
Fitzgerald, William E		Dec. 20, 1864	Dec. 20, 1864	Sub. M. O. July 19, 1865
Franning, William		Dec. 21, 1864	Dec. 21, 1864	Sub. M O. May 29, 1865
Franklin William G		Dec. 16, 1864	Dec. 16, 1864	Sub. Deserted June 6. 1865
Greenwalt, James			Dec. 8, 1864	Drafted. M. O. July 19, 1865
Garrison, David	Jefferson	Oct. 14, 1864	Oct. 14, 1864	Drafted. Supposed captured
George, Arson D	Mendota	Sept. 30, 1864	Sept. 30, 1864	Drafted. M. O. May 31, '65
Howard, Simes	Jefferson	Oct. 13, 1864	Oct. 13, 1864	Drafted. M. O. July 19, '65
Howard, John		"	"	Sub. M. O. July 19, 1865
Hawkins, J. L	Jefferson	"	"	Drafted. M. O. July 19, '65
Harmon, Joseph	"	"	"	" " "
Hayworth, Thomas			"	Sub. Absent, sick at M O. of Regiment
Huntington, Charles F		Dec. 15, 1864	Dec. 15, 1864	Sub. M. O. July 19, 1865
Hill, John		Dec. 20, 1864	Dec. 20, 1864	Sub. Never reported to Co.
Johnson, James		"	"	" " "
Kellinger, Christ		Oct. 18, 1864	Oct. 18, 1864	Sub. M. O. July 19, 1865
Klesser, John			Dec. 8, 1864	Drafted. M. O. July 19, 1865
Lemon, John		Oct. 15, 1864	Oct. 15, 1864	Sub. M. O. July 19, 1865
Lewis, Frederick		Dec. 21, 1864	Dec. 21, 1864	Sub. Never reported to Co
Ledrick, Christ				Never reported to Co
Linnes, James				Died Jan. 20, 1865
Leonard, James		Nov. 11, 1864	Nov. 11, 1864	Sub. Deserted Jan. 20, 1865.
McCormack, William		Oct. 17, 1864	Oct. 17, 1864	Sub. M. O. July 19, 1865
McCormack, John		Nov. 17, 1864	Nov. 17, 1864	" " "
Murray, James		Oct. 12, 1864	Oct. 12, 1864	" " "
Malay, Michael			Nov. 18, 1864	" " "
Murry, John		Dec. 20, 1864	Dec. 20, 1864	Sub. Never reported to Co.
Murphy, John		"	"	" " "
Myers, Theodore	Alton	Oct. 13, 1864	Oct. 13, 1864	Mustered out June 22, 1865
Merrill, William		Dec. 22, 1864	Dec. 22, 1864	Sub. Deserted June 6, 1865
Nicholson, George		Dec. 21, 1864	Dec. 21, 1864	Sub. Deserted June 27, 1865
Noble, Enoch	Akron	Sept. 27, 1864	Sept. 27, 1864	Drafted. M. O. May 31, '65
Reits, Peter		Dec. 2, 1864	Dec. 2, 1864	Sub. M. O. July 19, 1865
Ross, William C		Dec. 17, 1864	Dec. 17, 1864	Sub. Deserted June 27, '65
Stall, John M	Yorktown	Oct. 6, 1864	Oct. 6, 1864	Drafted. M. O. July 19, 1865.
Sekler, John		Oct. 18, 1864	Oct. 18, 1864	Sub. No discharge furnished
Smith, Peter		Dec. 20, 1864	Dec. 20, 1864	Sub. Never reported to Co.
Sullivan, Daniel		Dec. 24, 1864	Dec. 24, 1864	" " "
Sands, Casper	Loraine	Sept. 28, 1864	Sept. 28, 1864	Drafted. M. O. May 31, 1865
Spenser, Charles		Dec. 17, 1864	Dec. 17, 1864	Sub. Deserted June 27, 1865.
Taylor, John J.		Oct. 20, 1864	Oct. 20, 1864	Sub. M. O. July 19, 1865
Treister, Lot			Dec. 17, 1864	" " "
Thomason, John		Dec. 8, 1864	Dec. 8, 1864	Drafted. M. O. July 19, 1865.
Thompson, William C		Dec. 21, 1864	Dec. 21, 1864	Sub. Never reported to Co.
Thompson, William		Oct. 15, 1864	Oct. 15, 1864	Sub. Deserted June 27, 1865.
Vaughn, Thomas	Pickaway	Oct. 19, 1864	Oct. 19, 1864	Drafted. Died Jan. 9. 1865
Wimberly, James H		Oct. 15, 1864	Oct. 15, 1864	Sub. M. O. July 19, 1865
Walker, Charles		Dec. 14, 1864	Dec. 14, 1864	" " "
Wilburn, James		Oct. 21, 1864	Oct. 21, 1864	Sub. M. O. May 30, 1865
Williams, John R		Dec. 20, 1864	Dec. 20, 1860	Sub. M. O. July 19, 1865

COMPANY I

Name and Rank	Residence	Date of rank or en- listment	Date of muster	Remarks
CAPTAINS				
Edwin S. McCook	Pekin	Aug. 10, 1861	Sept. 18, 1861	Promoted Lieut-Colonel
Harry Almon	Pinckneyville	Feb. 17, 1862		Promoted Major.
Carroll Moore	Benton	Aug. 15, 1863		Mustered out Jan. 4, 1865.
Isaac Wert	Pekin	Jan. 4, 1865	Apr. 6, 1865	Mustered out July 19, 1865
FIRST LIEUTENANTS				
John Mooneyham	Benton	Aug. 10, 1861	Sept. 18, 1861	Resigned Mar. 13, 1862
Robert R. Townes	"	Mar. 13, 1862		Tr. to Gen. Logan's staff
John J. Curry	Pekin	May 2, 1862		Resigned Dec. 26, 1863
Isaac Wert	"	Jan. 5, 1864	April 20, 1864	Promoted
Francis W. Stickney	"	Jan. 4, 1865	April 7, 1865	Mustered out July 19, 1865
SECOND LIEUTENANTS				
Robert A. Bowman	Pekin	Aug. 10, 1861	Sept. 18, 1861	Resigned Mar. 29, 1862
Carroll Moore	Benton	Mar. 29, 1862		Promoted
David Wert	Pekin	July 18, 1865	Not Mustered	M. O. July 19, 1865, as Serg't
FIRST SERGEANT.				
Alexander H. Sutton	Delavan	Aug. 15, 1861	Sept. 18, 1861	
SERGEANTS.				
Carroll Moore	Benton	Sept. 10, 1861	Sept. 18, 1861	Promoted 2d Lieutenant
Edwin D. Lampet	Pekin	Aug. 15, 1861	"	Discharged May 10, 1862
CORPORALS				
James H. Miller	Pekin	Aug. 15, 1861	Sept. 18, 1861	Re-enlisted as Veteran
Charles Green	"	"	"	
Isaac Wert	"	"	"	Re-enlisted as Veteran
Chas. N. Emelton	"	"	"	Disch Oct. 31, 1861; disabil
John B. Reynolds	"	"	"	Re-enlisted as Veteran
MUSICIANS				
John I. Fuller	Pekin	Aug. 15, 1861	Sept. 18, 1861	Prom. Principal Musician
John Terrell	"	"	"	
WAGONER				
William Parker	Pekin	Aug. 15, 1861	Sept. 18, 1861	
PRIVATES				
Adams, John	Pekin	Aug. 15, 1861	Sept. 18, 1861	Re-enlisted as Veteran
Anthony, Benjamin H	Benton	Sept. 10, 1861	"	Disch. Aug. 10, '62; disabil
Barr, Hugh	Pekin	Aug. 15, 1861	"	Promoted Corporal
Benson, William	"	"	"	
Beckwith, John E	"	"	"	Re-enlisted as Veteran
Blanton, Thomas J	"	Sept. 10, 1861	"	
Brown, Charles W	"	Aug. 15, 1861	"	Died Nov. 16, 1862
Dickey, Jacob	"	"	"	Discharged Nov. 1, 1864
Drake, Edward	"	"	"	In Military Prison by sentence G. C. M
Dollins, John R	Benton	Sept. 10, 1861	"	Discharged
Drew, Benjamin M	"		"	Disch. May 21, '62; disability
Elson, Henry	Pekin	Aug. 15, 1861	Sept. 18, 1861	Re-enlisted as Veteran
Frasier, James	Benton	Sept. 10, 1861	"	Killed at Champion Hills, May 16, 1863
Gargus, Joseph	"	"	"	Died at Cairo
Glidewell, John	Cumberland co	"		Re-enlisted as Veteran
Guthrie, John	Benton	"	"	
Hoffman, Thomas	Pekin	Aug. 15, 1861	"	
Harris, William J	Benton	Sept. 10, 1861	"	Killed near Trenton, Tenn
Holman, Enoch	"	"	"	
Jones Henry	Pekin	Aug. 15, 1861	"	Deserted July 20, 1864
Jiles, William	Benton	Sept. 10, 1861	"	Discharged July 23, 1862
Kelly, John	Pekin	Aug. 15, 1861	"	Discharged May 10, 1862

Name and Rank	Residence	Date of rank or enlistment	Date of muster	Remarks
Keeton, Robert	Miss'ippi co., Mo	Sept. 10, 1861	Sept. 18, 1861	Detached at M. O. of Regt
Leanhart, Christopher	Fulton co	Aug. 15, 1861	"	
Martin, Isaac	Peoria co	"	"	Re-enlisted as Veteran
Marvin, Henry	Pekin	"	"	Disch. Mar. 8, 1862; wounds
Matthew, James	"	"	"	Re-enlisted as Veteran
Mickle, Jacob	"	"	"	" "
Moore, Riley	Benton	Sept. 10, 1861	"	
Murphy, John E	Canton	Aug. 15, 1861	"	Re-enlisted as Veteran
Murphy, Thomas	Pekin	"	"	
O'Brien, John	"	"	"	Died at St. Louis Mar. 14, '62
Rearden, James	"	"	"	Re-enlisted as Veteran
Roberts, Asa	Benton	Sept. 10, 1861	"	Disch. July 23, 1862; disabil
Roberts, William R	"	"	"	
Robinson, Jackson	"	"	"	Re-enlisted as Veteran
Ridley, Jonathan R	"	"	"	Died Feb. 22, 1863
Roney, James	Pekin	Aug. 15, 1861	"	Re-enlisted as Veteran
Roof, Robert	E. Palestine, O	"	"	Mustered out Sept. 27, 1864
Root, William M	Kewanee	"	"	Re-enlisted as Veteran
Sheen, Patrick	Peoria	"	"	Mustered out Nov. 10, 1864
Shidler, John	Pekin	"	"	Re-enlisted as Veteran
Spillman, John	"	"	"	Disch. May 14. '62; wounds
Stickney, Francis	"	"	"	Re-enlisted as Veteran
Strickland, Benjamin	Jerseyville	"	"	Killed at Grand Junction, Tenn. Jan. 18, 1863
Story, James	Ewing	"	"	Discharged May 10, 1862
Taylor, William	Tazewell co	Sept. 10, 1861	"	Died Dec. 6, 1861
Turman, Hodge B	Du Quoin	Aug. 15, 1861	"	Deserted June 14, 1862
Vankiper, Eden	Delavan	Sept. 10, 1861	"	Re-enlisted as Veteran
Warfield, Gilford	Lewistown	Aug. 15, 1861	"	
West, David	Pekin	"	"	Re-enlisted as Veteran
Whittington, F. M	Benton	"	"	" "
Whittington, Thomas	"	Sept. 10, 1861	"	" "
Whittington, Wm. J	"	"	"	Discharged; term expired
Winkey, John F.	Peoria	"	"	Discharged Dec. 16, 1862
Curry, John	Pekin	Aug. 15, 1861	"	Promoted 1st Lieutenant
Easland, Martin J	"	Sept. 10, 1863	"	Re-enlisted as Veteran
Fuller, Peter G	"	"	"	Deserted Dec. 1, 1861
Fuller, Philip B	"	"	"	Discharged Mar. 17, 1862
Melour, Elisha	Benton	"	"	Mustered out Sept. 28, 1864
Orwin, Thomas P	Pekin	"	"	Deserted Jan. 1, 1863
Pollock, William W	Clinton	"	"	Re-enlisted as Veteran
VETERANS				
Adams, John	Pekin	Jan. 5, 1864	Jan. 5, 1864	Corp'l. Absent without leave at M. O. of Regt
Beckwith, John E	"	"	"	Killed before Atlanta, July 21, 1864
Brown, Andrew J	Franklin co.	"	"	M. O. July 19, 1865, as Corp'l
Cousert, Elisha	Rose Clair	"	"	Mustered out June 7, 1865
Drew, Daniel C	Benton	"	"	Killed while at home Apr. 20, 1864
Easland, Martin J	Pekin	"	"	Mustered out June 17, 1865
Frazier, James M	Benton	"	"	Mustered out July 19, 1865
Gatewood, Isaac J	Saline co	Dec. 17, 1863	Dec. 17, 1863	" "
Guthrie, John	Benton	Jan. 5, 1864	Jan. 5, 1864	" "
Gargus, Benjamin	"	"	"	" "
Keisler, Jacob	"	"	"	Died May 16, 1864
Mathews, James	Pekin	"	"	Mustered out July 19, 1865
Martin, Isaac	Tazewell co.	"	"	" "
Murphy, John E	"	"	"	" "
Mikle, Jacob	Pekin	"	"	" "
Miller, James H	"	Dec. 17, 1863	Dec. 17, 1863	Died at Andersonville, June 20, 1864. Gr. 2257
Morris, Simeon	Franklin co	Jan. 5, 1864	Jan. 5, 1864	Killed before Atlanta, Ga., July 22, 1864
Pollock, William W	Tazewell co	"	"	Mustered out July 19, 1865
Rearden, James	Pekin	"	"	Died July 29, '64; wounds
Robinson, Jackson	Benton	Jan. 5, 1864	Jan. 5, 1864	Missing in action, near Watree river, S. C
Roney, James	Pekin	Dec. 17, 1863	Dec. 17, 1863	Mustered out July 19, 1865
Reynolds, John B	"	"	"	M. O. July 19, '65, as Sergt
Root, William M	Tazewell	"	"	" "
Shidler, John	Pekin	Jan. 5, 1864	Jan. 5, 1864	Killed before Atlanta, Ga., July 22, 1864
Smith, John	Alexander co	"	"	M. O. July 19, '65, as Corp'l

Name and Rank	Residence	Date of rank or enlistment	Date of muster	Remarks
Stickney, Francis W	Pekin	Dec. 17, 1863	Dec. 17, 1863	Promoted 1st Lieutenant
Simpson, Isaac	Franklin co	Jan. 5, 1864	Jan. 5, 1864	M. O. July 19, '65, as Serg't
Vankiper, Eden.	Tazewell co	Dec. 17, 1863	Dec. 17, 1863	Mustered out July 19, 1865
Whittington, F. M	"	Jan. 5, 1864	Jan. 5, 1864	"
Whittington, Thomas	Franklin co.	"	"	Killed before Atlanta, Ga., July 22, 1864
West, David	Tazewell co	"	"	M. O. July 19, 1865, as Serg't.
Wert, Isaac	"	"	"	Promoted 1st Lieutenant

RECRUITS

Name and Rank	Residence	Date of rank or enlistment	Date of muster	Remarks
Ackerman, Chas. E	Centralia	Sept. 20, 1862	Sept. 20, 1862	Tr. to Inv. Corps Oct. 27, 1863
Bennett, Joseph	Benton	Dec. 7, 1861		Died Aug. 29, 1862
Baxter, James	"			Discharged July 14, 1862
Bishop, James	Rose Clair	Dec. 10, 1861		Died Mar. 20, 1862
Brown, Andrew J.	Benton.	Dec. 28, 1861	Dec. 28, 1861	Re-enlisted as Veteran
Burke, William A	Walnut Grove	Dec. 30, 1863	Dec. 30, 1863	M. O. July 19, '65, as Corp'l
Bettis, Marion	Benton	Ap. 20, 1864	Apr. 20, 1864	Died Oct. 19, 1864; wounds
Brewer, William	Walnut Grove	Dec. 30, 1863	Dec. 30, 1863	Promoted 2d Lt. Co. I, 64th Ill.
Childers, Asberry	Benton	Nov. 23, 1861		
Cousert, Elisha	Rose Clair	Dec. 14, 1861		Re-enlisted as Veteran
Campbell, Josiah				Tr. to Inv. C'ps Oct. 27, '63
Drew, Daniel C	Benton	Aug. 15, 1861	Sept. 18, 1861	Re-enlisted as Veteran
DeGroat, Andrew	Rose Clair	Dec. 10, 1861		Deserted Dec. 1, 1862
Douglass, Thomas	"	Dec. 16, 1861		
Dunn, David M.	Bethalto	June 1, 1862	June 1, 1862	Prom. Hospital Steward.
Elledge, Joseph	Benton.	Sept. 10, 1862	Sept. 10, 1862	Died Feb. 27, 1863
Fargo, Frederick	New York	Nov. 2, 1861		Died Mar. 27, 1863.
Green, James B	Walnut Grove	Dec. 30, 1863	Dec. 30, 1863	Mortally wounded and left on field before Atlanta, Ga., July 22, 1864
Gargus, Mathias	Benton	Apr. 1, 1864	Apr. 1, 1864	Died July 23, '64; wounds
Giles, William				Discharged July 14, 1862.
Gatewood, Isaac	Equality	Aug. 15, 1861	Sept. 18, 1861	Re-enlisted as Veteran
Gargus, Benjamin				" "
Hopper, Berry R	Ewing	Nov. 23, 1861		" "
Huford, Benjamin	Rose Clair	Dec. 16, 1861		
Hughes, James H	"			Deserted July 1, 1865.
Ishmael, William	Benton	Aug. 15, 1861	Sept. 18, 1861	Killed near Vicksburg, May 27, 1863
Keisler, Jacob	"	Nov. 24, 1861		Re-enlisted as Veteran
Knights, Zina C	Walnut Grove	Dec. 30, 1863	Dec. 30, 1863	Mustered out July 19, 1865
Koons, Charles A.	"	"	"	" "
Kelly, Charles A	"			Died Aug. 27, 1864
Laughlin, Richard	"	Nov. 1, 1861		Tr. to Inv. Corps, Oct. 27, 1863
Moore, Thomas	Benton	Aug. 15, 1861	Sept. 18, 1861	
Morris, Simeon	"	Dec. 28, 1861	Dec. 28, 1861	Re-enlisted as Veteran
Miller, Andrew	Aurora	Jan. 1, 1863		Mustered out July 19, 1865
Montgomery, Isaac N	Walnut Grove	Dec. 30, 1863	Dec. 30, 1863	Abs't, sick, at M. O. of Reg.
McFall, Patterson	Makanda	Jan. 25, 1864	Jan. 25, 1864	Died Sept. 27, 1864
Peterson, Andrew	Princeton	Dec. 30, 1863	Dec. 30, 1863	Abs't, sick, at M. O. of Regt.
Perdew, James W	Walnut Grove	"	"	Died Aug. 8, 1864
Raymond, John B	Peru	Nov. 2, 1861		Promoted Serg't Major
Reed, William	Benton	Nov. 24, 1861		Discharged Sept. 29, 1862
Rea, Felix G	"	Sept. 6, 1862	Sept. 6, 1862	Killed before Atlanta, Ga., Aug. 8, 1864
Reeder, Edward R	Carbondale	Jan. 19, 1864	Jan. 19, 1864	Mustered out July 19, 1865
Storey, John	Spring Garden	Dec. 8, 1861		Died May 21, 1862
Stevens, Charles	Pekin	May 15, 1862	May 15, 1862	Mustered out May 31, 1865
Seaman, James W	St. Louis	Aug. 1, 1862	Aug. 1, 1862	" "
Summers, Sylvester	Benton	Sept. 18, 1862	Sept. 18, 1862	" "
Simpson, William				Died Mar. 14, 1863
Smith, John	Cumberland co Ky	Aug. 15, 1861	Sept. 18, 1861	Re-enlisted as Veteran
Simpson, Isaac				
Trout, Aaron	Illinoistown	Sept. 15, 1862	Sept. 15, 1862	Mustered out May 31, 1865
Townes, Robert R	Benton	Aug. 15, 1861	Sept. 18, 1861	Promoted 1st Lieutenant
Ward, Benjamin F	Belleville	Dec. 28, 1861	Dec. 28, 1861	
Walden, Eli	Benton	"	"	Died May 30, 1862
Wilson, James H	Chicago	Dec. 31, 1863	Dec. 31, 1863	Mustered out July 19, 1865
Yarder, Britton H	Rose Clair	Dec. 10, 1861		Discharged Dec. 31, 1862
Young, Alexander				Disch. Oct. 20, '62; wounds

DRAFTED AND SUBSTITUTE RECRUITS.

Name and Rank	Residence	Date of rank or enlistment	Date of muster	Remarks
Arment, Andrew			Oct. 12, 1864	Mustered out July 19, 1865
Bowers, Richard		Dec. 21, 1864	Dec. 21, 1864	Sub. Never reported to Co

NAME AND RANK	RESIDENCE	Date of rank or enlistment	Date of muster	REMARKS
Bennett, John		Dec. 17, 1864	Dec. 17, 1864	Sub. Never reported to Co.....
Burt, John		" "	" "	" " " "
Culver, Charles L	Peru	Sept. 27, 1864	Sept. 27, 1864	Mustered out June 3, 1865........
Carter, John				Deserted ....
Deans, Samuel D			Oct. 14, 1864	Sub. Under arrest at M. O. of Regiment................
Donaldson, Hugh		Dec. 23, 1864	Dec. 23, 1864	Sub. Never reported to Co.....
Davis, George		Dec. 19, 1864	Dec. 19, 1864	" " "
Dee, James		Dec. 17, 1864	Dec. 17, 1864	" " "
Haley, Michael	Meridian	Oct. 7, 1864	Oct. 7, 1864	Drafted. M. O. July 19, 1865..
Harst, Adolph		Oct. 21, 1864	Oct. 21, 1864	Sub. M. O. July 19, 1865 .....
Hemming, John		Dec. 20, 1864	Dec. 20, 1864	Sub. Never reported to Co ...
Johnson, James H		Dec. 21, 1864	Dec. 21, 1864	" " "
Knox, John		Oct. 14, 1864	Oct. 14, 1864	Sub. M. O. July 19, 1865 ......
Kerns, Michael	South Fork	Oct. 12, 1864	Oct. 12, 1864	" " "
Lewis, Noah K	South Fork	Oct. 13, 1864	Oct. 13, 1864	Drafted. M. O. July 19, '65...
Laymer, Joseph	Buckhart	" "	" "	" " "
Maddux, Ignatius	"	Oct. 17, 1864	Oct. 17, 1864	" " " "
McOsker, Edward		Oct. 18, 1864	Oct. 18, 1864	Sub. M. O. July 19, '65 ...
McFarland, Thomas	Logan	Oct. 14, 1864	Oct. 14, 1864	" " "
Marcheur, Ames		Dec. 7, 1864	Dec. 7, 1864	Drafted. M. O. July 19, '65 ...
McGovern, Thomas			Dec. 17, 1864	" " "
Mullen, Francis		Dec. 17, 1864	"	Sub. M. O. July 19, '65......
Morgan, Henry		Dec. 21, 1864	Dec. 21, 1864	Sub. Absent, sick, at muster-out of Regiment........
Murry, Thomas		Dec. 17, 1864	Dec. 17, 1864	Sub. Never reported to Co.....
Parks, Isaac		"	"	Mustered out, July 19, 1865 .....
Powers, Patrick		"	"	Sub. Deserted July 1, '65......
Rape, Butler	South Fork	Oct. 13, 1864	Oct. 13, 1864	Drafted. M. O. July 19, 1865...
Rasman, Joseph		Oct. 19, 1864	Oct. 19, 1864	Sub. M. O. July 19, '65......
Sherman, Henry J		Oct. 21, 1864	Oct. 21, 1864	" " "
Swift, John	Taylorville	Oct. 13, 1864	Oct. 13, 1864	Drafted. M. O. July 19, '65...
Scully, Michael		Dec. 17, 1864	Dec. 17, 1864	Sub. M. O. July 19, '65 ...
Salman, George		Dec. 20, 1864	Dec. 20, 1864	Sub. Never reported to Co.....
Smith, John		Dec. 21, 1864	Dec. 21, 1864	" " "
Worley, Caleb B	Taylorville	Oct. 13, 1864	Oct. 13, 1864	Drafted. M. O. July 19, '65.....
Warren, Luther	Meridian	Oct. 7, 1864	Oct. 7, 1864	" " "
Wilson, Alfred		Dec. 17, 1864	Dec. 17, 1864	Sub. Paroled prisoner. Discharged July 19, 1865..........

COMPANY K

NAME AND RANK	RESIDENCE	Date of rank or enlistment	Date of muster	REMARKS
CAPTAINS				
Alexander S. Somerville	Centralia	Sept. 8, 1861	Sept. 18, 1861	Dismissed May 8, 1862 ....
Thomas Hunter	DuQuoin	Feb. 15, 1862	Aug. 4, 1862	Died of wounds June 27, '64.....
John W. Stewart	Carlyle	June 27, 1864	Apr. 2, 1865	Mustered out July 19, 1865......
FIRST LIEUTENANTS				
Charles H. Capehart	Washington, D.C.	Sept. 8, 1861		Promoted Adjutant ... .
Henry T. Snyder	Patoka	Oct. 11, 1861	Sept. 18, 1861	Resigned Apr. 24, 1862..........
John S. Hoover	Newcastle, Ind	Apr. 24, 1862	Apr. 24, 1862	Resigned May 19, 1864...........
Henry C. Lewis	Patoka	May 19, 1864	Feb. 22, 1865	Mustered out July 19, 1865......
SECOND LIEUTENANTS				
Levi E. Morris	Marion	Sept. 8, 1861	Sept. 18, 1861	Resigned Apr. 16, 1862 ....
Pinkney K. Watts	Centralia	Apr. 16, 1862		Resigned Aug. 8, 1863 ....
Mitchell S. Barney	Richview	July 18, 1865	Not Mustered	M. O. July 19, '65, as Serg't...
FIRST SERGEANT				
Henry T. Snyder	Patoka	Aug. 10, 1861	Sept. 18, 1861	Promoted 1st Lieutenant..........
SERGEANTS				
Henry C. Brakeman	Harpersfield, O.	Aug. 10, 1861	Sept. 18, 1861	Deserted Nov. 12, 1862 ....
John B. Ricker	Quincy	"	"	Killed at Champion Hills, Miss., May 16, 1863 ....
William Fox	DuQuoin	"	"	Killed at Fort Donelson, Feb. 15, 1862.
William E. Langston	"	"	"	Re-enlisted as Veteran...........

Name and Rank	Residence	Date of rank or enlistment	Date of Muster	Remarks
CORPORALS				
Thomas Hunter	DuQuoin	Aug. 10, 1861	Sept. 18, 1861	Promoted Captain
John Vanhining	Centralia	"	"	Killed, Belmont, Nov. 7, '61
Robert L. Carpenter	Patoka	"	"	Reduced. Re-enlisted as Vet,
John McLaffiin	Janesville, Wis	Aug. 22, 1861	"	Reduced to ranks
John W. Stuart	Carlisle	Aug. 10, 1861	"	Re-enlisted as Veteran
Andrew N. Briscoe	Monroe co	"	"	Deserted June 13, 1863
Benjamin F. Brooker	Patoka.	"	"	Tr. to Inv. Corps Oct. 27, '63
Harrison Gordon	Aveston	"	"	Deserted Apr. 29, 1862
MUSICIAN				
Abraham Kesler	Easton, Pa	Aug. 10, 1861	Sept. 18, 1861	Disch. Oct. 24, '64; disabil.
John M. Bemis	Centralia	"	"	Deserted Jan. 11, 1862
WAGONER				
Samuel J. Braman	Hoylton	Aug. 10, 1861	Sept. 18, 1861	Died April 4, 1862
PRIVATES				
Alton, William A	Babcock Grove	Aug. 10, 1861	Sept. 18, 1861	
Barnet, William P	Centralia	"	"	
Burnett, Charles R	"	"	"	
Barber, Josiah A		Sept. 2, 1861	"	
Bryant, James	Lebanon	Aug. 10, 1861	"	Died Jan. 18, 1864
Boswell, John W	Middleton	"	"	Tr. to Co. F, 18th Ill. Inf.
Bell, Jacob R	Patoka	"	"	Re-enlisted as Veteran
Blalock. Wesley	Centralia	"	"	
Billings. Samuel D	"	"	"	Promoted Prin. Musician.
Bistole, Michael	Jacksonville	Aug. 22, 1861	Sept. 18, 1861	Killed at Fort Donelson, Feb. 15, 1862.
Brofield, James	Sandoval	"	"	Mustered out May 31, 1865
Barney, Mitchell S	Richview	Sept. 10, 1861	"	Re-enlisted as Veteran
Cooney, Patrick	Centralia	Aug. 10, 1861	"	" "
Carrier, Francis	Richview	"	"	" "
Christleich, Englebert	Philadelphia, P	"	"	Tr. to Inv. Corps Oct. 27, '63
Cole, James C	Shelbyville	Aug. 22, 1861	"	Deserted July 17, 1862
Campbell, George W	Patoka	Aug. 10, 1861	"	Died Mar. 11, 1862
Dougherty, Philip	Carlisle	"	"	Deserted Feb. 24, 1863
Doughtry, Benj. T	"	"	"	Re-enlisted as Veteran
Doughtry, John R	"	"	"	Disch. Dec. 23, '61; disabil.
Donohoe, Larkin	Centralia	"	"	Discharged Jan. 28, 1864
Dunham, George W	Carlisle	"	"	Corporal; Killed at Fort Donelson, Feb. 15, 1862.
Denney, William	Centralia	"	"	Mustered out Sept. 28, 1864
Earhart, Abraham L	Nashville	"	"	Re-enlisted as Veteran
Feegan, Henry	Jordan	Aug. 22, 1861	"	Deserted Sept. 28, 1862
Faulkner, Asa	Richview	Aug. 10, 1861	"	Deserted Feb. 11, 1863
Grogan, James E	Mt. Vernon	"	"	Deserted Aug. 4, 1862
Goold, Crayton	Nashville	"	"	Deserted twice
Gerrick, Jacob	Centralia	"	"	Killed at Fort Donelson, Feb. 15, 1862
Griffin, John	Chicago	"	"	Drowned Mar. 13, 1862
Gibson, Joseph	Carlisle	"	"	Deserted June 13, 1862
Graham, John R	Goose Island	Sept. 8, 1861	"	Tr to Co. D, 18th Ill. Inf.
Hutchraft, John	Central City	Aug. 10, 1861	"	Killed near Kenesaw Mt., June 27, 1864
Howerth, George	Alleghany, Md	"	"	Discharged June 13, 1862
Hoover, John S	New Castle, Ind	Sept. 2, 1861	"	Promoted Q. M. Sergeant
Hoover, —		"	"	
Kisner, David	Patoka	Aug. 10, 1861	"	Re-enlisted as Veteran
Lining, James C	Carlisle	"	"	Died March 12, 1862
Lewis, William H	Patoka	"	"	
Lewis, Henry C	"	"	"	Re-enlisted as Veteran
Morris, Henry A	DuQuoin	"	"	Promoted Corporal
Mosby, Aaron	Marion co	Aug. 19, 1861	"	Re-enlisted as Veteran
Matsler, Lafayette	Carlisle	Aug. 12, 1861	"	" "
Mallow, Alfred	Montreal, Can	Aug. 10, 1861	"	Tr. to Inv. Corps Oct. 27, '63
Nichols, Orson	Galesburg	"	"	Transferred to N. C. Staff.
Outhouse, James M	Carlisle	Aug. 12, 1861	"	Died March 16, 1862
Phelps, James	"	"	"	Deserted Feb. 24, 1863
Posey, Oliver		Aug. 10, 1861	"	Re-enlisted as Veteran
Payne, Joseph	Pittsfield	"	"	

Name and Rank	Residence	Date of rank or enlistment	Date of muster	Remarks
Petticord, Andrew N	Patoka	Aug. 10, 1861	Aug. 19, 1861	Re-enlisted as Veteran
Pearson, Robert N	Fayetteville	Sept. 18, 1861	Sept. 18, 1861	Promoted Adjutant
Patterson, Benj. F	Centralia	Sept. 2, 1861	"	Re-enlisted as Veteran
Rector, Elijah	Central City	Aug. 19, 1861	"	Promoted Adjutant
Sander, Samuel E	Centralia	Aug. 10, 1861	"	Re-enlisted as Veteran
Sanders, James A	"	"	"	" "
Simmons, William	Chandlerville	"	"	Killed at Thompson Hill, Miss., May 1, 1863
Simon, Walter	Patoka	"	"	
Shay, Timothy	Fall River, Mass.	Sept. 2, 1861	"	Died Feb. 9, 1862
Taylor, James	Camden, O	Aug. 10, 1861	"	Mustered out May 31, 1865
Temple, Thomas J	Decatur		"	Re-enlisted as Veteran
Teets, Edwards	Centralia	Aug. 22, 1861	"	
Turner, Jeremiah	Cairo	Sept. 2, 1861	"	Deserted Apr. 29, 1862
Weaver, Thomas B	Marion	Aug. 10, 1861	"	Died Dec. 10, 1864
Weaver, James	"	"	"	Re-enlisted as Veteran
Waterhouse, Thomas	Patoka	"	"	Missing in action July 22, '64

VETERANS

Name and Rank	Residence	Date of rank or enlistment	Date of muster	Remarks
Bell, Jacob R	Patoka	Jan. 5, 1864	Jan. 5, 1864	Mustered out June 9, 1865
Barney, Mitchell S	Richview	"	"	M. O. July 19, '65, as Serg't
Burnes, James E	Marion	"	"	Mustered out July 19, 1865
Cooney, Patrick	Centralia	"	"	Absent. wounded, at M. O. of Regiment
Carrier, Francis	Richview	"	"	Absent, under arrest at M. O. of Regiment
Carpenter, Robert L	Centralia	Mar. 1, 1864	Mar. 1, 1864	Mustered out July 19, 1865
Dougherty, Benj. F	Carlisle	Jan. 5, 1864	Jan. 5, 1864	Deserted Feb. 11, 1864
Earhart, Abraham L	Marion co	"	"	Mustered out July 19, 1865
Kissner, David	Patoka	"	"	M. O. July 19, '65, as Serg't
Langston, William	DuQuoin	"	"	Absent, sick, at M. O. of Regt.
Lewis, Henry C	Patoka	"	"	Promoted 1st Lieutenant
Mosby, Aaron	Marion co	"	"	Mustered out July 19, 1865
Matsler, Lafayette	Carlisle	"	"	M. O. July 19, '65, as Corp'l
Petticord, Andrew M	Patoka	"	"	Mustered out July 19, 1865
Patterson, Benj. F	Centralia	"	"	" " "
Posey, Oliver	Carlisle	"	"	
Robinson, William	Marion	"	"	M. O. July 19, '65, as Serg't
Stewart, John W	Carlisle	"	"	Promoted Captain
Sanders, James A	Clinton co	"	"	Mustered out May. 30, 1865
Sanders, Samuel E	"	"	"	Mustered out July 19, 1865
Temple, Thomas J	Decatur	"	"	Dishonorably dismissed, sentence of G. C. M
Weaver, William	Marion	"	"	Killed by a mob
Weaver, James	"	"	"	Mustered out July 19, 1865

RECRUITS

Name and Rank	Residence	Date of rank or enlistment	Date of muster	Remarks
Allbright, John J		Feb. 29, 1864		Mustered out July 19, 1865
Arterberry, Nathaniel		Dec. 17, 1861		" " "
Burnes, James E	Marion	Feb. 11, 1865	Feb. 11, 1865	Re-enlisted as Veteran
Branch, James H	Marion co	"	"	Mustered out July 19, 1865
Barnes, Leander		Apr. 5, 1865	April 5, 1865	Absent, wounded, at M. O. of Regiment
Bailey, Bennett	Chicago	"	"	Mustered out July 19, 1865
Burnett, William				Discharged Apr. 25, 1865
Crew, Joseph	DuQuoin	Oct. 22, 1862		
Clark, Thomas J		Feb. 29, 1864		Mustered out July 19, 1865
Childers, Joel		Sept. 26, 1862	Nov. 4, 1862	" "
Childers, John A				Discharged Apr. 22, 1865
Childers, Robert		Sept. 2, 1862	Nov. 4, 1862	Mustered out July 16, 1865
Dero, Francis J	Carbondale	Apr. 11, 1864	April 11, 1864	Died Oct. 31, '64; wounds
Foot, Andrew	Jackson	July 16, 1862		Mustered out May 31, 1865
Ginn, James	Marion	Nov. 17, 1861		Died June 29, 1862
Gibbons, Marion	"	Dec. 17, 1861		Killed near Vicksburg, May 21, 1863
Grider, James V		Feb. 29, 1864		Mustered out July 19, 1865
Grogan, Ambrose B		Sept. 28, 1862	Nov. 4, 1862	" "
Hopper, Thomas J	Marion	Oct. 21, 1861		
Henlin, Joab		Feb. 15, 1864		Mustered out July 19, 1865
Kelly, James	Centralia	Nov. 16, 1861		Deserted June 13, 1862
Kirk, James M		Mar. 8, 1864		Mustered out July 19, 1865
Laflin, John	Centralia			Disch. Apr. 17, '62; disabil
Lowry, Thomas J		Feb. 29, 1864		

Name and Rank	Residence	Date of rank or enlistment	Date of muster	Remarks
McQuirter, Henry	Cloverport, Ky	Nov. 1, 1861		Disch. Nov. 11, '62; disabil......
Moore, James	Springfield	Jan. 11, 1862		Deserted July 20, 1862...........
Mason, John B				Mustered out July 19, 1865 ....
Mills, James N	Marion co	Feb. 9, 1865	Feb. 9, 1865	" "
Milham, Martin T	"	Feb. 11, 1865	Feb. 11, 1865	Mustered out June 5, 1865 ....
Patterson, John M	Carbondale	May 23, 1864	May 23, 1864	Mustered out July 19, 1865.....
Posey, Jubilee J	Centralia	Mar. 9, 1864	Mar. 9, 1864	" "
Phelps, John	Marion co	Feb. 9, 1865	Feb. 9, 1865	Died June 30, 1865................
Robinson, William	Marion	Dec. 17, 1861		Re-enlisted as Veteran...... ...
Staddon, Hiram V	DuQuoin	Sept. 15, 1862		Deserted Feb. 14, 1863
Stround, Robert				Mustered out July 19, 1865.....
Smith, Amos				" " "
Stephens, Joab				" " "
Teets, Alexander	Chicago	Apr. 5, 1865	Apr. 5, 1865	" " "
Usselton, William		Mar. 8, 1864		" " "
Weaver, William	Marion co	Jan. 1, 1862		Re-enlisted as Veteran ....
Williams, Isham		Feb. 15, 1864		Mustered out July 19, 1865......
Walker, George				Died, Andersonville, Sept. 19, '64; wounds. Gr. 9218.........
Watts, Pinkney K	Centralia	Sept. 16, 1861	Sept. 18, 1861	Promoted 2d Lieutenant...........

DRAFTED AND SUBSTITUTE RECRUITS

Name and Rank	Residence	Date of rank or enlistment	Date of muster	Remarks
Brown, James H			Dec. 16, 1864	Sub. Deserted June 6, '65......
Clark, Charles			Dec. 16, 1864	Never reported to Co ....
Drown, Theodore			Dec. 17, 1864	Sub M. O. July 19, 1865 ......
Dunn, James		Dec. 17, 1864	"	Sub. Never reported to Co......
Einspach, August	Worth	Sept. 29, 1864	Sept. 29, 1864	Drafted. M. O. July 19, 1865..
Gordon, George			Mar. 15, 1864	Never reported to Co.............
Holeman, Willis B		Dec. 17, 1864	Dec. 17, 1864	Sub. M. O. July 19, 1865......
Henderham, John		Dec. 16, 1864	Dec. 16, 1864	Sub. Never reported to Co .....
Johnson, William				Never reported to Co .....
Keoler, Fritz			Dec. 1, 1864	Drafted. M. O. July 19, '65...
Kiddle, James G		Oct. 11, 1864	Oct. 11, 1864	Sub. M. O. July 19, 1865......
Klisker, Edward			Oct. 18, 1864	Drafted. M O. July 19, 1865..
Kiddle, Richard	Bremen	Sept. 28, 1864	Sept. 28, 1864	Drafted. M. O. May 31, '65...
Lanz, Henry	Richland	Oct. 19, 1864	Oct. 19, 1864	Drafted. M O. July 19, 1865..
Lentz, Henry			Dec. 2, 1864	Drafted. Absent, sick, at M. O. of Regiment................
Martin, John		Oct. 15, 1864	Oct. 15, 1864	Sub. M. O. July 19, 1865......
Murphy, Dennis		Dec. 17, 1864	Dec. 17, 1864	Sub. Never reported to Co .....
Murphy, Patrick		"	"	" " " "
Morgan, Thurman	Jefferson	Oct. 15, 1864	Oct. 15, 1864	Died Dec. 24, 1864 ....
Newman, William		Oct. 11, 1864	Oct. 11, 1864	Sub. Died Dec. 2, 1864 ....
Pelton, A. D	LaSalle	Dec. 15, 1864	Dec. 15, 1864	Sub. M. O. July 19, 1865......
Perris, George W		Dec. 16, 1864	Dec. 16, 1864	" " " "
Robinson, Thomas		Dec. 17, 1864	Dec. 17, 1864	Sub. Never reported to Co....
Rodgers, John	Walnut	Dec. 21, 1864	Dec. 21, 1864	" " " "
Schrader, Henry		Oct. 13, 1864	Oct. 13, 1864	Sub. M. O. July 19, 1865. ....
Snare, William		Dec. 15, 1864	Dec. 15, 1864	" " " "
Stiles, John		Dec. 17, 1864	Dec. 17, 1864	Sub. Never reported to Co....
Scott, Thomas			Dec. 16, 1864	Never reported to Co ....
Taylor, John W		Dec. 17, 1864	Dec. 17, 1864	Sub. M. O. July 3, 1865......
Tash, William		"	"	Sub. M. O. June 9, 1865...
Toombs, Richards	Orland	Sept. 28, 1864	Sept. 28, 1864	Drafted. M. O. May 31, '65...
Wilderker, John A		Dec. 14, 1864	Dec. 14, 1864	Drafted. M. O. July 19, '65...
Williams, Joseph		Oct. 13, 1864	Oct. 13, 1864	Sub. M. O. July 19, 1865......
Wagner, Frederick		Dec. 15, 1864	Dec. 15, 1864	Sub. Absent, under arrest at muster out............
Welch, John		Dec. 20, 1864	Dec. 20, 1864	Sub. Never reported to Co.....
Wisner, Isaac N	Hurricane	Dec. 10, 1864	Dec. 10, 1864	Died March 11, 1865 ....
York, Frank		Dec. 20, 1864	Dec. 20, 1864	Sub. Never reported to Co.....

UNASSIGNED RECRUITS.

Name and Rank	Residence	Date of rank or enlistment	Date of muster	Remarks
Booth, John C	Marion	Jan. 23, 1864	Jan. 23, 1864	Deserted ....
Brunis, Crlas	Carbondale	Jan. 30, 1864	Jan. 30, 1864	....
Doyle, Harvey A. P	Moweaqua	Dec. 30, 1863	Dec. 30, 1863	....
Doyle, Benjamin F	"		"	....
Davis, William B	Blainsville	Jan. 19, 1864		Deserted ....

Name and Rank	Residence	Date of rank or en- listment	Date of muster	Remarks
Emilton, Charles N	Henry	Dec. 16, 1863	Dec. 16, 1863	Rejected
Goodman, Talbert	Anna	Jan. 23, 1864	Jan. 23, 1864	
Goodman, Allen L	" "	Jan. 12, 1864	Jan. 12, 1864	Died, Camp Butler, Feb. 19,'64.
Gulley, Robert ..				
Harpendy, John C	Anna	Feb. 7, 1864	Feb. 7, 1864	Deserted
Hicks, James F	" "	Feb. 22, 1864	Feb. 22, 1864	Died
Huntington, Dan'l J. C	North Fork	Apr. 13, 1865	Apr. 13, 1865	Mustered out May 14, 1865.
Jones, Henry	Flora	Jan. 24, 1865	Jan. 24, 1865	Deserted Feb. 3, 1865
Lewis, William	DeSoto	Feb 29, 1864	Feb. 29, 1864	Deserted
Maxey, John	Clyde	Mar. 1, 1865	Mar. 1, 1865	
Nelson. Alfred	Delvin	"	"	Died at Camp Butler, Ill
Neely, Thomas J	Sulpher Springs	Jan. 5, 1864	Jan. 5, 1864	
Owens. Ellery	Alabama	Feb. 4, 1864	Feb. 4, 1864	Deserted
Rice, Henry	Harrisburg	Mar. 5, 1864	Mar. 5, 1864	
Rose, Wiley A. J	Vienna	Feb 9, 1864	Feb. 9, 1864	Rejected
Stewart, Samuel	Moweaqua	Dec. 30, 1863	Dec. 30, 1863	
Smith, John	Flora	Jan. 24, 1865	Jan. 24, 1865	
Smith, Joseph W	Carbondale	April 11, 1864	Apr. 11, 1864	
Verner, Thomas	Moweaqua	Dec. 30, 1863	Dec. 30, 1863	
Williams, John H	Centralia	Feb. 2, 1864	Mar. 16, 1864	
Weir, Robert G	Carbondale	Feb. 20, 1864	Feb. 20, 1864	Rejected
Wilhelm, Henry F	Anna	Feb. 26, 1864	Feb. 26, 1864	
Wilson, Andrew	Lost Prairie	Apr. 7, 1865	Apr. 7, 1865	

UNASSIGNED, DRAFTED AND SUBSTITUTE RECRUITS.

Name and Rank	Residence	Date of rank or en- listment	Date of muster	Remarks
Armbruster, Peter		Sept. 22, 1864	Sept. 22, 1864	
Anderson. Henry	Vermont	Oct. 3, 1864	Oct. 3, 1864	
Blair, Dennis		Dec. 21, 1864	Dec. 21, 1864	Substitute
Clesbey, Edward	Prairie ..	Oct. 18, 1864	Oct. 18, 1864	
Greene, James	Saratoga	Oct. 19, 1864	Oct. 19, 1864	Substitute
Hays, John	Wythe	Oct. 8, 1864	Oct. 8, 1864	
Herveth, Thomas C	Licking	Oct. 15, 1864	Oct. 15, 1864	Substitute
Kennedy, Edward B	Jefferson	Oct. 12, 1864	Oct. 12, 1864	"
Little, William H	New Jersey	Sept. 30, 1864	Sept. 30, 1864	
Mehr, James		Dec. 22, 1864	Dec. 22, 1864	Substitute
O'Brien, John		Dec. 21, 1864	Dec. 21, 1864	"
O'Neil, William		Dec. 13, 1864	Dec. 13, 1864	
Sponly, Michael		Dec. 17, 1864	Dec. 17, 1864	Substitute
Smith, John		Dec. 23, 1864	Dec. 23, 1864	"
Sedgwick. Christopher	Fairfield	Dec. 21, 1864	Dec. 21, 1864	"
Techner, Frank		"	"	"
Wright, William	Evans	Dec. 15, 1864	Dec. 15, 1864	"
Welch, Patrick	Chicago	Aug. 19, 1864	Aug. 19, 1864	"
Young. Augustus		Dec. 6, 1864	Dec. 6, 1864	
Jenden, William		Dec. 22, 1864	Dec. 22 1864	Substitute

THE Thirty-first Regiment of Illinois Infantry, except Companies I and K, was mainly composed of men from the southern part of the State, the counties of Williamson, Perry, Franklin, Jackson, Johnson, Saline and Union furnishing the larger number. Its rendezvous was at Camp Dunlap, Jacksonville, Illinois; but it was organized at Cairo by John A. Logan, and was there mustered into the service by Captain Pitcher, U. S. A., on the 18th of September, 1861, and went into camp of instruction in the brigade of General McClernand.

With less than two months' drill, the regiment took part in the battle of Belmont, Mo., November 7, 1861, cutting its way into the enemy's camp, and with equal valor, but less hazard, cutting its way out again. On the 7th of February, 1862, the regiment was at Ft. Henry, Tenn.; and after emerging from the muddy environments of that stronghold, it traversed the hills to Fort Donelson, and there, amid winter snows, on the 15th of the same month, it lost 260 men killed and wounded—the regiment having performed, in this engagement, the difficult evolution of a change of front to rear on tenth company, in the heat of battle, among tangled brush and on uneven ground. From Donelson the regiment was transported by steamer to Shiloh, Tenn., and thence it moved towards Corinth, Miss., with the main body of the army, and reached that place only to find it evacuated by the enemy. From Corinth the Thirty-first marched to Jackson, Tenn., and the summer of 1862 was spent in guarding railroads, skirmishing in the country of the Forked Deer River, and scouting in the direction of Memphis, to Brownsville and beyond. Ordered to the support of General Rosencrans, at Corinth, the regiment reached that place in time to follow the retreating foe to Ripley, Miss., where the men fed on fresh pork, without salt, or crackers, or coffee. On this expedition it was engaged in the skirmishes of Chewalla and Tuscumbia, ending the 6th of October, 1862. The regiment was with Grant in the first campaign against Vicksburg, sometimes called the Yokona expedition, and passed through Holly Springs to Coldwater, at which place the men, destitute of rations in consequence of the capture and destruction of supplies at Holly Springs by the enemy, showed their characteristic adaptability by carrying out at once the suggestion of Logan to convert the timber into ashes, and, by means of the ashes, the corn of the surrounding country into hominy.

Upon the termination of this campaign the regiment, with the army under Grant, was transferred to a new field, that of the operations which finally resulted in the downfall of Vicksburg. On the 15th of January, 1863, it set out for Lagrange, Tenn., and thence went to Memphis, by way of Colliersville. Leaving Memphis March 10, 1863, it embarked for Lake Providence, La.; and after assisting in the attempts to open a route by water to a point below Vicksburg, it moved, upon the abandonment of these attempts, to Milliken's Bend, and thence to Waynesborough. Having crossed the Mississippi below Grand Gulf, April 30, 1863, the next day the regiment, without waiting for rations, though hungry and weary enough, hurried forward to the support of the comrades then engaged in battle at Thompson's Hill, near Port Gibson, and quickly forming on McClernand's left, under the eyes of Generals Grant and Logan, it moved upon the right wing of the enemy at the charge step, routing him completely, and helping to secure a speedy victory. Governor Yates, in civilian garb of swallow-tail coat and high shirt collar, and overflowing with enthusiasm and patriotism, witnessed this charge. After crossing the Bayou Pierre, the men of the Thirty-first again met and dispersed their foes at Ingram Heights, May 3, 1863, and pushed on to Raymond where on the 12th the regiment hurled from its front the fragments of a brigade which the enemy had thrown against the advance of Grant. Moving onward, in almost ceaseless march, it took part in the battle of Jackson, Miss., May 14, 1863, and thence at midnight, on the 15th, through drenching rain, it marched toward Vicksburg, to meet the enemy anew. About ten o'clock in the morning of the 16th the men spread their cartridges to dry in the sun, in an old field about five miles from Champion Hills, from which latter point was soon after heard the sound of battle. The men hastily gathered up their ammunition and seized their muskets, and the regiment followed the head of the column at double-quick, effecting a formation with its brigade on the right of our embattled line, where it rested for a moment, the men lying on their faces while the hostile shells whistled and shrieked and exploded above them. At the command "attention" the line stood erect, with bayonets fixed; the brigade-commander, General John E. Smith, gave the word; McPherson said with a smile, "give 'em Jesse!" and Logan shouted "remember the blood of your mammies! give 'em hell!" and then the brigade sprang forward, broke and routed the two column formation over which waved the Confederate flag, captured the opposing battery, turned its guns upon the retreating enemy, and took as many prisoners as there were men in the charging brigade. In this encounter there was crossing of bayonets and fighting hand to hand. Sergeant Wick, of Company B, used his bayonet upon his foe, and Sergeant Hendrickson, of Company C, clubbed his musket in a duel with one of the men in gray.

From this point the regiment, with the main army, followed the retreating enemy to his entrenched lines at Vicksburg, where it took part in the bloody assaults on the 19th and 22d of May; its gallant Lieutenant-Colonel, Reece, meeting death by the explosion of a grenade while planting the regimental colors upon the ramparts. Here the flag received 153 bullets, and the staff was shot asunder in four places.

During the siege the regiment took a prominent part in the operations against Fort Hill, and when the fort was blown up, on the 25th of June, by the explosion of a mine beneath it, there came a time that tested the stuff the men were made of. Here in the night, in that crater remembered as the "slaughter-pen," the soldiers fighting by reliefs, and within an armslength of the enemy—some had their muskets snatched from their hands—under a shower of grenades and of shells lighted by port-fires, while the voices of Pearson, Goddard, Mooningham and others, rising at times above the terrific din of combat, cheered on their men—were deeds of valor performed which would adorn the heroic page.

On the morning of July 4, 1863, the place of honor having been assigned to the brigade, the Thirty-first regiment marched proudly across the rents and chasms of Fort Hill into Vicksburg.

Having made the expedition to Monroe, La., under General Stephenson, the regiment went into camp at Black River, Miss., the scene of Lawler's splendid victory, and here, on the 5th of January, 1864, three-fourths of the men again enlisted in the service. That night the men, formed in line, with lighted candles held in the shanks of their bayonets, marched to the quarters of General Force, commanding the brigade, who appeared before his tent and catching the splendor from the candles full in his face, cried out with enthusiasm, "Three cheers for the Thirty-first!" But the "boys" were not going to cheer for themselves and there were no others present to do it, they stood in their ranks, silent

and with military air, and cheered not nor stirred; where-
upon the general shouted, "Cheer yourselves, boys! hip! hip!"
and then the cheers were given with a will, followed by a
'tiger" for the Union, and three groans for the Confederacy.

The regiment was with General Sherman in the campaign against Meridian, Miss., after which the re-enlisted men
—the "Veterans"— took their furlough, starting for home
the 19th of March, 1864. Having returned to the front, by
way of Cairo, the regiment camped from the 6th to the 15th
of May at Clifton, on the Tennessee River, and thence marching by way of Rome, Ga., sometimes collecting, herding and
driving beef-cattle, and sometimes skirmishing with the
enemy, it joined Sherman's army at Ackworth Station. It
was in the skirmishes at Big Shanty, and at Brush Mountain—the assault upon Kenesaw on June 27, 1864; also in
the battles around Atlanta, on the 21st, 22d, and 28th of
July, of which that on the 22d was the most terrible, the
men fighting sometimes on one side of the earthworks, sometimes on the other. The regiment was also engaged in the
battles of Lovejoy Station and Jonesborough, and was with
Sherman in the mock pursuit of Hood upon his invasion of
Tennessee. Retracing its steps, the regiment reached Atlanta on the 13th of November, and on the 15th it there began with Sherman the triumphant march to the sea, and on
through tangled forests, bridging streams for the passage of
troops, tearing up railroad-tracks, twisting the rails "as
it marched, with that magnificent army, cutting roads
crooked as rams' horns," "discovering" and devouring sweet

potatoes and other provender, surging over the country "from Atlanta to the sea," "shouting the battle cry of freedom," and proceeding by way of Millen, it arrived the 10th of December, 1864, at Savannah. Here the regiment went into camp on the rice plantation of Dr. Owen, where the rice was consumed for food, the husks being beaten off by means of wooden mortars and pestles appropriated from the slave quarters near by. One of the incidents of the day was the encountering of a battery mounted on a flat car, pushed along the railroad by a locomotive.

On the 4th of January, 1865, the Thirty-first bade farewell to Savannah, and shipped on the steamer Harvest Moon, and after the novel experience and sights of a sea voyage, disembarked at Beaufort, S. C., where it remained, enjoying the luxury of fresh oysters at low prices, until the 13th. To this succeeded some skirmishing at Fort Pocotaligo—"Poke-'em-till-they-go," as the men called it—which was evacuated by the enemy.   On the 30th of January the march began through the Carolinas, by way of Salkahatchie, Orangeburg— which was captured, after some fighting by the regiment's skirmishers,—Columbia—scourged by destroying flames— Winsborough, Cheraw, Fayetteville—captured by foragers— and Bentonville—scene of the last great struggle of John ston's army, and the regiment came out of the swamps, out of the pine forests, "out of the wilderness," the men ragged, dirty, many of them barefooted, to Goldsborough, N. C., where it arrived the 24th of March, 1865, and where letters from home and news from the world were received. These and the prospect of the nearing of the end were cheering and refreshing to men who for 54 days had been without communication with home or the world, and were weary with long marching and fighting.

On the 14th of April, 1865, the regiment was with the army at Raleigh, N. C. Signs of the ruin of the Confederacy and the dispersion of its armed forces were apparent on every hand. Soon came the surrender of Johnston's army—the only force which could oppose the onward march of the Union troops to Richmond, and the regiment formed a part of the host to which that army surrendered.

On the 9th of May the regiment was at Richmond, on the 19th at Alexander; and on the 24th of May, with faded and tattered uniforms, but with martial step and bearing, in column of company, eyes front, it marched through the principal avenues of the capital, in that grand review of the returning armies in presence of the great leaders, civil and military, of the republic—the most magnificent and imposing spectacle ever witnessed by the city of Washington. The end had been attained!

Soon afterwards the regiment was moved to Louisville, Ky., arriving at that place on 11th of June, where it was assigned to provost-guard duty. On the 19th of July, 1865, it was mustered out of the service, by Lieutenant Aug. P. Noyes, A. C. M., 3d Division 17th Corps. It was then moved to Springfield, Ill., where it arrived on the 23d of July, 1865; and there on the 31st of the same month, the men received their final discharge, and separated for their homes—those who were left of them.

At the time of the discharge there were present 25 officers and 677 enlisted men. When first organized the regiment numbered 1,130 men. It had recruited 700. The casualties, including men discharged before the final muster out, amounted to 1,128. In the course of its existence the regiment had been commanded by four colonels, and had had five lieutenant-colonels and six majors. Of the twenty-five officers discharged at the final muster-out, all save the chaplain had risen from the ranks.

In the campaigns of Sherman this regiment had marched 2,076 miles. This part of its history is included in that of the brigade to which it belonged—the 1st brigade, 3d Division, 17th Corps, Army of the Tennessee. The regiment marched 2,000 miles under Grant, and on expeditions other than those of Sherman. It served in the hostile States of Missouri, Kentucky, Tennessee, Mississippi, Louisiana, Georgia, Alabama, North Carolina, South Carolina and Virginia. Before January 1, 1863, the history of the regiment is comprised in that of the 1st brigade, 3d Division, Reserve Army of the Tennessee.

Always efficiently commanded, and evincing soldierly qualities in its first battle, the regiment became in the days of its "veteran" existence, one of the best drilled in the service. It was while encamped at Black River, Miss., after the Vicksburg campaigns, that the regiment, under the skillful management of Lieutenant-Colonel Pearson, attained that

high degree of discipline and proficiency in drill for which it
became known, and towards which it had been directed, under Logan and White, in the earlier days of the war. The
latter fell at Donelson and deserved the title "The bravest of
the brave."

Colonel Pearson had seen service under General Prentiss
before the organization of this regiment, and early showed an
aptitude for tactics and drill which made him a favorite with
the field and staff, while his soldierly qualities displayed at
Henry and Donelson endeared him to the rank and file.
Hence he rapidly rose from the ranks, being promoted to
commissary sergeant March 1, 1862; to adjutant, May 16,
1862; to Major, February 24, 1863, by the unanimous vote of
the officers; to Lieutenant-Colonel July 1, 1863; and to
Colonel September 26, 1864. On the 13th of March, 1865,
he was breveted Brigadier-General of Volunteers, for gallantry during the war.

Many of the officers and soldiers of the regiment deserve
special mention and lasting remembrance, but the space al-
lotted forbids a more extended account. To some of the men
were awarded medals for gallantry; among them Sergeant
George W. White, of Company C, who, severly wounded in
the battle of Atlanta, July 22, 1864, resolutely and persistently refused to be carried to the rear.

The fighting qualities of this regiment were displayed in
fourteen battles and twenty-five skirmishes, of various de-
grees of importance. It witnessed the surrender of Buckner
and the garrison at Donelson, the capitulation of Pemberton

and his army at Vicksburg, the humiliation of Johnston and his force at Bentonville, and their final surrender near Raleigh. And a brilliant gem in its crown of glory is the fact of its organization as a "veteran" regiment, at a time when the Union cause stood so much in need of trained and tried soldiers to complete the overthrow of armed rebellion, and to establish upon the ruins of anarchy and slavery "a government of the people, by the people, for the people."

Shawnee Classics: A Series of Classic Regional Reprints for the Midwest